The Great Mental Models: Systems and Mathematics

The Great Mental Models

Systems and Mathematics

SHANE PARRISH
Rhiannon Beaubien,
and Rosie Leizrowice

Cornerstone Press

5 7 9 10 8 6 4

Cornerstone Press
One Embassy Gardens
8 Viaduct Gardens
London SW11 7BW

Cornerstone Press is part of the Penguin Random House group of companies whose addresses can be found at global.penguinrandomhouse.com.

A portion of this work has appeared online at fs.blog.

First published in Canada by Latticework Publishing Inc., Ottawa, in 2021
This updated and revised edition first published in the US by Portfolio, an imprint of Penguin Random House LLC, New York, and in the UK by Cornerstone Press in 2024

www.penguin.co.uk

A CIP catalogue record for this book is available from the British Library.

ISBN 9781529945713

Book design by Daniel Lagin

Printed and bound in Great Britain by Clays Ltd, Elcograf S.p.A.

The authorised representative in the EEA is Penguin Random House Ireland, Morrison Chambers, 32 Nassau Street, Dublin D02 YH68

www.greenpenguin.co.uk

Penguin Random House is committed to a sustainable future for our business, our readers and our planet. This book is made from Forest Stewardship Council® certified paper.

Contents

MATHEMATICS

Introduction

An individual understands a concept, skill, theory, or domain of knowledge to the extent that he or she can apply it appropriately in a new situation.

—HOWARD GARDNER[1]

We learn so much from the world if we are willing to take the time to let it teach us. Each discipline we study contains fundamentals that provide insight into many of the common challenges we face. These fundamentals make up *Farnam Street*'s latticework of mental models, a way of approaching new ideas and situations, problems, and challenges with a toolkit of valuable knowledge.

In volume 1 of *The Great Mental Models,* we introduced nine general thinking concepts to get you started on the journey of building a framework of timeless knowledge. Time and again those models have proven indispensable in both solving problems and preventing them in the first place.

In volume 2 of *The Great Mental Models,* we continued the journey and explored fundamental ideas from physics, chemistry, and biology. The truths about the physical world, from the forces that allow us to manipulate energy to the behaviors that drive the actions of all organisms, are constants that can guide our decisions so that our actions are aligned with how the world works.

> How much you know in the broad sense determines what you understand of the new things you learn.
>
> —HILDE ØSTBY AND YLVA ØSTBY[2]

In this book, volume 3, we will consider the core ideas of systems thinking and mathematics. Although these subjects can appear abstract, as soon as we start taking them apart, we quickly see that they describe many of the behaviors and interactions that govern our lives. We hope you are excited about embarking on this next step of the journey.

> The more moving parts you have in something, the more possibilities there are.
>
> —ADAM FRANK[3]

About the Series

The *Great Mental Models* series is designed to inspire and challenge you. We want to give you both knowledge and a framework for using it in everyday life.

One of our goals for the series is to provide you with a set of tools built on timeless knowledge that you can use again and again to spot opportunities others miss, avoid problems before they happen, and live a better life. It is a guide to dozens of mental models, spread across multiple volumes, that define and explore the foundational concepts from a variety of disciplines. We then take the concept out of its original discipline and show you how you can apply it in less obvious situations. We encourage you to dive into new ideas not only to augment your knowledge toolbox but also to leverage what you already know by applying it in new ways to gain a different perspective on the challenges you face.

In the first book, we explained that a mental model is simply a representation of how something works. We use models to retain knowledge and simplify how we understand the world. We can't relearn everything every day, so we construct models to help us chunk patterns and navigate our world more efficiently. *Farnam Street*'s mental models are reliable principles that you can see at work in the world time and again. Using them means synthesizing across disciplines and not being afraid to apply knowledge from different areas far outside the domain they usually cover.

Not every model applies to all situations. Part of building a latticework of mental models is educating yourself regarding which situations are best addressed by which models. This takes some work, and you're likely to make some mistakes. It's important to constantly reflect on your use of models. If something didn't work, you need to try to discover why. Over time, by reflecting on your use of individual models, you will learn which models will best help you tackle which situations. Knowing why a model works will help you know when to use it again.

> Systems thinking is a discipline for seeing wholes. It is a framework for seeing interrelationships rather than things, for seeing patterns of change rather than static "snapshots."
>
> —PETER SENGE[4]

About This Book

Volume 3 examines some of the core mental models from systems and mathematics.

Systems are everywhere, and we live our lives as part of many of them. Mathematics too explains the dynamics of how a great deal of our world works. We start each chapter by explaining the theory behind the concept and then situate it in real-world examples. We want you to see each concept in action and be inspired to find analogous uses in your own life. To achieve this goal, we show how using the model as a lens will help you see stories and themes in history in a new way.

As you go through this book, you will begin to see just how interconnected systems and mathematics are. Although we have broken the components apart to consider them separately, by the end you will be making connections between the models yourself. A lot of the work of this series is helping you reach these connections yourself. For example, you will start to see how bottlenecks connect to surface area and how feedback loops underpin the behavior of so many system interactions. Often the lessons and insights are relevant at both an individual and organizational level. As you learn the models, you will start to see the principles they cover in almost any situation in which you find yourself. You'll see things others don't and avoid costly mistakes.

Some of the models in this book function like metaphors, especially in the mathematics section. We aim to show you how to use these models to uncover the dynamics in a variety of challenging situations you may face and give you insight on how to harness the suggested ideas to positively influence your outcomes. The more you know, the easier it is to design solutions that will work.

Other models, especially from systems, have a more literal application. Because systems are so ubiquitous, it's not useful to try to apply these models outside them. Instead, we offer ideas for considering just how much of life is part of a system so you can expand your application of systems thinking.

When looking at historical examples through the lens of a model, it's important to remember we are not attempting to demonstrate causation. We are not saying that what happened in a particular moment in history can be explained by, for example, a mathematical formula or that a certain historical figure used the described model to guide their decisions. We are simply showing you how you might understand that bit of history differently when you use a particular model as a lens or giving you a different perspective on why a particular person's decisions led to the outcomes they did. You therefore will get inspiration for applying the same model to nonintuitive situations in your own life.

Finally, all these models, as with those covered in the previous books, are value-neutral. They can be used to illuminate both the positive and negative aspects of any situation. They might work well in one situation but not in another. We try to balance use of the models with noting some of their limitations so you have ideas for when you might want to take an alternate approach.

You will learn the differences in how to apply each model through the stories we have chosen to explain them. Each example is crafted to give you insight into where the model can apply. You can take the elements of each story as a signpost directing you to find similar situations in your life where the lens of a particular model will be most useful.

The most important thing to remember is that all models are tools. You are meant to try them out, play with them, and learn what you can use each of them to fix. Not all tools are useful for all problems, and just as a traditional toolbox has a hammer when you need to pound a nail and a wrench for when you need to turn a bolt, you'll learn through practice which tools are useful in which situations in your life. The best way to do that is to start by being curious. As you begin each chapter, be open to learning and updating your knowledge. Then, practice. Pick a new model every day, apply it to a situation you are in, and see if you can improve your understanding and decision making. Finally, reflect. Take some time to evaluate your successes and failures. In doing so, you will begin to learn the full potential of the toolkit you are building.

Time to get started.

SYSTEMS

In spite of what you majored in, or what the textbooks say, or what you think you're an expert at, follow a system wherever it leads. It will be sure to lead across traditional disciplinary lines.

—DONELLA H. MEADOWS[1]

Feedback Loops

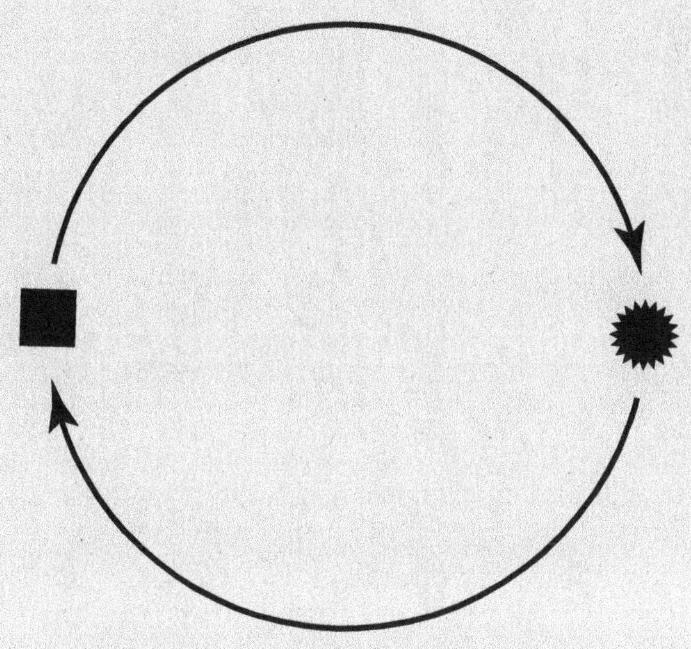

Listen and incorporate.

The key to the feedback loop is the information it provides. You need to know whether you are moving toward your goal or away from it, and you need to know if your actions are having the intended effect.

–JAMES CLEAR[1]

Feedback loops are everywhere in systems, making them a useful mental model.

Think of feedback as the information communicated in response to an action. Whether we realize it or not, we give and receive different forms of feedback every day. Sometimes feedback is more formal, as is the case with performance reviews. Other times, it is less so. Our body language is a form of feedback for people interacting with us. The tone you use with your kids is feedback for them.

A feedback loop is a process in which the output of a system also acts as an input to the system, helping to refine and improve the system over time. It's like a conversation in which each reply helps to shape the next question and answer, making the discussion better and more focused.

Once you start looking for feedback loops, you see them all over the place, giving you insight into why people and systems react the way they do. For example, much of human behavior is driven by incentives. We want to take actions that lead to us getting something good or avoiding something bad on a range of timescales. The incentives we create for ourselves and other people are a form of feedback, leading to loops that reinforce or discourage certain behaviors. If you get visibly upset whenever someone at work offers you constructive criticism, you'll incentivize your colleagues to only tell you when you're doing something well—thereby missing out on chances to improve.

The challenge in using this mental model is that the ubiquity of feedback loops can become overwhelming. How do you know which ones to pay attention to? Or which ones to adjust to improve your outcomes?

We are constantly offering feedback to others about our feelings, preferences, and values. Others, in turn, communicate feedback on the same things, but we don't necessarily receive it or interpret it correctly. A critical requirement is learning how to filter feedback. Not all of it is useful. The quicker you learn to identify feedback that helps you progress, the faster you will move toward what you want to achieve.

Learning to communicate feedback in a way that makes it easy for others to receive is a valuable skill to develop. Feedback is crucial to relationships of all kinds. The skill is in giving feedback in a kind and clear way, in hearing it without getting defensive, and in partnering with people who can receive it on a regular basis. If you feel you can't communicate important thoughts and feelings, you won't be happy in that relationship or situation long-term. Much of relationship therapy consists of a therapist helping a couple tell each other things they have been afraid to say—when that feedback should have been free-flowing for years.

There is a larger implication here about working with the world. The world offers us feedback, but do we listen and incorporate, or do we just keep wanting it to work differently than it does?

The technical definition of a feedback loop comes from systems theory.

A *feedback loop* is a process in which the outputs (information) of a system affect that system's behaviors. Depending on the complexity of a system, there may be a single source of feedback or multiple, possibly interconnected sources. It helps to first consider feedback in a simple system as we do in the following, but keep in mind, we are part of many large systems that contain many interconnected feedback loops.

Feedback loops are a critical model because they are a part of your life whether you are aware of them or not. Understanding how they work helps you be more flexible with the variety of feedback you receive and incorporate, and then you can offer better feedback to others.

There are two basic types of feedback loops: balancing and reinforcing, which are also called negative and positive. Balancing feedback loops tend toward equilibrium. Your thermostat and heating system run on a balancing feedback loop. Information about the temperature of the house is communicated to the thermostat, which then adjusts the output of the furnace to maintain your desired temperature.

Reinforcing feedback loops amplify a particular process. They don't counter change, like your thermostat does. Instead, they keep the change going, as with the popularity of trends in fashion (in which styles become ubiquitous within months, only to disappear soon after) or the loops usually involved in poverty (in which different but related circumstances can compound the problem). Breaking out of reinforcing loops often requires outside intervention or a new change in conditions. Or, as with fashion, they simply burn themselves out after a while.

Within complex systems, feedback is rarely immediate. It can take a long time for changes in flows to have a measurable impact on how the system works. This delay complicates establishing cause and effect. In our lives, problems arise when the feedback for our actions is delayed or indirect, as is often the case.

A challenge to improving our decision making is getting accurate feedback on decisions. On one hand, consequences may take a long time to become apparent or may be hard to directly attribute to a particular decision. On the other, we may trap ourselves in maladaptive behaviors when something we do receives positive short-term feedback but has negative long-term consequences. Thus, it's important to remember immediate feedback isn't the only feedback. When you eat junk food, there is an instant hit of pleasure as your body responds to fat and sugar. After a little while, though, you receive other feedback from your body that indicates your choice of junk food has negative consequences. And over longer periods, conditions such as type 2 diabetes and high blood pressure provide more feedback from your body about the effects of your eating habits.

The faster you get useful feedback, the more quickly you can iterate to improve. Yet feedback can cause problems if it's too fast and too strong, as the system can surge. It's like when you press the gas or brake too heavily when first learning how to drive.

Feedback loops are a useful mental model because all systems have them, and we operate in a world of systems and subsystems.

Adam Smith and the Feedback Loop of Reactions

You probably know Adam Smith as one of the most influential economists of all time, notable for his notion of the "invisible hand" of the market. But Smith's first book, *The Theory of Moral Sentiments*, is a work of philosophy.[2] In it, he describes a different sort of invisible force that guides us: how the approval and disapproval of others, real or imagined, influences our behavior.

We are, by nature, selfish. We value ourselves above all other humans. Smith illustrates his point by suggesting that the news that your little finger must be amputated would likely be more stressing than the news of the deaths of a huge number of strangers overseas. Yet despite our inherent selfishness, the majority of people the majority of the time are cooperative and kind to one another. Smith believed our interactions with others are responsible for our well-established reciprocity. He saw others' responses to our behavior as feedback guiding how we act in the future. To do something selfish usually warrants a disapproving reaction. To do something selfless usually merits an approving one.

The feedback loop of others' reactions to our actions is the basis of civilization. Russ Roberts writes in *How Adam Smith Can Change Your Life*, "Smith's vision of what sustains civilization is the stream of approval and disapproval we all provide when we respond to the conduct of those around us. That stream of approval and disapproval creates feedback loops to encourage good behavior and discourage bad behavior."[3]

This type of feedback doesn't just cover formal punishments and prohibitions according to the law where we live. It also covers the ways people respond to behavior that is just considered the norm. If a friend says hello to you on the street and you fail to acknowledge them, you haven't broken any laws, but they're likely to respond in a negative fashion. So you adhere to the norm. Smith writes: "When Nature formed man for society, she endowed him with a basic desire to please his brethren and a basic aversion to offending them. She taught him to feel pleasure in their favorable regard and pain in their unfavorable regard. She made their approval most flattering and most agreeable to him for its own sake, and their disapproval most humiliating and most offensive."

Smith asked readers to imagine a person who grows to adulthood without any interactions with other people. He believed such a person would have no awareness of their character and no notion of the right or wrong way to act.[4] Our desire to be loved and accepted prompts moral behavior relative to the standards of our society. We in turn respond with approval of the same behavior on the part of others.[5]

Everyday Loops

We can address many of the challenges we face every day by adjusting feedback loops. Figuring out how to change behavior (ours and others'), dealing with inaccurate information, and building trust are ongoing challenges. How to get customers to buy your product and not the competitors'; how to sort through information to find what's relevant to your decision; how to cooperate effectively with others: these are common situations many of us face.

All these dynamics play out on the larger social scale as well. How do societies incentivize the behavior they want and disincentivize the behavior they don't want? How do they get people to trust one another enough to keep society functioning?

Any system with an unchecked reinforcing feedback loop is ultimately unsustainable and destructive. Balancing feedback loops are more common in systems because they are sustainable—they maintain a system long-term, whereas reinforcing loops can crash and burn. In many societies, a legal system has historically served to stop reinforcing feedback loops from crumbling the social infrastructure and to promote balancing feedback loops that support desired dynamics. How they do it suggests options for addressing similar issues with feedback loops in our own lives.

Let's explore four aspects of social systems through the lens of feedback loops:

1. Creating the right future incentives
2. Influencing behavior at the margins
3. Dealing with information cascades
4. Building trust

Creating the Right Future Incentives

We want to minimize, as much as possible, making a choice today that creates a negative reinforcing feedback loop down the road. So, we consider the future incentives a decision will create.

A classic example of today's solution inadvertently creating a reinforcing feedback loop of future problems is paying off kidnappers. The immediate problem is someone being kidnapped and a ransom being demanded. If you have the resources to meet the kidnappers' demands, you might want to pay the money right away. You save a life and solve the problem.

However, your response communicates to the kidnappers that you will meet their demands. You thus create an incentive for them to kidnap again, as well as signal to other would-be kidnappers that there is money to be made. By paying a ransom, you create a powerful reinforcing feedback loop that causes more problems in the future.

In many legal systems, each decision by a court becomes a bit of information that moves via a feedback loop into the stock of legal options to influence both how the system responds to future cases and how judges form future decisions. Each decision becomes legal precedent. In *The Legal Analyst*, Ward Farnsworth explains that in making decisions courts will consider "what incentives people will have after the case is over."[6] Courts need to be careful. If they compensate for a wrong now, they could create a climate that increases the chances of that wrong happening again.

One set of issues courts often face is questions of liability. If something bad happens to me, then does someone else need to pay to compensate? Sometimes the answer is yes, but not indiscriminately so. If we go back to the kidnapping example; let's say an

American citizen is kidnapped overseas and the kidnappers demand the government pay for release. Is the government liable to compensate the victim's family for the loss of life if they choose not to pay the ransom? Most courts will answer no. If I am held liable, it incentivizes me to pay in the future, and we are back in the same reinforcing feedback loop. When considering certain instances of liability, Farnsworth explains, "Instead of looking back and deciding who should bear the suffering, [a court] can look ahead and decide what ruling will make the suffering less likely to occur later."[7]

In some situations, choosing an immediate benefit creates reinforcing feedback loops that remove the possibility of future benefits. For cases like these, laws are designed to support balancing feedback loops, such as protecting attorney-client privilege, or copyright and patent laws. Although one could argue for the immediate benefit of, say, forcing a defense attorney to testify about what their client disclosed, the feedback loop created would make clients disinclined to disclose things to their attorney. As Farnsworth summarizes concerning copyright protection, "Once books and music exist... there's a great case for free distribution of them. But then they are less likely to exist at all next time."[8]

People look around and often see what they view as unfairness—but they don't realize that unfairness sometimes has a greater purpose. Unfairness in specific cases creates fairness on the whole, as in the aforementioned cases. Often things happen that look like an injustice to the individual, and they may be so. But those things may create greater justice for the collective. Think of someone being "excessively" punished; that may seem unfair to them, but if it is successful in deterring others from committing the same infractions, it's not always such a bad idea.

Influencing Behavior at the Margins

Not everyone is likely to change their behavior in response to pressures, such as social or economic changes, at the same intensity and rate. Some people need more convincing; others need more time.

A good customer retention strategy doesn't lump all customers into one group. It might, for example, treat customers of ten years better than customers of six weeks. These are examples of margins. "Margins" can mean a lot of things in economics; in this case we mean "by increments," or "small changes"—shades of gray instead of all or nothing. Farnsworth explains thinking at the margin as "looking at problems not in a total, all-or-nothing way . . . but in incremental terms: seeing behavior as a bunch of choices about when to do a little less along one dimension and a little more along another."[9]

Let's consider the consumption of sugary drinks. Influencing behavior at the margins means that you won't see the problem as a binary of consumption or no consumption. Instead, you look at how you can influence people's behavior to help nudge them toward a particular choice you consider better for them without preventing them from making the opposite choice. The idea is to make it easier to choose one option and harder to choose another.

Maybe you want people to consume fewer drinks. Maybe you want them to substitute sugar-free drinks as a healthier option. If we were thinking about putting in rules to reduce the consumption of sugary drinks, we could tax them, or limit where they could be consumed or sold, or limit the age of people who can buy them. Farnsworth writes, "The activities of individual people have margins . . . and then groups of people have marginal members," and often a legal rule is created with "the hope, realistic or not . . . that it cuts down on the practice at the margin."[10]

Using feedback loops as a lens, we can understand influencing behavior at the margins as instituting a series of incentives that create loops. Over time this feedback changes the system to produce the desired outcomes. We can tailor our feedback to adjust to nuances in behavior that, when combined across a large population, can have significant positive impacts on our system.

Another reason to pay attention to the margins is that they are often the place where reinforcing feedback loops start. A loyal customer of twenty years is not likely going to be the first to leave after a price hike. It's probably going to be the person who just purchased recently. However, when they leave to go to a competitor or even just buy less, there is a danger of setting off a negative reaction that sees sales plummet, which makes reinvestment in the product harder, which leads to more customers leaving.

Criminal law has to work at the margins in terms of deterring unwanted behavior. This means any additional (incremental) crime must be met with appropriate punishment. For example, if a criminal "faces execution for the crime he already has committed, he pays no additional price for adding a murder to it."[11] We don't want thieves to get a death sentence, or there would be no incentive for them not to kill people in the course of their thievery. Farnsworth explains, "The designers of criminal penalties have to worry about preserving *marginal deterrence*—scaling penalties so that there is always something more to fear by doing a little worse."[12] In essence, this creates a balancing feedback loop that responds with appropriate consequences depending on the severity of the crime.

One of the issues as systems get larger is that there are more margins on which to adjust behavior. Adjusting a feedback loop in an attempt to balance it may create an undesirable reinforcing feedback loop somewhere else. For example, if you make it more difficult for people to consume sugary drinks in public, do you then force them into consuming in private indoor spaces? If you do, there is the danger that consuming sugary drinks in the home could lead to increased consumption with fewer judgmental eyes around. It could also normalize the behavior for children in the household, leading to another generation of sugary drink consumers.

> The concept of feedback opens up the idea that a system can cause its own behavior.
>
> —DONELLA H. MEADOWS[13]

Dealing with Information Cascades

Information cascades happen when people make decisions based on the observations or actions of others, which often leads to a convergence of behavior. Many investors selling a particular stock might trigger a cascade in which others sell the same stock, not because of something being wrong with the company but rather because others are selling. Or consider social media virality. A small number of people rapidly liking a post makes the algorithm show the post to more people, who, seeing everyone else liking it, engage with it as well—often without evaluating the content.

Information cascades are a reinforcing feedback loop. They can be evaluated as either positive or negative, depending on the information they communicate. Information cascades occur because we rarely have perfect information, and in many situations, especially in situations of uncertainty, we look to others to determine what we ought to do.

In his book *Kitchen Confidential,* Anthony Bourdain offers a lot of advice to would-be restaurant-goers based on his years working in the industry—useful tips such as try the local food and never ask for your steak well done. Another insight: when choosing which restaurant to go to, pick the one that looks the busiest. If lots of people are eating there, the food must be fairly good.[14]

Restaurateurs are aware of the effects of signaling. They know that the more customers you seat, the more will come in the door. This is why they will seat the first patrons of the evening close to the window and why they don't mind a line of people waiting to be seated. They understand that the more people there are signaling their interest in the restaurant, the greater the reinforcing feedback loop communicating how wonderful their restaurant is. Farnsworth explains, "People draw inferences from what they see others doing and do the same; now even more people are doing it, and they create a still stronger impression on the rest."[15] People who were on the fence about the restaurant will be drawn in by the apparent interest. As they join the queue, the interest of the next threshold level (the next number of customers) gets piqued.

There are other information cascades, some of which can be damaging if left to grow unchecked. Many legal systems have rules designed to interrupt reinforcing feedback loops of illegal activity. Most of us think we are law-abiding citizens. But we break the law more often than we realize. Just think of speeding. When was the last time you drove under the speed limit for your entire car journey? When it comes to things like speeding—or consuming pirated media, insider trading, or paying someone under the table—we often draw inferences about acceptable behavior from the people around us. However, a legal system cannot prosecute everyone who speeds. So how does it interrupt the loop?

Farnsworth writes, "Ignorance and uncertainty are the best soil for a cascade; people rely on what others think when they have no strong knowledge of their own, and the fragility of the consensus that results makes it easily disrupted by shocks."[16] Thus two common legal solutions for dealing with a negative information cascade are laws that require public disclosure of information and prosecuting in certain high-profile situations to make a visible example.

Sometimes having more easily available and accurate information can interrupt a cascade. Think of the disclosure of financial information for publicly traded companies. Not only does the prosecution of high-profile cases act as a deterrent, but the publicity involved often provides more information about the legal territory. The prosecution of Al Capone for tax evasion probably did a lot to educate people about their basic tax responsibilities.

Ultimately these types of actions by the courts are "meant to send signals stronger than the ones people get by watching each other."[17] And it is those signals that interrupt the reinforcing feedback loop of an information cascade.

Building Trust

Complex societies require trust among members to function. Look at how much trust we place in the other drivers on the road every time we get into a car. We trust that they will stop at red lights and stay in their lane. We are vigilant for the occasional mistake, but we drive as if other drivers will obey the same rules and quickly notice when they don't. We place trust everywhere—from the people of our children's school system to those who work in our food and safety systems. For relationships without direct interaction, the law facilitates trust. Farnsworth writes, "Law often amounts to a substitute for trust in situations too complex or dispersed for trust to arise."[18]

There is an experimental game that is widely performed and cited that explores the building of trust in social interactions: the Prisoner's Dilemma. To understand some of the dynamics of the feedback loops involved in trust, it's helpful to look at that game, as well as one of the strategies for playing it, tit for tat.

A \ B		Prisoner B	
		Cooperation	Defection
Prisoner A	Cooperation	A: 1 year B: 1 year	A: 5 years B: 0 years
	Defection	A: 0 years B: 5 years	A: 2 years B: 2 years

Numerous tournaments have been held in which participants use different strategies to compete to win the most points in the iterated Prisoner's Dilemma. The results show how repeated interactions between self-interested agents can lead to cooperative behavior.

The thought experiment goes as such: Two criminals are in separate cells, unable to communicate. They've been accused of a crime they both participated in. The police do not have enough evidence to sentence both, though they are certain enough of their case to wish to ensure both suspects spend time in prison. So they offer the prisoners a deal. They can accuse each other of the crime, with the following conditions:

- If both prisoners say the other did it (both defect), each will serve two years in prison.
- If prisoner A says the other did it (defects) and prisoner B stays silent (cooperates), prisoner A will serve zero years and prisoner B will serve five years (and vice versa).
- If both prisoners stay silent (both cooperate), each will serve one year in prison.

In game theory, the altruistic behavior (staying silent) is called "cooperating," while accusing the other is called "defecting."

What should they do? If they were able to communicate and they trusted each other, the rational choice is to stay silent; that way, each serves less time in prison than they would if the other defects. But how can each know the other won't accuse them? After all, people tend to act out of self-interest. The cost of being the one to stay silent is too high. The equilibrium outcome when the game is played is that both accuse the other and serve two years. In a one-off game of the Prisoner's Dilemma, you are always better off defecting, which means not trusting the other player. Your outcomes are not usually great, but defecting prevents them from being horrible.[19]

We can imagine, however, in iterated versions of the game, that defecting might not always be the best choice. If you have to face the same situation over and over, figuring out ways to trust is worth the investment.

Feedback loops are one of the key mechanisms that provide the information we use to make trust-based decisions. What happened before in your interaction with a person provides feedback that may cause you to modify your behavior, as does someone's reputation.

The loop of information is the basis for the classic strategy of the Prisoner's Dilemma, tit for tat. In a repeated Prisoner's Dilemma, the best solution, based on experiments conducted by Robert Axelrod, is to cooperate first, and then in subsequent rounds, to do what the other player did in the previous round. You start off trusting, and more important, you create a feedback loop that says you are capable of and willing to trust.

The law has a couple of mechanisms that help in encouraging a basic level of trust. The first mechanism is that legal systems often enforce contracts. Knowing that there are repercussions for defecting on our agreement might dissuade me from defecting the first time we work together. Consequences also increase the costs of defecting, even if we will never work together again. In addition to protecting individuals in the one-off, contract enforcement also helps to create feedback loops that promote and incentivize trust. Farnsworth explains, "Contracts . . . give everyone a convenient way to beat prisoner's dilemmas and enjoy the gains that come from cooperation."[20] The point here is that we can trust the feedback loops of the system to enforce micro-interactions so we can establish trust. We can imagine that after a few interactions, the gains that come from cooperation contribute to a feedback loop that encourages people to prioritize cooperation in those situations.

The law can also impose rules and associated penalties for noncompliance in situations where contracts are not possible. Paying your taxes is a way of participating in a sort of contract with your fellow citizens, and most countries have laws that penalize people for not paying. Rules can also govern the use of common or public stocks to incentivize people to cooperate for the common good.

This is often the intent with rules governing fishing quotas. To prevent all those who fish for a living from acting in their self-interest and depleting the stock beyond sustainable levels, laws regulate how much each company can fish. Enforcing quotas is a way of forcing a level of cooperation to maintain a common good.

As we can easily imagine, if no one cooperates, that quickly becomes a reinforcing feedback loop with negative consequences in many situations. The less people cooperate, the less incentive there is for future cooperation. To prevent that loop from beginning, the law can impose rules that discourage the initial defection.

Kandinsky's Iterations

We learn from our efforts. Our first try at anything is rarely any good, but the experience of trying gives us feedback. If we pay attention to it, this feedback can help us improve in our next effort. Through many iterations, by paying attention to and incorporating feedback, we end up becoming more capable. Too often we remove the learning process, including the inevitable failures and disappointments, in success stories. In particular, when it comes to artistic creation, we look at the final product of a painting or piece of music without seeing all the iterations that came before.

In *How to Fly a Horse*, Kevin Ashton tells the story of how Wassily Kandinsky created one of his most famous works, *Painting with White Border*. The piece was not the single output of a flash of inspiration, but from a series of small changes and adjustments based on the feedback he received from each iteration.

The artist started with what would be called *Sketch I for Painting with White Border*. Based on the feedback he received from looking at the effort, he continued to iterate. As Ashton describes it, "His second sketch, barely different, diffused the lines until they were more stain than stroke . . . More sketches followed. . . . He made twenty sketches, each no more than one or two steps different from the last. The process took five months."[21]

Ashton describes Kandinsky as trying to solve certain problems in his painting (these can also be understood as artistic goals). Each iteration Kandinsky produced gave him feedback on whether he was closer to solving his problems. Eventually he had enough information from the feedback on multiple iterations to produce the painting he wanted. The finished work is Kandinsky's twenty-first iteration.

Conclusion

Feedback loops are the engines of growth and change. They're the mechanisms by which the output of a system influences its own input.

Complex systems often have many feedback loops, and it can be hard to appreciate how adjusting to feedback in one part of the system will affect the rest.

Using feedback loops as a mental model begins with noticing the feedback you give and respond to every day. The model also gives insight into the value of iterations in adjusting based on the feedback you receive. With this lens, you gain insight into where to direct system changes based on feedback and the pace at which you need to go to monitor the impacts.

Feedback loops are what make systems dynamic. Without feedback, a system just does the same thing over and over. Understand them, respect them, and use them wisely.

Equilibrium

Dynamic balance.

A system can be said to be at equilibrium when it is in a stable state. All the forces acting upon it and within it are in balance. Nothing changes until something disturbs the equilibrium.

Usually when systems stray too far from their equilibrium, they fall apart. When we consider just the pure functioning of a system, equilibrium is a good thing. Using this model as a lens helps us understand where we might intervene to promote equilibrium, but it also cautions us that in complex systems, anticipating what is needed for equilibrium is exceptionally difficult.

Think of equilibrium as a system's comfort zone—in static equilibrium, everything is at a standstill, perfectly ordered and unchanging. But that's rare. What's common is dynamic equilibrium, in which things aren't frozen but dance within a certain range, adjusting constantly. It's the system's way of self-correcting through feedback loops, nudging anything that drifts too far back into its rhythm.

One way to conceptualize the idea of equilibrium is to imagine a hypothetical family whose overall household forms a system. For the household to run in the way that's best for everyone on average, many variables need to stay within the desired range. If they get out of that range, the family makes adjustments to restore balance. For instance, to cover their living costs, the family needs a certain amount of money to flow into the household each month as well as to keep their money for emergencies at a comfortable level. When they decide to start paying for piano lessons for one of the children, they may cut down on dining out to maintain equilibrium. The family also needs their home to remain within a certain cleanliness range for them to remain happy and healthy. When they decide to get a dog, remaining at equilibrium means they have to spend more time cleaning to compensate for the mess the dog makes. When one family member is away for the week, the others reduce how many groceries they buy. If you imagine your household—even

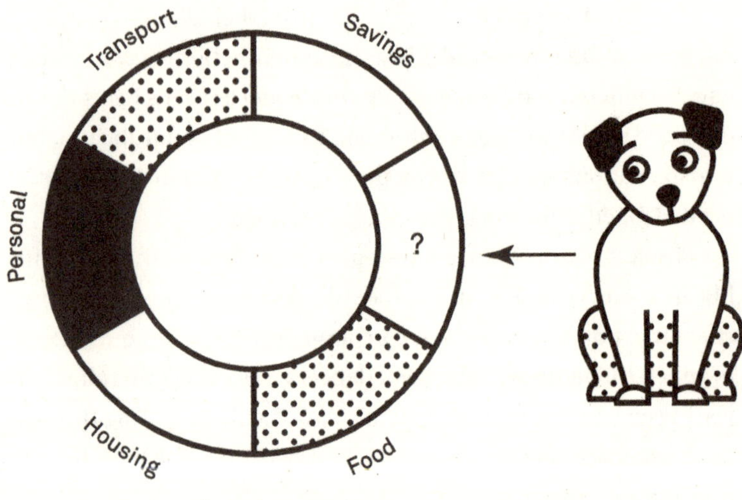

There are only so many hours in a day and so much money available to spend. Adding in new commitments means adjusting our current equilibrium.

if it's just you—you can think of innumerable variables you're always tweaking to keep things as you like them.

Homeostasis is the process through which organisms make continual adjustments to bring them as close as possible to their ideal conditions. Changes in external conditions lead to changes in internal conditions, which may shift a system away from what it needs to work well.

Physician Walter Cannon coined the term "homeostasis" in his iconic 1932 book, *The Wisdom of the Body.* He marveled at the many variables our bodies manage to keep within narrow parameters, including blood glucose, body temperature, and sodium levels. Although systems theory did not exist as a field of study at the time, Cannon was espousing a view of the human body as a whole system that needed to maintain a stable internal state in response to its ever-changing environment.[1]

An important point is that systems can have multiple equilibriums. Just because a system is at equilibrium, that doesn't mean it's functioning as well as it can. It just means things are stable. Sometimes systems achieve equilibrium in inefficient ways. If you're feeling ill one week and struggling to focus on work, you might work extra hours each day to get your usual work done. You've maintained equilibrium, but you would have probably been better off overall if you'd done less.

Short-term deviations from equilibrium are often what is needed to maintain it in the long term. An argument with a sibling that takes work to resolve might shift your relationship with that sibling away from its equilibrium for a few weeks, but in the long run, it could make things more stable between you by helping you resolve tension and agree on new ways to treat each other.

A Different Look at Homeostasis

In his book *The Strange Order of Things*, Antonio Damasio explores the role of homeostasis in evolution. He explains that homeostasis "ensures that life is regulated within a range that is not just compatible with survival but also conducive to flourishing, to a projection of life into the future." He further clarifies the concept by saying, "Homeostasis refers to the process by which the tendency of matter to drift into disorder is countered so as to maintain order but at a new level, the one allowed by the most efficient steady state."[2]

Individuals, organizations, and countries–all are systems that must respond to environmental changes with modifications intended to bring them closer to a desired state. When we go through external challenges, whether it be a breakup, job challenges, or extreme weather, homeostasis kicks in to help us return to a point where the surrounding system functions at its best. Sometimes that can simply be a matter of what feels good rather than a precisely definable set of conditions. Unlike biological systems, we as humans can change the state we aim for, such as when we realize something else would work better–we can be quite happy alone, in a smaller house, or at a different job.

Damasio argues that feelings act as the key to understanding the biological role of homeostasis. Our feelings are a feedback loop that provides information to our body system about how we are doing. You have to be able to monitor the adjustments and responses to make changes that put you back on track. We do this through the value judgment of feelings. After a disaster, for instance, homeostasis does not need to (and frequently doesn't) return the system to its previous state. Instead, it's more useful to think of homeostasis returning a system to a place where it "feels good" under new conditions.

Therein lies the potential of homeostasis. How systems define themselves as "feeling good" will have a huge impact on their ability to adapt to stress and change. In biological systems, feelings are a critical component of how we assess problems. When your blood glucose drops, you feel terrible, which causes behavior that seeks to bring you back to where you feel OK. But that level of OK is a range, and Damasio's idea is that homeostasis normally keeps us at the end of the range that allows us to develop. As variables under- and overshoot and external conditions change, systems can never stop making adjustments. Homeostasis is never a static state.

When Information Can Help

When we look at biological systems, we can easily see that information is required to maintain homeostasis, or dynamic equilibrium. In our bodies, various components are constantly receiving and communicating an incredible amount of information about everything from the sensations on our skin from the external temperature to the potassium levels in our blood. Without accurate information, our bodies cannot work properly. Using this model as a lens, we can understand which situations might benefit from information to maintain equilibrium. One such situation is the modern approach to doctor-patient communication in many medical systems.

The doctor-patient relationship is universally unbalanced in terms of power and knowledge. Doctors have more knowledge about both medicine and the system used to treat patients. This dynamic has led to patients being passive participants in their health care, given neither the knowledge nor the opportunity to make decisions regarding their treatment. Now, in some places, the relationship has started to change, with patients becoming more active participants. There is growing recognition in some medical systems that the experience of treatment (and consequently sometimes health outcomes) improves when patients are more active participants in making treatment-related decisions. To facilitate this participation, in some medical systems patients are now given much more extensive information about their condition and the various treatment options, including associated risk.

Part of the reason for the change to more patient participation is the acknowledgment that diagnostics and treatments are rarely black-and-white. In a paper called "Tolerating Uncertainty," the authors write, "Doctors have to make decisions on the basis of imperfect knowledge, which leads to diagnostic uncertainty, coupled with the uncertainty that arises from unpredictable patient response to treatment and from health care outcomes that are far from binary."[3] It doesn't make sense for a doctor to make treatment decisions for a patient in isolation, because any treatment is going to have consequences that the patient will disproportionately bear. Involving a patient in the discussion of their care options also serves to minimize blind spots and bias. Explaining options to a patient means that a doctor must at least acknowledge the options that exist, and coming to a solution through dialogue with a patient helps to make the solution situation-specific.

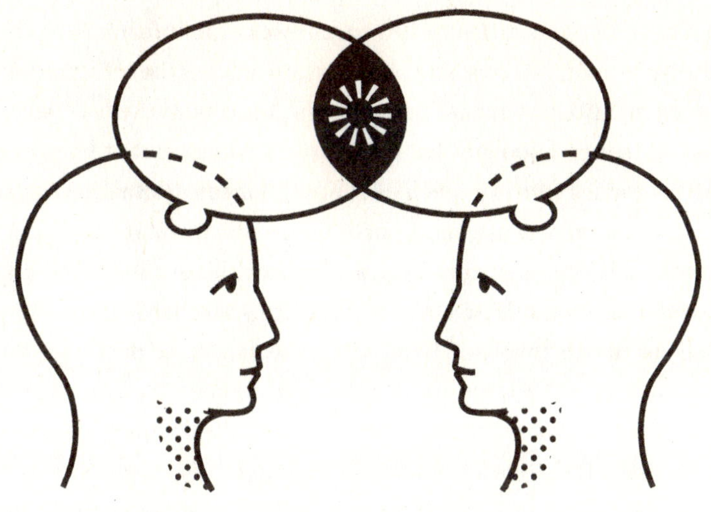

People who are actively supported in making decisions about their health care often experience more favorable health outcomes, including less anxiety and a quicker recovery.

One of the methods for increasing the information availability of treatment options in the doctor-patient relationship is a process called "shared decision making" (SDM). SDM does not put the responsibility for a decision on one party or the other but instead provides the resources necessary for the doctor and patient to come to an acceptable decision together. In a 1997 paper, the authors explain that SDM is "seen as a mechanism to decrease the informational and power asymmetry between doctors and patients by increasing patients' information, sense of autonomy and/or control over treatment decisions that affect their well-being."[4]

For patients to make an informed choice about their care, they need to understand the benefits and harms of the various treatment options. They might also require the support of a loved one, multiple opportunities to hear and assess the information, the ability to ask questions, and some time to process the information. In one definition of dynamic equilibrium, the condition exists "when the system components are in a state of change, but at least one variable stays within a specified range."[5] A medical situation is just such a system because many parts are usually in a state of change, specifically the exact parameters of the health issue itself. Usually too, in more complicated health situations, there are many doctors and specialists involved. In addition, the needs and desires of the patients are not always static. SDM tries to keep the information variable within a range that allows for both the doctor and patient to navigate the situation in an informed way.

For information to be closer to equilibrium for both patient and doctor in medical treatment situations, it's important to recognize the elements that might affect the flow of information. It's not enough to share raw information. Doctors and patients also must build trust that will allow that information to be accepted and processed. In a 2014 analysis of parent experiences in neonatal intensive care units (NICU), the authors explain, "When families voice their dissatisfaction with the NICU, it is often not because they think their baby has not received good medical care. Instead, it is because the parents' needs have not been acknowledged and addressed."[6] Small things like using a baby's name and acknowledging the parents' caregiving role help create a communication environment where the information needed for good decision making can be heard and understood.

Medical situations are often complex. They can involve a lot of people and a lot of uncertainty. In addition, they almost always include very powerful emotions. Allowing information to come as close as possible to equilibrium in these types of situations can provide enough structure to support positive functioning in a changing environment.

Exploiting Assumptions

If you become too dependent on a particular equilibrium to perform well, you make yourself vulnerable to being thrown off by changing circumstances. Being able to function in a wider range of conditions makes you more versatile and flexible. It's also useful to have homeostatic processes in place to enable you to get back to what you find optimal after any sort of disruption. In competitive situations, those who flounder when they're thrown off their equilibrium by something unexpected without having the mechanisms to reorient often suffer. Sometimes you can transcend your abilities by thinking about what an opponent expects or considers normal. You can also achieve more by rethinking what the equilibrium is in your field.

Take the case of card tricks. When an audience watches a magician perform a trick, they start with certain assumptions and expectations. The same is true for professional magicians watching other magicians perform a trick. Their equilibrium consists of a set of assumptions that enables them to identify how a trick works by watching it or to reverse-engineer it from the end point. Professional magic includes all sorts of conventions and assumptions. One unspoken assumption is that a magician performing a particular named trick does it the same way every time, using the same technique. To figure out how the trick works, you need to identify that technique.

One American magician, Ralph Hull, managed to invent a card trick no one–not even the smartest expert magicians–could fathom by rethinking the equilibrium of card magic. He called it "The Tuned Deck."[7] Hull would show the audience a pack of cards, claiming he could sense the location of any card in the deck by detecting minute vibrations. He would then allow an audience member to pick a card, look at it, then put it back into the pack. Hull moved the cards around, shuffling them one way and another, then pulled out the correct card. Its unique vibrations revealed its location, or so he said.[8]

No one managed to figure out how he did the trick, despite expert magicians watching him perform it again and again. Only at the end of his life did Hull reveal the secret: The Tuned Deck didn't have one, single secret. Hull would use a mixture of different techniques, moving between them depending on whether an audience seemed to be twigging what he was doing. If a professional magician were watching, he might use a few different consecutive methods until he threw them off the scent.[9] The real trick was that Hull shifted away from the equilibrium assumption that a trick with a name had to be done the same way every time.

The Complexity of Equilibrium

Beginning in the 1960s, scientists began to ask questions such as: How could humans survive for a long time in space—or even form permanent settlements on other planets? What does it take to sustain life within a sealed environment, like a spaceship or underground bunker on Mars? How can we create an ecosystem in a closed environment, capable of reaching an equilibrium necessary to keep people alive?

In asking these questions, scientists recognized that our planet is itself a closed system. Innumerable complex processes come together to enable humans to survive. Beginning with experiments in which samples of microbial life were sealed permanently into flasks (some of which are still alive today),[10] researchers demonstrated ways in which closed systems could sustain themselves. Such experiments, on a modest scale, formed an important part of the Russian and US space programs. But the project known as "Biosphere 2" (with planet Earth being Biosphere 1) was on a scale unlike anything that had come before it, and few experiments since have matched its sheer scale, audacity, and ambition.

Biosphere 2 consists of a 180,000-square-meter structure located in the desert near Tucson, Arizona. Its aboveground structure is made of almost 204,000 cubic meters of glass supported by a steel framework with a maximum height of 27.7 meters.[11] Parts of the building are rectangular, parts are pyramid-shaped, parts are domed. Inside, Biosphere 2 contains the following five separate ecosystems mimicking key environments in the outside world:

1. Coastal fog desert
2. Tropical rainforest

3. Savanna grassland
4. Mangrove wetland
5. Ocean

Biosphere 2 also includes areas for agriculture, as well as underground areas for housing the equipment necessary to keep the whole thing functioning. It was the brainchild of John Allen and Ed Bass. Allen was a metallurgist and Harvard MBA who, following a psychedelic trip in the 1960s, founded a commune called Synergia Ranch in Santa Fe County, New Mexico.[12] Successful relative to similar projects at the time, Synergia attracted the attention of Ed Bass, a young billionaire heir to an oil fortune.[13] Together they launched several ambitious projects before deciding in 1984 to set out and discover what it would take to form a Mars colony that humans could live in. With Bass's fortune and Allen's ambition at hand, they assembled a team of experts and began the monumental task of creating Biosphere 2.

In 1991, the "Biospherians"—a team of eight individuals who'd spent years preparing—were sealed inside Biosphere 2 for two years. The aim was for them to maintain a functioning ecosystem with nothing (not even air) coming in from the outside. They would farm all of their food, grow plants and raise animals, and strive to maintain all conditions necessary for their survival. By the time they emerged, the Biospherians had endured a great deal. Oxygen levels had sunk drastically, to the point where it proved necessary to bring in outside oxygen to keep them alive. They struggled to meet their caloric requirements while engaging in so much physical work, though this lifestyle left them healthier than before and they suffered no major health problems during the experiment.

The Biospherians frequently fell out with one another and with those controlling the experiment.

Much of the contemporary media coverage of Biosphere 2, as well as its representations in popular culture, depict the whole thing as a failed experiment replete with fraud and trickery. But this is the result of a gross misunderstanding of both the aims of the project and indeed the nature of science. Experiments aren't meant to "succeed." They're meant to provide us with data about the world that we can use as the basis for future experiments. None of the people who worked on Biosphere 2 expected everything to run perfectly from the first day. They understood that for a system—in this case, the biosphere within the dome, consisting of plants, animals, and people as well as air, water, and more—to achieve an equilibrium, a lot of variables need to be right. Only by trying out the experiment could they discover what all those variables were. They couldn't preempt everything, and it would have been hubris to think they knew everything an ecosystem needed to function well.

As a voyage of discovery, Biosphere 2 excelled. It showed us that maintaining life in a sealed environment is almost infinitely challenging because ecosystems are complex adaptive systems. Under natural conditions, they have countless feedback loops in place to maintain equilibrium. An artificially created ecosystem requires humans to maintain those feedback loops, in part by preempting what they'll need to control but also in part by learning to sense when something is going wrong so they can create a new feedback loop.

When left alone in their typical conditions, systems are pretty good at reaching equilibrium. But when we try to control them or we disrupt their conditions, it takes a lot of effort to bring them to a desirable balance. Despite the early stage of the project, the achievements of the Biospherians were remarkable. They did manage to produce almost all their food, get enough clean water, and keep hundreds of plant and animal species alive. Anyone who has ever tried to grow vegetables at home or even keep a few houseplants alive can appreciate the scale of the experiment. Those who view the project as a comical failure have arguably neglected to think about the sheer complexity of getting a system like that to an equilibrium. Just maintaining the level of balance the Biospherians achieved was a monumental act deserving of acclaim.

Not only that, but Biosphere 2 is an important reminder of the effects of human activity on ecosystems. It highlights how small, misguided interventions can have catastrophic domino effects and just how much damage we can do anytime we interfere with nature. Everything that went into Biosphere 2 required careful examination of ways in which it might both be unable to maintain its equilibrium and also disrupt the overall balance of the ecosystem. Linda Leigh, who helped develop Biosphere 2 and was one of the participants sealed inside, described the complexity of choosing animal species to include.[14] Every animal needed to be evaluated for how it might interact with everything else. For example, they consulted a bat specialist to choose a species that could pollinate some of the plants. Yet when they looked at the consequences of including that species, they were huge:

> One of those bats would nightly have needed to eat twenty two-centimeter-long night-flying moths, and would have had to [have] encounters with over a hundred per night in order to catch the twenty. Where would all of the moths come from? What would their larvae eat, and could we have enough and the correct habitat for the moths' eggs? In addition, the air handlers, as designed, would have sucked the moths in and killed them. Engineers suggested a fine screen

> over the opening to the fans in order to give the moths a chance to survive the pull. That screen would increase the electricity needed to pull the air through, a budget increase that was not supported.[15]

In another example, an expert tried to find a hummingbird species that could live inside Biosphere 2.[16] They had to ask lots of questions about each option, which a casual observer might not consider. What shape is this type of hummingbird's bill? Will it be the right size to pollinate enough plants? What kind of mating display does this type of hummingbird exhibit? Will it be at risk of colliding with the glass during this display? And so on. The considerations were endless.

Even the most seemingly inconsequential things had the potential to compound and endanger the lives of everything in the ecosystem. As professor and filmmaker Shawn Rosenheim explained, "Part of the point in building a self-sustaining world was to make the unimaginably rich interconnections of the actual Earth newly vivid."[17] The initial two-year closure experiment was meant to be the first of fifty such experiments, with the aim of improving incrementally each time. As a starting point, the first closure went better than expected. For instance, 30 percent of the species inside went "extinct," but researchers had predicted up to 70 percent.

At the time of writing, Biosphere 2 still stands, having been donated to the University of Arizona in 2011. From the outside, it looks like a shadow of its former self. The windows are murky without sufficient funds to employ a full-time crew to keep them clean, and rust accumulates on the structure. But inside, Biosphere 2 remains full of life. Many of the microcosms within it are thriving, having found the equilibrium they need to function as they would in the outside world. Researchers still utilize it as a unique place for valuable controlled experiments they can't easily do anywhere else.

Conclusion

Equilibrium is the state of balance, the point where opposing forces cancel each other out. It's the calm in the center of the storm, the stable point around which the chaos swirls. In a system at equilibrium, there's no net change. Everything is in a steady state, humming along at a constant pace.

However, systems are rarely static. They are continuously adjusting toward equilibrium, but they rarely stay in balance for long.

Equilibrium is a double-edged sword, both stability and stagnation. In our lives we often act like we can reach an equilibrium: once we get into a relationship, we'll be happy; once we move, we'll be productive; once X thing happens, we'll be in Y state. But things are always in flux. We don't reach a certain steady state and then stay there forever. The endless adjustments are our lives. The trick is to find the right balance, to strive for equilibrium where it's needed, but to also know when to break free, to embrace the disequilibrium that drives progress.

Bottlenecks

The limiting factor.

All systems have parts that are slower than others. The slowest part of a system is called the "bottleneck" because, as the neck of a bottle limits the amount of liquid that can flow through, bottlenecks in systems limit the amount of outputs they can produce. Viewing systems through the lens of their bottlenecks offers us a powerful perspective: these constraints can either stifle our progress or serve as a strategic choke point that, when managed wisely, can compel efficiency and innovation.

No one wants to be a bottleneck, which is easily conceptualized as that person who makes everyone else wait. We see this behavior in people who can't delegate. If you insist on making every decision yourself, there's likely a long line of people twiddling their thumbs as they wait for you to move their projects forward while you are overwhelmed.

Bottlenecks tend to create waste as resources pile up behind them. In manufacturing, they limit how much you can produce and sell. If you work in an industry that depends on timely information, then you risk inputs becoming irrelevant before they make it through the bottleneck.

A bottleneck is also the point that is most under strain. It can be the part that is most likely to break down or has the most impact if it does. In trying to improve the flow of your system, focusing on anything besides the bottleneck is a waste of time. You will just create more pressure on the bottleneck, further increasing how much it holds you back by generating more buildup.

Every system has a bottleneck. You cannot completely eliminate them because once you remove one, another part of the system becomes the new limiting factor. You can, however, anticipate bottlenecks and plan accordingly. Or you can leverage the need to overcome them as an impetus for finding new ways of making a system work. Sometimes you can overcome bottlenecks by adding

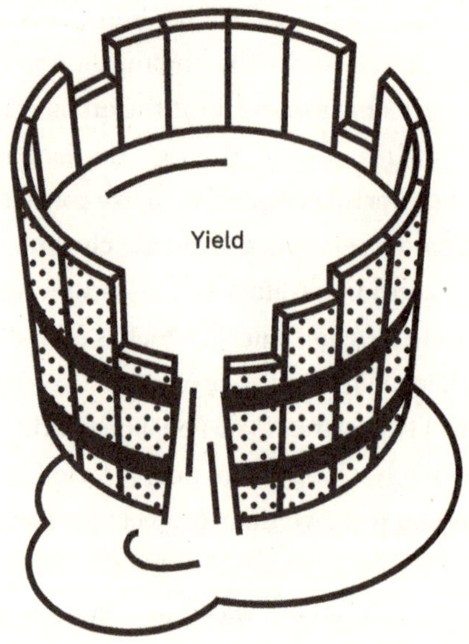

Liebig's law of the minimum refers to the idea that a plant's growth will be limited by the nutrient that is least available. Yield is thus constrained by resource limitation.

more of the same, such as dedicating more resources to ease the pressure on a bottleneck. But sometimes the sole solution is to rethink that part of the system.

What you want to avoid is opening one bottleneck only to create additional, worse ones for yourself later. If bottlenecks are unavoidable, we at least want them to be in a less disruptive place.

Although the terms are sometimes used interchangeably, a bottleneck is different from a constraint. A bottleneck is something we can alleviate; a constraint is a fundamental limitation of the system. So a machine that keeps breaking down is a bottleneck, but the fact that there are twenty-four hours in the day is a constraint.

Be vigilant for masqueraders in the system—those false dependencies that pose as bottlenecks. Like the illusionists of the machine, they divert attention and resources as if they hold sway over the throughput, when in reality they're just specters of constraint, not its substance. We often hear explanations in the form of: "I won't do X before Y." Most statements of this type are only in place to make you feel good about procrastinating when you are the bottleneck. For example, you might say you will start writing every day once you move and have a dedicated desk for it. If the bottleneck is a lack of a suitable workspace, then moving will alleviate it. But if the bottleneck is something else, like time or ideas, you're setting up a false dependency. The bottleneck will still be there once you move. Even if the problem is your workspace, you could still find ways to make progress, such as by going to the library or reading source material. Anything you do now will make it easier to get into the habit of daily writing.

If you think you've identified a bottleneck, it's a good idea to do what you can to validate that this is indeed the limiting factor. Otherwise, you might end up solving the wrong problem.

The Trans-Siberian Railway

How you deal with your bottleneck can have huge impacts on the overall quality of your system. Often, we tend to just take care of the bottleneck no matter the cost. But there is always one in every system. Some bottlenecks are better to have than others because they are easier to organize the rest of our system around.

The building of the Trans-Siberian Railway (TSR) was a complicated project with many moving parts that borrowed from future resources to address its bottleneck. It is both an inspiring and cautionary tale, as sometimes dealing with bottlenecks in the most expedient way possible can cause significant issues later. Part of solving a bottleneck is anticipating the consequences.

The TSR was a massive undertaking. Not only is it the longest railway in the world, but the challenges in building over that distance were unmatched at the time. The railway spans the entirety of Russia from Saint Petersburg in the west, close to Finland, to Vladivostok on the Sea of Japan just east of North Korea.

As W. Bruce Lincoln describes in *The Conquest of a Continent*, there were multiple challenges to building the TSR:

> Construction crews would have to work thousands of miles away from their bases of supply. Rails and bridge iron would have to be brought to Siberia from foundries as far away as St. Petersburg and Warsaw, ties would have to be cut in European Russia and shipped across the Urals because almost no hardwoods grew in the steppe or the taiga, and stone for bridge piers and abutments would have to be transported from quarries on the western frontier of Mongolia. Then, as the tracklayers moved deeper into Siberia, terrain and climate would magnify the obstacles. Then endless forest, the

> gorges cut from solid rock, the mountains of the Transbaikal, the treacherous permafrost, the short winter days, and the deep, deep Siberian cold all presented obstacles on a scale that the world's builders had yet to face.[1]

Given the scope of the undertaking—9,458 kilometers, two to three times longer than the transcontinental railways that had been built in North America at the time—it's not surprising that addressing a bottleneck could have far-reaching consequences.

One critical point about bottlenecks is they can move around systems. You fix one only to introduce another. In *The Chip,* T. R. Reid gives an example of shifting a bottleneck that threatened an entire system. He describes a textile factory that started falling far behind its normal production rate. To figure out what was going on, the factory manager followed the output process on the production floor. They found the employees constantly had to rethread their sewing machines because a cheaper thread they'd bought kept breaking. To save fifteen cents per spool, they were losing $150 per hour in production output.[2]

The TSR was a complex undertaking, so attempts to alleviate a bottleneck could easily cause unanticipated consequences. Problems beset the project. There was a continual shortage of local supplies. There were limits to construction schedules caused by the seasonal weather. The fact that all decisions about the railway had to go through a central committee in Saint Petersburg with a weeks-long communication delay created uncoordinated short-term solutions to problems.

In addition, the deepest lake in the world sits in the middle of the route. Originally the main line stopped on one side of the lake and goods were ferried across to the rail continuation on the other shore. This created a huge physical bottleneck in terms of the movement of goods and people until a track was completed around the lake's southern shore decades after the main line was built.

Finally, and perhaps most critically for the actual construction, an extreme shortage of labor created a bottleneck that had significant impacts on the functioning of the other parts of the system.

The railway was built as five separate projects that were worked on simultaneously. One of the consequences of deciding to work this way was that the railroad wasn't treated as one project when it came to labor. Each of the five projects competed with the others for the same pool of resources.

The desire to shorten the total building time resulted in a trade-off that augmented the labor bottleneck. As Christian Wolmar explains in *To the Edge of the World,* this construction approach created a competition for resources that, combined with a low local population density, meant there weren't enough locally available workers. They had to be imported.[3] In order to ease the pressure on the labor bottleneck, skilled workers were imported from all over Europe to work along the length of the TSR. For the eastern section, thousands of workers were brought in from China, Japan, and Korea. And on all parts except the middle section that ran through the Siberian prison camp area, convicts were used in the construction of the track.

The enormous time pressures placed on the men charged with building the railway meant that the labor bottlenecks were often addressed with excessive sums paid to contractors. Thus labor absorbed most of the money available for the project. As Wolmar describes, local peasant contractors were unsupervised, and there was no competitive tendering process. Contractors "often asked for extra payment, once work had begun, as they knew that there was no alternative supplier because the imperative was to get the job done quickly."[4]

The problem with easing the pressure on the labor bottleneck by subcontracting the work to those without sufficient experience manifested on the train track itself. The incentive for the contractors was to pocket money in the short term. The labor shortage could be solved with money, yet there was only so much funding available. Something had to give. What got sacrificed was safety. "With very little supervision of the work, contractors boosted their profits by skimping on material or building below the required standard, resulting in embankments that were too narrow, insufficient ballast, inadequate drainage and a host of other failings."[5] To save money on building materials because the labor was so expensive (and the cut directly pocketed by the subcontractor so high), the inclines in many places were too steep and the curves too tight. It was a dangerous railway.

For the TSR, solving the labor shortage created a materials bottleneck because the money used to solve the labor problem meant there wasn't enough left over to purchase quality materials. The central committee thousands of miles away could not keep up with the demands to solve workmanship and safety issues. They were unable to react fast enough, so the integrity of the track was compromised.

Despite the remarkable achievement of building the TSR, the cost-cutting on materials and the shortening of the route through unsuitable terrain with steep grades and tight corners meant it had problems from the start. Wolmar explains, "Almost as soon as each section of the line was completed, improvements had to be made to ensure it was functioning properly."[6] Even with the sustained effort, the locomotives wore out quickly, goods were shipped painfully slowly, and accidents and deaths occurred all the time.

Spending money without quality assurance only moves problems into the future. Russia effectively had to build the same railroad multiple times because the first track was almost unusable.

On a project with the scope of the TSR, bottlenecks are inevitable. Identifying them and planning how to manage them is part of the process of construction. The lesson here is to be careful how we address bottlenecks so that we don't create huge problems for ourselves later on.

Often when we encounter a bottleneck, we patch it over, and it bounces back to being a bottleneck again. On the TSR, the money used to solve the labor shortage also created incentives to keep that shortage going. Throwing money at the problem without understanding the system is unlikely to yield the intended benefits.

Instead of addressing bottlenecks as they appear, your time might be better spent on a root-cause fix that makes a foundational improvement that leads many bottlenecks to disappear indefinitely. One way to achieve foundational improvement is to simulate conditions you are likely to face to try to find bottlenecks ahead of time. Instead of merely fixing the problem, we can solve a bottleneck by asking how the system could be designed to not have that problem in the first place. Addressing bottlenecks is a never-ending job and must always be factored into your planning.

Bottlenecks and Innovation

Bottlenecks inspire innovation. When a limit emerges, we're often forced to try something new to alleviate it. Many inventions come about as the result of shortages that prompt us to find alternatives.

Innovating as a response to bottlenecks is common during wars, when default materials may be unobtainable. Looking at the past century, many things we now use regularly were invented in times of conflict to alleviate bottlenecks in supply.

Nylon was the first synthetic fiber, and today we use it in everything from swimwear and fishing nets to seat belts and tents. It's light, strong, and waterproof—in other words, versatile and practical.[7] Nylon was invented in the early 1930s as an alternative to silk and began commercial production toward the end of the decade. The United States obtained most of its silk from Japan at the time but risked losing access due to rising tensions between the two nations. Nylon eliminated that bottleneck by providing an alternative material manufactured in the United States.

While it was invented in response to a shortage, it proved to have advantages over silk in common products as well as new uses. In particular, nylon stockings were popular during the early 1940s, before nylon's production was diverted for military purposes. It served an essential wartime role as parachute and tent material. DuPont, the inventors of nylon, decided not to trademark it so it would seem like a material in itself, not a brand.[8] By being in the public domain and available for experimentation and development, nylon continues to find many uses.

Similarly, the United States had difficulties obtaining rubber during World War II due to conflict with Japan. Ameripol, a synthetic rubber that didn't rely on access to Asian natural resources, was invented by chemist Waldo Semon as an alternative.[9] Not having any rubber would have been disastrous for the war, as it was integral for practically every item and device used in the fighting, in particular tires. Without rubber, as innocuous as it seems, vehicles like planes and tanks wouldn't have been able to operate. It's very possible that without the rapid effort to invent a viable form of synthetic rubber and develop the capacity to produce almost a million tons of it, the Allies would have lost the war.[10] Now most rubber is synthetic.

Medical science tends to advance the fastest during wars. Facing new demands and shortages of essential supplies, people find creative ways to deal with injuries and diseases. During the American

Civil War, dozens of new types of prosthetic limbs were invented, and surgeons became more adept at using ligatures. At the start of the war, the mortality rate from infections was 60 percent. By the end, it was 3 percent.[11] During World War II, production capabilities for penicillin skyrocketed.[12]

During World War I, many people became malnourished or undernourished due to food rationing. Nutrients became a bottleneck. Lack of adequate food was problematic for children, many of whom developed rickets (soft bones due to vitamin D deficiency). Many soldiers suffered serious bone breakage. Kurt Huldschinsky, a doctor working in Berlin, discovered he could cure rickets by seating children in front of an ultraviolet lamp. Research after the war identified why this worked: a sun lamp simulates sunlight and prompts the body to produce vitamin D, thereby helping to alleviate the bottleneck in access to nutritious food caused by the war. Today sun lamps are a common medical tool for everything from skin conditions to seasonal affective disorder.[13]

The need to overcome the effects of a lack of nutritious food led to the invention of an alternative way of meeting people's nutritional needs. Wartime medical innovations that developed as a response to bottlenecks have, in many cases, ended up benefiting everyone.

Conclusion

Bottlenecks are the choke points, the narrow parts of the hourglass where everything slows down. They're the constraints that limit the flow, the weakest links in the chain that determine the strength of the whole. In any system, the bottleneck is the part that's holding everything else back.

The tricky thing about bottlenecks is that they're not always obvious. It's easy to focus on the parts of the system that are moving quickly and assume everything is fine. But the real leverage is in finding and fixing the bottlenecks. Speed up the slowest part, and you speed up the whole system.

This is the theory of constraints in a nutshell. Figure out what your bottleneck is and focus all your efforts on alleviating it. Don't waste time optimizing the parts that are already fast. They're not the limiting factor.

However, bottlenecks aren't always the villains we make them out to be. Sometimes, they're a necessary part of the system. Think of a security checkpoint at an airport. It slows everything down, but it's there for a reason. Remove it, and you might speed things up, but at the cost of safety.

The key is to be intentional about your bottlenecks. Choose them wisely, and make sure they're serving a purpose. A deliberate bottleneck can be a powerful tool for focusing effort and maintaining quality. An accidental bottleneck is just a drag on the system.

Bottlenecks are the leverage points, the places where a little effort can go a long way.

Scale

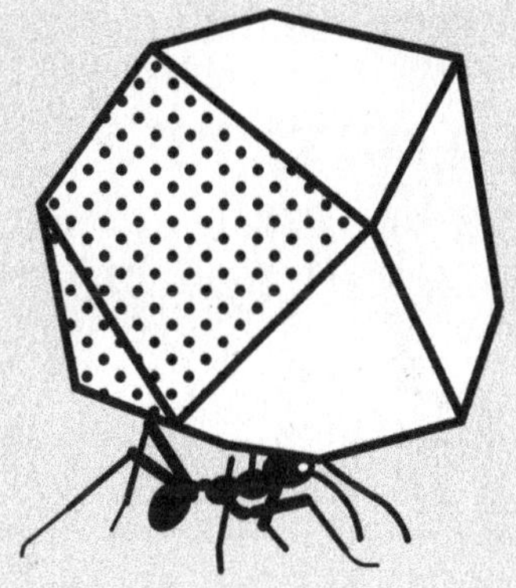

Bigger or smaller = different.

If you do not look at things on a large scale, it will be difficult to master strategy.

—MIYAMOTO MUSASHI[1]

Systems come in a variety of sizes, and they change as they scale up or down. Staying small can sometimes be a strategic choice, a way to avoid the growing pains that would force unwanted changes.

Scaling up is rarely simply a matter of multiplication. Take baking as an example: double the dough doesn't mean double the bread. The geometry of growth affects the pace of fermentation. Size influences function, a principle as true in baking as in building businesses. Understanding scale means recognizing that what works in a small setup may falter when magnified.

When we study a complex system, it's beneficial to consider how its functioning behaves differently at different scales. Looking at the micro level may mislead us about the macro, and vice versa. As systems expand, complexity does too; more connections breed more potential blockages. Thus, it's important to combine scale with bottlenecks. As systems become larger, different parts might struggle to keep up. Imagining your business scaling up in some areas faster than others lets you anticipate breakages and bottlenecks.

To give an example of how things change as they scale, consider a company at two different sizes. For a small company with a handful of people with close personal relationships working together in a garage, there's no need for an HR department or management consultants. They can work together and solve problems face-to-face. Proximity can discourage them from letting too much tension build up. No one is going to steal a coworker's lunch from the fridge because it's a tight-knit group and the culprit would be obvious.

Fast-forward a few years and the company is larger, with six hundred employees in several offices. Many have never met, and few are friends. Scaling up means the system has completely changed. It's now necessary to hire people whose entire job is to organize and make sure everyone gets along. To avoid communication bottlenecks, the company divides into teams, meaning they are better able to manage social dynamics. Provided links remain between parts, systems can safely scale in this fashion: by dividing into parts. But things will always be different as a system scales, and a collection of teams within a company will never be able to communicate like individuals in a small company. The larger the company grows, the more work it takes to ensure information flows to the right places.

As companies increase in scale, parts of the system break because what works for ten people doesn't typically work for a thousand. As changes to the system are implemented in response to growth, the question always is: How will this system fare in the next year? Ten years? A hundred years? In other words, how well will it age?

As growth occurs, resilience can be increased by keeping a measure of independence between parts of a system. Macro dependencies tend to age poorly because they rely on every one of their micro dependencies aging well.

Economies of Scale

In economics, production processes change as they scale. The more of something that is produced, the more the marginal cost of each additional unit tends to shrink. As more people can afford a product, demand tends to increase. Owning it may become a norm or habit. Economies of scale work because they enable cost-cutting measures, such as purchasing materials in bulk. Systems do not scale indefinitely; economies of scale begin to break after a certain point. Eventually, saving any more money becomes impossible, or there may be no more possible customers. In addition, limitations exist when there are dependencies on finite resources, such as energy, raw material, or computing power.

Long-Lived Japanese Family-Run Companies

Success often sows the seeds of its own destruction. Sometimes getting bigger means becoming more vulnerable, and some things are most apt to survive if they stay small. After all, the majority of species on this planet are insects—tiny, simple creatures that move quickly when a potential threat arrives.

In business, scaling is often seen as inherently good. The bigger a company gets, the more successful we consider it. We hear laudatory stories of how fast new companies grow—hiring more people, opening new offices, and spreading their products or services to vast new audiences. But getting bigger can make companies more fragile. During difficult economic times, companies that scaled too fast can struggle to sustain themselves. Sometimes, when longevity is the goal, staying small and simple can be a superpower.

Most businesses fail in the first few years. The largest companies around at any given point in time, however mighty they may seem in the moment, don't last long. The average life span of an S&P 500 company is twenty-four years, and this number is decreasing over time.[2] In most parts of the world, a company lasting a few decades is remarkable. Yet in Japan, that's not the case. The country is home to an astonishing number of incredibly old companies, known as *shinise*.[3] Over 50,000 Japanese companies are more than a century old, with nearly 4,000 dating back over 200 years.[4]

Why are long-lived companies more common in Japan than in the rest of the world? It's impossible to know for certain. But most of the oldest companies have something in common: the way they scale. Or rather, the way they *don't* scale.

Long-lived Japanese companies tend to be small. They're owned and run by relatives and people with close relationships. They usually have fewer than a hundred employees and trade within a small area in Japan. Durable, loyal customer relationships are integral to their business models. Also, they are driven by a strong internal philosophy that goes beyond their products and services, enabling them to adapt to changing times.

By staying small, long-lived Japanese companies can hold on to their traditional values. Being no larger than necessary benefits them during less favorable economic conditions. In a small team where a job may last a lifetime, diffusion of responsibility is less of a problem, as there's nowhere to hide. Employees may be more invested and take their work as a point of pride.

Take the case of perhaps the most famous long-lived Japanese company, Kongo Gumi. A construction company specializing in high-quality Buddhist temples, it operated independently from 578 AD to 2006. Today it exists as a subsidiary of a larger company. At the time of Kongo Gumi's liquidation, it was the oldest company in the world, having built Japan's first-ever Buddhist temple. All that time, it remained in the hands of the same family—forty generations of them. Each owner passed the company on to his oldest son.[5] However, to ensure this close-knit succession system worked no matter what, it had some flexibility. If the oldest son didn't have the right leadership potential, a younger son would take over. If none of the sons were suitable or an owner had no male children, they would choose a suitable husband for a daughter and then adopt him. Adult adoption for business purposes is a common practice in Japan even today, enabling companies to stay within a single family for many generations.[6] At one point, the widowed wife of an owner took charge of Kongo Gumi.[7]

To give context for the length of time Kongo Gumi remained in operation building iconic temples, at the time of its founding, the Roman Empire had just collapsed. The prophet Muhammad was not yet a decade old.[8] The world changed a great deal between then and 2006. Kongo Gumi survived numerous wars, periods of immense political upheaval, economic crises, and other disasters. It managed this by adapting to the times. For instance, during World War II, demand for Buddhist temples was low. The company switched to making coffins.

Other notable long-lived Japanese companies also keep things small and within a single family. The same family has owned the Tsuen Tea shop for twenty-four generations and the Nishiyama Onsen Keiunkan inn for fifty-two. In some cases, even the staff pass on their jobs to their children. Other companies of comparable ages may not have remained in the possession of their founders' descendants but were under the ownership of the same families for long periods.

Scaling up is not always advantageous. Systems change as they get bigger or smaller, and so, depending on your goals and desires, staying small and flexible might be the ideal choice to realize them.

> Scaling up from the small to the large is often accompanied by an evolution from simplicity to complexity while maintaining basic elements or building blocks of the system unchanged or conserved.
>
> —GEOFFREY WEST[9]

On Being the Right Size

In 1928, British-Indian scientist J. B. S. Haldane published an essay titled "On Being the Right Size," which explores the role of scale in biology. Different animals are of different sizes. What's less obvious is the link between an animal's size and its appearance. In general, it would be impossible for a species to become much bigger without changing its appearance.

For instance, Haldane imagines what would happen if a gazelle became much larger. The only way its long legs would be able to support its weight would be by either becoming short and thick, or long and spindly but with a smaller body. Incidentally this is how rhinoceroses and giraffes manage.

Not only does changing an animal's scale require it to look different, but it also transforms the impact of gravity on it. "You can drop a mouse down a thousand-yard mine shaft," Haldane writes, "and, on arriving at the bottom, it gets a slight shock and walks away, provided that the ground is fairly soft. A rat is killed, a man is broken, a horse splashes." The reason is air resistance, which prevents a mouse from falling too fast due to the ratio between its weight and surface area.

The Story of Illumination

We often think linearly: If we double our inputs, we'll get double the outputs. It's hard for us to imagine that double our inputs will give us half the amount of outputs, or four times the amount. Understanding that systems can scale nonlinearly is useful because it helps us appreciate how much a system can change as it grows.

Since the dawn of time, humans have had to contend with one of our greatest foes: the dark. Once the sun goes down, without artificial light our eyes are ill-equipped to see our surroundings, and we cannot keep watch for danger. Nor can we carry out useful daytime activities like making tools or foraging for food. For this reason, throughout history people have been willing to put a remarkable amount of effort and ingenuity into developing artificial light and making it better, safer, cheaper, and accessible to more people. Each time the technology available to supply us with light has improved, there have been two interesting results. We've had to scale up the infrastructure necessary to fuel it, and we've changed our productivity scale.

The first attempts humans made at illumination, around forty thousand years ago, were simple unworked pieces of limestone with a smidgeon of burning animal fat, held in cupped hands. As time progressed, people used shells, then fashioned lamps out of pottery, making incremental improvements to the design.[10] Early lamps took little work to power, but their light had a tiny range and went out easily. They extended the range of human activity only a little, though it was enough to allow us to make art on the walls of caves.

While the Romans likely made the first beeswax candles, cost considerations meant that for many more centuries, most people used any available form of oil for lighting.[11] There were no elaborate systems behind this activity; people made their own fuel. It was labor-intensive to make and maintain, and still only brightened the night a fraction, but it was enough that the value of artificial light was evident.

It can be hard for us to imagine how lacking an effective means of artificial light limited the scale of human activity. Light allowed productive time to scale. People could work longer and produce more.

There was a time when all the women in a village would cluster in one cottage at night, sit in a tiered circle around a single lamp, and share its rays as they sewed, made lace, and the like.[12] They were limited to whatever work they could manage with their share of the light. Outside, the streets would remain dark until the seventeenth century. Most activities outside the home were restricted to daylight hours, which kept the world small. Unless you were rich, brave (or foolhardy), or doing something illegal, the night was off-limits for most activities. In cities throughout Europe in the Middle Ages, night meant a total shutdown. The city gates closed, chains ran across roads to prevent movement, and a night watch patrolled the streets to ensure no one was out.[13]

Moving into the eighteenth century, whale oil became a widespread choice for lamp fuel. This led to a drastic change. For the first time, people fueled their lights with something they hadn't made themselves. Whale oil came from far away and was purchased in its prepared form. The system required to make whale oil was a huge increase in scale from people producing their own forms of fuel. It took elaborate, dangerous operations aboard ships to find, kill, and extract oil from whales, each of which could yield up to eighteen hundred gallons of the fuel.[14] Light was an industry for the first time. For individuals, purchasing fuel was more efficient than making it themselves.

However, the light produced by burning whale oil was still no brighter than that from older forms of oil. The next change in artificial lighting would require a giant change in the scale of the surrounding systems. The transition from candles and oil lamps to gas also enabled human affairs to scale up, transforming areas such as factory work.[15]

The production of coke (a type of coal-based fuel) created a byproduct of burnt gas, which made for a much clearer, stronger flame than anything to come before it.[16] Factories embraced it first, for it offered a way to approximate the kinds of precise work previously possible only in daylight. In *Disenchanted Night,* Wolfgang Schivelbusch says, "Modern gas lighting began as industrial lighting." The new artificial light, he explains, "emancipated the working day from its dependence on natural daylight . . . Work processes were no longer regulated by the individual worker . . . In the factories, night was turned to day more consistently than anywhere else."[17] Factories could scale up production and run at any time of day, all year round.

Though the first gas systems were built for individual factories and dwellings, inventor Frederick Albert Winsor came up with the idea of a centralized supply connected via underground pipes to all the buildings in an area.[18] This would be cheaper, decreasing the marginal price of adding more users, as well as cementing gas's place as an essential utility for the modern home.

Here we see another increase in the scale of the systems surrounding lighting. Not only did gas have its own production system outside the home, it also had its own distribution system, further removing people from the process of making their light. They didn't even have to tend gas lamps to keep them working; they just turned them on and off.[19]

Jane Brox writes in *Brilliant* that "gaslight divided light—and life—from its singular, self-reliant past. All was now interconnected, contingent, and intricate." People's homes became part of a larger system.[20]

Two consequences of this increased scale were, as Schivelbusch argues, the loss of autonomy for individual households and the regulation of utilities in geographical areas. Houses became part of an infrastructure that increased the scale of the city. Gas lighting provided for households many of the same benefits it gave to industries—activities were no longer bound by the availability of daylight or constrained by the cost and coverage of a candle. But households became dependent on infrastructure they had very little say in.

Gas also scaled up what people could do during the night out on the city streets. Gas streetlamps soon became widespread in cities in England and the United States. No longer did people have to hide away at night while armed watchmen prowled the streets. Now "nightlife" came into existence as a concept.[21] New activities or better versions of old ones became possible: coffeehouses and taverns stayed open late as patrons socialized, shops lit up their windows so people could window-shop their wares, areas of cities grew famous for their beautiful appearance at night, and theaters could create visual effects and better distinguish the stage from the audience.[22]

Artificial light increased the scale of what we could see at night and thus opened up new businesses and new ways of conducting one's day. Festivities and holiday celebrations began to move later and later into the evening.

With the advent of electricity—a means of making light without fire—nighttime activity was able to further scale up by an order of magnitude. Once electric technology progressed, it was much cheaper, safer, and easier to use for the end consumer, and it could evenly light a whole space as well as the sun could.

Electric light was at first an oddity that seemed to possess no practical value. Humphry Davy discovered the arc light, which used carbon sticks, but it faced the problem of being too bright and short-lived to be practical. Inventing the incandescent bulb would take several more decades of problem-solving, with Thomas Edison and his lab finding the right filament material for bulbs that could scale.[23]

Having solved that problem, Edison needed a way to supply electricity to homes. As Jane Brox explains it, gas was both a rival and an inspiration. Edison copied the concept of a central supply with a grid connecting houses. As with gas, factories proved eager customers, especially those that used flammable materials.[24] Manufacturers soon learned that with electric light, they could operate all the time, increasing profits by running shifts during the night. Time of day ceased to matter in the factory.[25] Every moment of the day could be productive, eliminating one of the biggest limitations on human activity.

Achieving the ambition of supplying as many people as possible with electric light required creating supporting systems on a whole new scale. It meant digging tunnels for cables and building power stations. Generating electricity meant massive-scale engineering undertakings, like utilizing the power of the Niagara Falls.[26] The electric grid, which continues to connect ever more people around the world by transmitting electricity from power plants via power lines, would end up being one of humanity's greatest ideas.[27]

As light coverage increased, new concerns emerged. As Schivelbusch notes, "The twentieth century was to experience this relentless light to the full. The glaring and shadowless light that illuminates H. G. Wells' negative Utopias, no longer guarantees the security of the individual. It permits total surveillance by the state." As the coverage of artificial light has scaled up, the opportunities for and constraints on individuals have changed. As wonderful as artificial light is for navigation and safety, most of us realize it has limits. To banish darkness suggests "a nightmare of a light from which there is no escape."[28]

Artificial light changed the scale at which human activities can happen. In many ways, the limits of our lights are the limits of our world. There are still places where we lack the means to eradicate darkness, such as outer space and the deepest parts of the oceans.

When you scale up a system, the problems you solved at the smaller scale often need solving again at a larger scale. In addition, you end up with unanticipated possibilities and outcomes. As the scale increases, so does its impact on other systems. Increasing the size of a system does not result in just more of the same; there are often new impacts and requirements as the system develops new capabilities.

Looking at the development of artificial light through the lens of scale, we see how important it is to be aware of how scale changes might impact the system as a whole. A more interconnected, larger system may be able to handle variations better, but it may also be vulnerable to widespread failures. Increasing the scale of a system might mean using new materials or incorporating methods like the ones that worked on a smaller scale. Or it might mean rethinking your whole approach.

Conclusion

Systems change as they scale up or down, and neither is intrinsically better or worse. The right scale depends on your goals and the context. If you want to scale something up, you need to anticipate that new problems will keep arising—problems that didn't exist at a smaller scale. Or you might need to keep solving the same problems in different ways.

Think about a recipe. If you're making a cake for four people, you use a certain amount of ingredients. But if you want to make a cake for four hundred people, you don't just multiply the ingredients by one hundred. That's not how scale works. You need to change the process, use bigger mixers, bigger ovens. You need a system that can handle the increased volume without breaking down.

The challenge with scale is that it's not always obvious how to achieve it. What works for a small system often breaks down at larger volumes. You have to anticipate the bottlenecks, the points where the system will start to strain under the increased load. And you have to be ready to re-engineer your processes as you grow.

If you're building something, always be thinking about scale. How will this work when you have ten times as many customers? One hundred times? One thousand times? Build with scale in mind from the start, and you'll be ready for the growth when it comes.

Margin of Safety

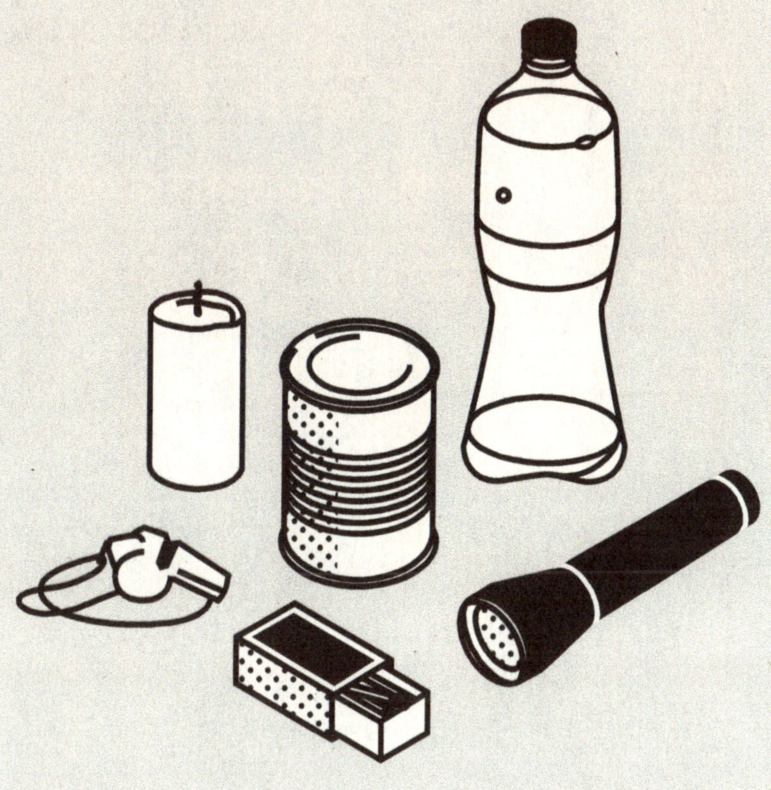

Expect the unexpected.

This world of ours appears to be separated by a slight and precarious margin of safety from a most singular and unexpected danger.

—ARTHUR CONAN DOYLE[1]

When we interact with complex systems, we need to expect the unexpected. Systems do not always function as anticipated. They are subject to variable conditions and can respond to inputs in nonlinear ways.

A margin of safety is necessary to ensure systems can handle stressors and unpredictable circumstances. This means there is a meaningful gap between what a system is capable of handling and what it is required to handle. Think of the margin of safety like a buffer zone or extra space on a busy highway; it's the wiggle room you keep between you and the car in front, so you have time to react if something unexpected happens. It's the extra bit you don't use unless you really need it, ensuring you stay safe even when things get a bit wild. A margin of safety is a buffer between safety and danger, order and chaos, success and failure. It ensures a system does not swing from one to the other too easily, causing damage.

Engineers know to design for extremes, not averages. In engineering, it's necessary to consider the most something might need to handle—then add on an extra buffer. If five thousand cars are going to drive across a bridge on an average day, it would be unwise to construct it to be capable of handling precisely that number. What if there were an unusual number of buses or trucks on a particular day? What if there were strong winds? What if there were a big sports match in the area, and twice as many people want to cross the bridge? What if the population of the area is much higher in a decade? Whoever designs the bridge needs to add on a big margin of safety so it stays strong even when many more than five thousand cars cross it in a day. A large margin of safety doesn't eliminate the possibility of failure, but it reduces it.

For investors, a margin of safety is the gap between an investment's intrinsic value and its price. The higher the margin of safety, the safer the investment and the greater the potential profit. Because intrinsic value is subjective, it's best this buffer be as large as possible to account for uncertainty.[2]

Margin of safety is the wisdom of having an emergency fund, health insurance, and friends you can call on if needed. You need it the most when you don't have it. It's wise to build in margins of safety in all areas of life, and the more you cultivate them, the safer and more prepared you'll feel for anything life throws your way.

When calculating the ideal margin of safety, we always need to consider how high the stakes are. The greater the cost of failure, the bigger the buffer should be.

To create a margin of safety, complex systems can utilize backups—in the form of spare components, capacities, or subsystems—to function when things go wrong. Backups make the system resilient. If an error occurs or something gets broken, the system can keep functioning. One way to think of backups is as an alternate path, like how you might have multiple routes to your office in mind so you can still get there if there's a car accident blocking one road. A system can't keep working indefinitely without anything breaking down. One without backups is unlikely to function for long.

As with margins of safety, the higher the stakes, the greater the need for backups. If a part in your pen breaks, it's not a big deal. If a critical part in an airplane breaks, it's a different story. If you're going to the local shops, taking your phone in case you need to communicate with anyone is sufficient. If you're going hiking in the wilderness alone, you might want more than one communication method. You're safer in an airplane than in a car, in part because it has so much backup; after all, the cost of failure is higher.

We have to be careful with margins of safety, as they can make us overconfident. If we get too reckless, we cancel out the benefits. When humans are involved in a system, too much margin of safety or backup can lead to risk compensation. For instance, we all know we should wear a seat belt in a car, but do they make us safer? Some research suggests they might not reduce car accident fatalities because people drive with less care, feeling there is a margin of safety between them and injury. This puts pedestrians and passengers at a higher risk even if drivers are safer.[3] Still, seat belts save lives, and most of us would feel at least slightly uncomfortable riding in a car with a driver or front-seat passenger not wearing one.

The risk of a system failure is not fixed. Failure rates can remain consistent when humans are involved because margins of safety sometimes create perverse incentives. If we change our behavior in response to the knowledge that we have a margin of safety in place, we may end up reducing or negating its benefits. Setting your watch fifteen minutes ahead could help you be on time more often. If you follow the time it displays, you'll have a buffer in case of delays. But if you remember the time is wrong and amend it in your head, it won't make any difference to your punctuality.

Conversely, margins of safety and backups can also make us too cautious. Not all situations we face are like building a bridge, in which it either stands or doesn't and collapsing results in death. There is a difference between what's uncomfortable and what ruins you. Most systems can be down for an hour. Our bodies can go without food or water for days. Most businesses can do without revenue for a little while. Too much margin of safety could be a waste of resources and can sow the seeds of becoming uncompetitive. If you know it's impossible to fail, you get complacent. But too little margin of safety can lead to destruction. You won't be able to weather inevitable shocks.

Minimum Effective Dose

The difference between medicine and poison is in the dose. Too much of a beneficial substance can be harmful or lethal, and a tiny amount of a harmful substance can have beneficial effects. It's necessary for doctors to give patients doses of medication that are high enough to be effective but not so high as to be dangerous. However, prescribing a bit less than the harmful amount isn't much good; a patient could take too much or take their doses too close together.

So pharmacologists calculate the minimum effective dose: the lowest possible amount of a medication to achieve a meaningful benefit in the average patient. Then they calculate the maximum tolerated dose: the largest amount an average patient could take without suffering harm. For example, a vaccine contains the minimum possible dose of a virus necessary to get the body to produce an immune response. Too much could cause actual illness; too little would not be protective. Knowing this window means doctors can ensure a margin of safety by starting with a low dose they know is still likely to work.

Learning as a Margin of Safety

How can we develop a margin of safety in our lives?

Things go wrong, at least once in a while, and it would be ideal to increase our resilience in the face of dramatic change by having a built-in margin of safety. One way of applying this model on an individual level is learning.

The more we learn, the fewer blind spots we have. Blind spots are the source of all mistakes. While learning more than we need to get the job done can appear inefficient, the corresponding reduction in blind spots offers a margin of safety. Knowledge allows us to adapt to changing situations.

The best way to learn? Books, nonfiction or fiction. Books offer vicarious experience—they put you in a character's shoes, so you experience the consequences of their mistakes without making them yourself. Most people have been tempted to cheat on their partners, but through Anna Karenina you experience the dissolution of family that an affair causes. Most people are tempted to punish thieves, but through Bishop Myriel in *Les Misérables,* you learn that one act of kindness can be transforming. It's infinitely easier to learn these lessons through a book than by living them out in real life.

One profession that demands that an individual have far more knowledge than they will ever use is astronaut. Carrying out your job in the hostile environment of space means that you have to prepare for as many variables as possible in order to have the best potential response to any challenge. Learning is a way for an astronaut to develop a large margin of safety, giving them the chance to deal with the unexpected in space. The human capacity for not only learning but also the ability to flexibly apply knowledge in novel situations is one of the main reasons we need astronauts in space. They respond to new information, use creativity, and make assessments in a way that only humans can.

In his book *An Astronaut's Guide to Life on Earth,* Chris Hadfield explains how and why astronauts learn as much as they can. They don't stop at what they need to know but continue lifelong learning to prepare for any eventuality they can think of. They reduce blind spots. He says of astronauts, "No matter how competent or how seasoned, every astronaut is essentially a perpetual student."[4] They are "trained to look on the dark side and to imagine the worst things that could possibly happen."[5] And then they train for them. Hadfield describes hours in simulators and classrooms, constantly training and preparing for an incredibly vast array of potential scenarios.

The culture of the space program is one of constant debriefs about every detail. The point of these is not to be pedantic or shame anyone but to get the information necessary to learn and to improve the program. Thus for both the individual astronaut and the space organization they are a part of, there is a recognition that ongoing learning is the key element in creating a margin of safety in space operations.

Although astronauts are well educated and very experienced, they come into the space program with an incredible amount to learn. Hadfield says of his early career, "Training in Houston, I hadn't been able to separate out the vital from the trivial, to differentiate between what was going to keep me alive in an emergency and what was esoteric and interesting but not crucial." Throughout the program, working both in space and on the ground, he says of his development, "Over time, I learned how to anticipate problems in order to prevent them, and how to respond effectively in critical situations."[6] Hadfield's experience demonstrates why it's important for astronauts to learn meta skills: they always need to know something, they just don't know ahead of time what knowledge they will have to use in the variety of situations they will face on a space mission.

In the space program, learning is critical to success. "Our core skill," Hadfield writes, "the one that made us astronauts—the ability to parse and solve complex problems rapidly, with incomplete information, in a hostile environment—was not something any of us had been born with. But by this point, we all had it. We'd developed it on the job."[7]

While the space missions get all the attention, the job of an astronaut is so much more. If all someone wants to do is be in space, they aren't a good fit for the program, because there is no guarantee of any one individual getting the go-ahead for a mission. Rather, most of the job of an astronaut is performed on Earth, doing things like learning Russian and practicing mechanics in a spacesuit while submerged in a pool. The training is ongoing, with a mission to space only a possibility.

Hadfield spent six months commanding the International Space Station (ISS). There are three to seven people on the ISS at any given time, and when things go wrong, at least one, but preferably two, of them can deal with it. There isn't any time for someone to be flown in to solve a problem.

Although astronauts can communicate with the ground to get insight and advice, they have to rely on the group up in space to fix any problem. That is why, Hadfield says, "having 'overqualified' crewmates is a safety net for everyone."[8]

Astronauts need to be good at everything. That redundancy is necessary in case one of them is incapacitated or in need of help. This means that time on Earth is best spent learning as much as possible that might be relevant to a space mission. "The more you know and the keener your sense of operational awareness, the better equipped you are to fight against a bad outcome, right to the very end."[9]

Our ego gets in the way of capitalizing on the margin of safety that is produced by knowing more than you need to. Often we learn enough to solve today's problem but not enough to solve tomorrow's. There is no margin of safety in what we know. Another way our ego gets in the way is that we tend to coast on our natural strengths, too afraid or intimidated to dive into being the worst at something. But as Hadfield explains, "Early success is a terrible teacher. You're essentially being rewarded for a lack of preparation, so when you find yourself in a situation where you *must* prepare, you can't do it. You don't know how."[10] Life will throw at you challenges that require capabilities outside your natural strengths. The only way to be ready is to first build as vast a repertoire of knowledge as you can in anticipation of the possibilities you'll face, and second to cultivate the ability to know what is relevant and useful.

Hadfield concludes that in space and on Earth, "truly being ready means understanding what could go wrong—and having a plan to deal with it."[11] Even if the plan is just knowing how you deal with uncertainty, these plans, based on learning, are your margin of safety. Astronauts train in simulators all the time for all sorts of disasters that may come to pass on a mission. Instead of being disheartening, Hadfield suggests, they have incredible value because they teach the astronaut how to think clearly in real-life situations.

After decades in the space program, Hadfield offers this perspective on life: "If you've got the time, use it to get ready. . . . Yes, maybe you'll learn how to do a few things you'll never wind up actually needing to do, but that's a much better problem to have than needing to do something and having no clue where to start."[12]

After all, "When the stakes are high, preparation is everything."[13] The more you know, the more you will be able to anticipate and avoid problems. Knowledge then can be conceptualized as a margin of safety, a buffer against the inevitable unexpected challenges you will have to face.

> The professionals plan for "mild randomness" and misunderstand "wild randomness." They learn from the averages and overlook the outliers. Thus they consistently, predictably, underestimate catastrophic risk.
>
> —JAMES GLEICK[14]

Anticipating the Worst

We cannot have a backup plan for everything. We do too much in a day or a year to devote the resources necessary to plan for dealing with disaster in all our endeavors. However, when the stakes are high, it is worth investing in a comprehensive margin of safety. Extreme events require extreme preparation.

"To lead is to anticipate" was the motto of Jacques Jaujard, director of the French National Museums during World War II.[15] If this is true, Jaujard was a perfect leader.

Before the war started, many French people refused to believe the Nazis would target Paris and disturb the cultural treasures contained within its museums and galleries. But Jaujard was less optimistic. Considering the irreplaceable work in his care, he wanted to err on the side of caution. Jaujard had seen things most French people hadn't that impressed upon him the role of art in conflict. During the Spanish Civil War of the 1930s, he assisted with the transportation of artwork from the Museo Nacional del Prado in Madrid, Spain, to Switzerland. Artworks are vulnerable to destruction from bombing, fire, and so on during wars. They're also vulnerable to seizure by a country's enemy—for profit, as a means of subjugation, and to erode culture. Jaujard's experiences had taught him it was best to move Paris's treasures away if there was any risk whatsoever of attack.[16] That way, no matter what, France could hold on to a piece of its pride knowing part of its culture was safe.

Anticipating that invasion by the Germans was inevitable, Jaujard developed a plan. What turned out to be mere days before the war reached France, he announced that the Louvre would close for three days for maintenance. But once the doors opened again, it was empty. Where had the thousands of pieces of artwork gone?

While the Louvre was closed, a team of hundreds of its staff, art students, and other volunteers packed up every piece for transportation.[17] Some paintings could be rolled into tubes; others were large enough to need transporting in trucks intended for theatrical sets.[18] Then a crew of vehicles, including everything from taxis to ambulances, slipped through the night and left Paris for the countryside. Before the war even began, the artwork was installed in the basements and other safe storage spaces of castles around France.

By starting before the threat was imminent, Jaujard and his team ensured a margin of safety for the Louvre's treasures. His forethought was wise. The Nazis stole an estimated five million works of art,[19] around one hundred thousand of which came from France.[20] One of Hitler's ambitions was to build the Führermuseum in Austria, featuring artwork plundered from other nations.

To reduce the risk of the Nazis discovering the hidden artwork, Jaujard and his team had dispersed it across multiple locations. If the Nazis found any of these stashes, it would be only a small portion of the total. Jaujard built in extra safety mechanisms at every point, supplying equipment to maintain the right temperature and humidity conditions and relocating pieces anytime he doubted their safety. Should some disaster compel someone to choose the most important pieces to save, Jaujard labeled the cases with colored circles denoting levels of importance.[21]

For years, the collection remained in hiding. The Louvre's treasures were moved repeatedly. As the Nazi occupation progressed, Louvre curators sometimes resorted to sleeping next to the most important pieces.

One notable figure among the hundreds involved in the Louvre operation was Rose Valland. She worked in the Nazis' art-theft division recording the whereabouts of the thousands of stolen paintings that left France. But she was not loyal to the Nazis, and she used her position to make copies of the information on French artwork. Her unassuming nature allowed her to spy on the Nazis without them suspecting her of anything. They didn't even know that she could speak German and was eavesdropping on their conversations.

After the war her records helped with the repatriation of many works that might otherwise have been lost, including more than twenty thousand items hidden in Neuschwanstein Castle in the Bavarian Alps. Up until her death, Valland continued to work to help bring home French art and cultural items.[22]

Due to the extreme prudence of Jaujard and his team, by the end of the war, not one item from the Louvre's collection had been lost or damaged. The collection stayed safe from the Nazis, as well as avoiding damage by fire or water, or even theft. Acting early and being cautious worked.[23]

After the war ended, the Louvre reopened its doors at last. The survival of the museum's collection symbolized the resistance of many French citizens to Nazi occupation.[24] We could say what Jaujard did was a waste of effort and irrelevant to the outcome of the war for the French. But he was simply doing his job as the director of the French National Museums: helping to preserve the country's soul, the heritage and history that made it worth fighting for and part of what made France special.

Of course, the Nazis lost in the end. But many of the artworks they took from other museums were never returned or were damaged beyond repair. The Louvre and other French museums still host around eight hundred that never made it back to their original owners.[25] We can learn from Jaujard's removal of artworks from Paris during the war the importance of building in a significant margin of safety when the risk of failure is high. The future is seldom predictable, and so the greater the threat, the more important it is to plan for the worst.

Conclusion

Margin of safety is a secret weapon. It's the buffer, the extra capacity, the redundancy that you build into a system to handle unexpected stress. It's the difference between a bridge that can just barely handle the expected load, and one that can handle ten times that load without breaking a sweat.

You can apply margin of safety to any area of life where there is uncertainty and risk. The key is to always be asking yourself: What if I'm wrong? What if things don't go as planned? How much extra capacity do I need to build in to handle the unexpected?

But here's the rub: building in a margin of safety often isn't free. It means spending more upfront, investing more resources, taking on less risk. In the short term, it can feel like you're leaving money on the table, like you're being too conservative. But in the long run, it's what separates the winners from the losers. It's what allows you to survive and thrive in an uncertain world.

Margin of safety is the unsung hero of long-term success. It's not flashy. It's not exciting, but it's the foundation on which everything else is built. Master it, and you'll be well on your way to navigating the uncertainties of life with confidence and stability.

Churn

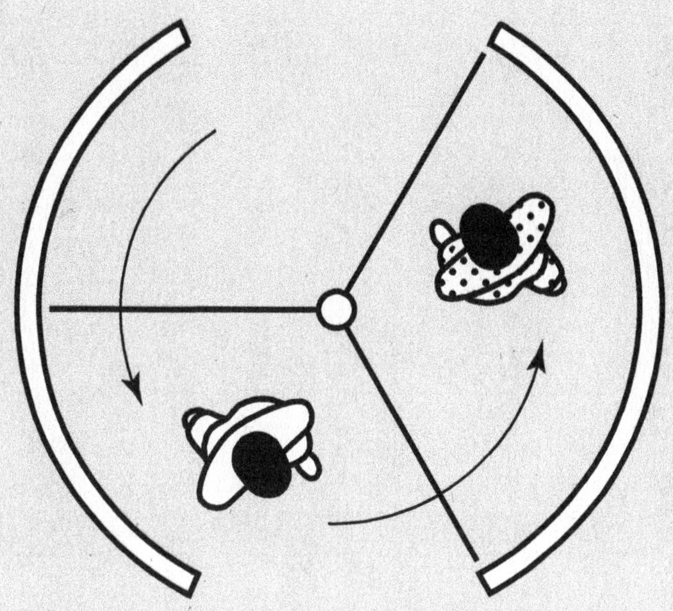

There's always movement.

Within systems, components are constantly wearing out and getting used up. This includes both the material and information within a system and the parts of the system itself. Keeping a system functioning requires ongoing replenishing of both the stocks and the parts used to maintain them. We call this process of attrition "churn."

There are examples of churn everywhere. For example, your favorite sneakers wearing out after lots of use. The skin cells on your body being constantly replaced. Trees in a forest die and new ones grow. The parts in a car deteriorate with time; some need replacing, and some render the car unfixable once they break. People move in and out of cities. System components are never static, and to run a successful system you need to understand how and why parts wear out. The churn model is a lens through which you can look at that kind of system change and learn how to work with it.

In business, churn refers to the loss of a customer, whether that's because they canceled a subscription, stopped buying a product, moved away from a store, or something else. No business can retain every customer forever. However, the rate of churn varies depending on factors like the availability of alternatives, ease of switching, and overall satisfaction. Often given as a percentage, churn is an indicator of whether a product fits its market.

Growth may be good in business, but churn is also important to consider. It doesn't matter how many new customers a company gets through the door if those customers don't stick around long enough for the company to earn back the cost of acquisition. If churn is high, a company may run out of money acquiring new customers.

Churn can also refer to the turnover of employees, something that varies between industries because of the varying costs for both employees and employers. If hiring and training new employees is costly, a company has an incentive to keep churn low, and vice versa. Fast-food restaurants, for instance, have a higher employee churn rate than governments. A certain level of churn, even just

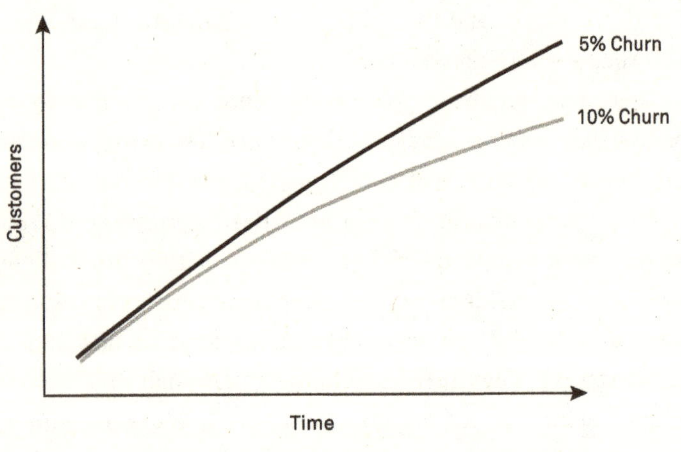

When we have a customer retention rate of 90 percent, we may think we're doing great. But over time, the 5 percent difference between us and our competitor means we have less growth and have to work a lot harder to keep up.

from people retiring, helps bring in new perspectives and experiences. Too much churn prevents expertise from accumulating.

When churn is too high in a system, replacing what is lost or used up becomes a process of running to stay in the same place. Once we get stuck in the trap of keeping up with churn, it's time to step back and reassess if it's worthwhile or if there's another way.

Because churn is inevitable in all systems, it's useful to ask how we can use it to our benefit. Is it worth going through contortions to keep every customer, or should we let a certain percentage go and focus on the core customers who keep our business going? Is it worth trying to retain employees who have lost interest in the job or who would experience more professional growth elsewhere? Understanding your situation through the lens of churn can help you figure out how to harness the dynamics that drive it.

Cults

We can never eliminate churn in groups of people. When the purpose of an organization becomes preventing members from leaving, it turns into a cult. A cult is a group that does everything possible to control its members. Avoiding churn becomes the whole purpose, as opposed to whatever the initial aim was. Every detail is intended to entrap members further. Even if the initial purpose was positive, this process can only ever end up harming members.

"Today is the first day of the rest of your life." These words might be a motivational quote, but their origins are somewhat more sinister. Charles Dederich, founder of the cult Synanon, is the originator of this quote. Synanon is one of the most notable cults in US history for several reasons. Its success in attracting members lent it a place in popular culture, earning mentions in well-known songs and books between the 1950s and 1990s. It gained support from political figures like Senator Thomas J. Dodd and First Lady Nancy Reagan. Synanon was also practically unrivaled in the intensity of its efforts to prevent members from leaving or the outside world from impeding its activities. It was an efficient churn-minimizing machine. Though the organization began with positive intentions, the goal of holding on to members became all-encompassing.

Synanon began in 1958 as a drug addiction rehabilitation program. Dederich, a former alcoholic, started the group in his small apartment, using a thirty-three-dollar (about three hundred dollars today) unemployment check.[1] By its demise in 1991, Synanon had progressed to an incomprehensible level considering its inauspicious origins; it had morphed into a full-blown cult with thousands of indoctrinated members.[2]

When Dederich founded Synanon, treatment options for people with addictions were limited in the United States. Having dropped out of college and failing to hold down a job or make relationships work due to his own out-of-control drinking, he knew the cost of uncontrolled addiction for individuals and their families. Although Alcoholics Anonymous existed at the time, rehabilitation facilities were not widespread, and the belief that addiction is a personal failure was prevalent. Based on his own experiences, Dederich believed addiction was curable, provided an individual changed their social context and helped others.[3] He saw it as the result of a combination of systemic issues. Although we now know that environment and relationships do play a significant role, his belief ended up being a means of control and not of treatment.

A decade after Synanon's founding, Dederich changed his mind about the nature of drug addiction. He decided it was impossible for people with addictions to ever make a full recovery and go on to live regular lives. Synanon members were now expected to stay in the group. Forever.

Dederich began using brainwashing techniques to eliminate churn while using the threat of force to deter potential defectors. To grow Synanon further, he started accepting new types of members, including middle-class people in search of personal growth and young people sent to him by court order—showing that the organization had mainstream approval at the time.

Synanon's control over members to prevent them from churning was total, using a combination of brainwashing, denial of autonomy, and threats of violence. Synanon members shaved their heads, wore overalls, and quit smoking and drugs cold turkey. As they went about their day in dedicated Synanon buildings, they listened to Dederich repeat his views over radio stations for hours on end. Married couples who joined together had to divorce. Members were not permitted to have children.

Perhaps the most extreme mind-control technique was "the Game."[4] During lengthy sessions, members were encouraged to criticize one another and air grievances with anyone in the group. In theory the purpose was to ensure no secrets were held and no hierarchies emerged. In reality it served to break members down emotionally before rebuilding them with support from others. The Game is best viewed as a deliberate form of traumatic bonding in which cycles of abuse appear to strengthen relationships. Synanon also had a paramilitary group equipped with hundreds of guns and capable of attacking anyone who opposed Dederich or left. A lawyer who sued Synanon found a live rattlesnake in his mailbox, its rattle removed.

When Synanon came under legal scrutiny for operating without medical licensing, Dederich declared it was no longer an addiction treatment program and was now a religion. Once again this move allowed more control over members. A rehabilitation or personal development program has an end point. A religion does not.

Dederich had a stronger justification for preventing the churn of members.

Synanon met its end when the IRS revoked its tax-exempt status and ordered it to pay millions in back taxes.[5] Its story teaches us that churn is inevitable within any system and seeking to eliminate it perverts the goals of a system. Regardless of initial intentions, a group that tries to stop *anyone* from leaving can only end up violent and coercive. People being able to leave when they wish places checks on abuses of power. The same is true for countries or companies. People need the freedom to vote with their feet if things get too bad. In this sense, lack of churn can be a powerful indicator that something is not right.

Using Churn to Innovate

> Like a duck on the pond. On the surface everything looks calm, but beneath the water those little feet are churning a mile a minute.
>
> —GENE HACKMAN[6]

At the right level, churn is a healthy part of systems. Components need to change and be refreshed. In some cases, when churn isn't naturally high enough, it can be necessary to build it into a system as a deliberate process. People leaving a business can be good. New people bring in fresh ideas. And if you mandate a degree of churn, you can make it less likely that people will stay for the wrong reasons or that you'll do harmful things to prevent them from leaving.

The value of churn varies with the kind of group you are trying to create, but for organizations wanting to invent and innovate, having a fixed tenure with no bonuses or promotions can keep the focus where it needs to be. This is what a group called Bourbaki did with its members: it ensured a regular turnover to allow for the flow of ideas and inspiration.

In 1935 a group of eminent young French mathematicians met in a Paris café.[7] Among them were André Weil (a foundational figure in number theory and algebraic geometry), Henri Cartan (a major advancer of the theory of analytic functions), Claude Chevalley (a significant figure in many mathematical theories), Charles Ehresmann (best known for the concept of the Ehresmann connection), and Szolem Mandelbrojt (who received recognition for his mathematical analysis work). As a collective, they had an ambitious goal—though it was a realistic one, considering their credentials. They wanted to compile all existing mathematical knowledge into a single overarching theory, then produce comprehensive textbooks covering it.[8]

They decided that everything they produced should be a group effort and not the work of any particular individual. How else could it be a unified theory reflecting the best of mathematical knowledge at the time and not the opinions of one person? So the mathematicians created a fictional persona to whom they attributed their work: Nicolas Bourbaki of Poldevia. They took pains to make him seem like a real person.[9] Many of the students who used their textbook never had any idea that Bourbaki was a group.

Aside from a break during World War II, the members of Bourbaki met for a week two or three times each year to work on their textbook series. It was a truly collaborative effort. The mathematicians debated every single sentence until everyone was at least reasonably satisfied. Each textbook took years of criticism and rewriting to complete. To a casual observer, the approach looked chaotic. There was no discernible system to it. But it meant their work was rigorous. Sometimes, amid a heated disagreement, they would come up with a new way of doing things. The resulting textbooks did indeed have a significant impact on mathematics. By some accounts, the approach they took to conveying knowledge has become the standard.[10]

Bourbaki is relevant to the mental model of churn because of the context in which the group began. Unlike other countries, France did not exempt certain professions, including academics, from military service during World War I. This meant that distinguished mathematicians were as much at risk of dying on the front lines as anyone else.[11] Those who survived that war tended to have been over forty-five years of age at the time of Bourbaki's founding—old enough to be excused from service in World War II. With the deaths of so many young mathematicians in the First World War, many of those teaching and writing textbooks in 1935 tended to be reasonably elderly. Though experienced, they were not always entirely up-to-date with the latest research. The field missed out on the usual regular influx of new figures with new ideas. Having lost a generation of mathematicians, no doubt with many potential geniuses among them, the field stopped progressing at its usual speed in France.[12]

Part of what made Bourbaki such a revolutionary collective was its insistence that members churn at regular intervals. This ensured an inflow of new perspectives and knowledge. Bourbaki members were asked to retire at the age of fifty and invite new, younger mathematicians to join in their place. While we may decry this as ageist today, it was not a critique of their expertise. The intention was to keep bringing people who had studied the latest theories into the fold. Anyone who wanted to leave the group at any point for any reason could without impediment. If a mathematician lost interest, they didn't stay. Only those who wanted to remain part of Bourbaki stayed. Its membership was never static.

Bourbaki still exists in name and runs seminars, although the group no longer publishes anything. This vibrant, ever-shifting group played an important role in mathematical history in the twentieth century. There may be a time one day that calls for it to rise and once again revitalize the field.

Using the lens of churn on the story of Bourbaki demonstrates there can be value in constant change. Harnessed and directed appropriately, churn brings in new ideas and increases our adaptability. It's what allows for evolution by selecting for beneficial traits. Within Bourbaki, the churn of members selected for those with up-to-date knowledge of mathematics and enthusiasm for the project. Within any system, parts need replacing from time to time in order to keep the whole functioning well and to remove anything that proves a hindrance. Churn helps systems improve over time, and it is both undesirable and unrealistic for all the parts to stay the same. However, no matter how often the parts are replaced, no system can function forever. Bourbaki no longer exists in its original form as a producer of textbooks. Its environment changed, and it ceased to be the thing best suited to that task. But while it pursued its original goal, churn helped Bourbaki stay relevant and useful.

Conclusion

Churn is the silent killer of businesses. It's the slow leak, the constant drip of customers slipping away, of users drifting off to find something new. It's the attrition that eats away at your growth, that forces you to keep running just to stay in place. The thing about churn is that it's often hidden. It's not like a sudden crisis that grabs your attention. It's a slow, quiet process that happens in the background.

Churn can present opportunity. Like a snake shedding its skin, replacing components of a system is a natural part to keeping it healthy. New parts can improve functionality.

When we use this model as a lens, we see that new people bring new ideas, and counterintuitively, some turnover allows us to maintain stability. Replacing what is worn out also gives us a chance to upgrade and expand our capabilities, creating new opportunities.

Some churn is inevitable. Too much can kill you.

Algorithms

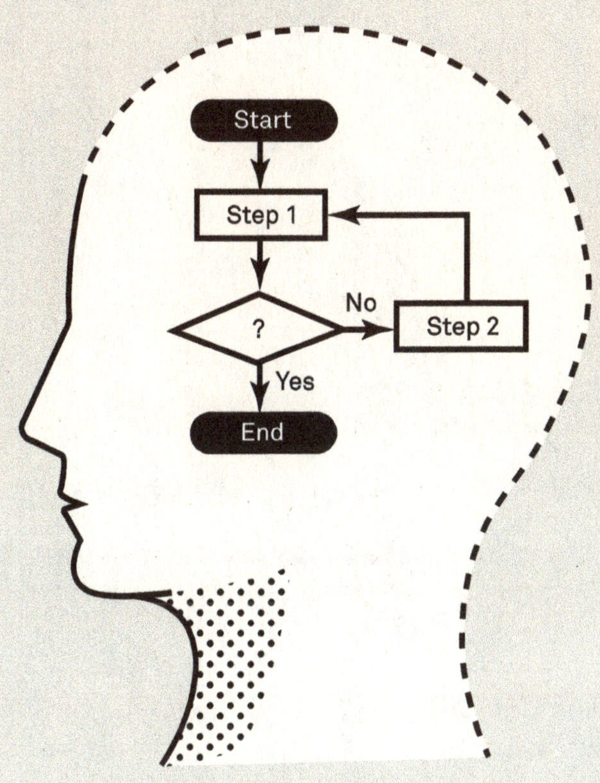

Recipes for success.

"Algorithm" is arguably the single most important concept in our world. If we want to understand our life and our future, we should make every effort to understand what an algorithm is, and how algorithms are connected with emotions. An algorithm is a methodical set of steps that can be used to make calculations, resolve problems, and reach decisions. An algorithm isn't a particular calculation, but the method followed when making the calculation. For example, if you want to calculate the average between two numbers, you can use a simple algorithm. The algorithm says: "First step: add the two numbers together. Second step: divide the sum by two." When you enter the numbers 4 and 8, you get 6. When you enter 117 and 231, you get 174.

—YUVAL NOAH HARARI[1]

Algorithms turn inputs into outputs. An algorithm is like a recipe for a computer, giving it a step-by-step guide to solve a problem or complete a task. It's a set of rules or instructions that if followed precisely lead to a predictable end, just like following a recipe leads you to a tasty dish.

One reason they are worth understanding is because many systems adjust and respond based on the information provided by algorithms. Another reason is that they can help systems scale. Once you identify a set of steps that solve a particular problem, you don't need to start from scratch every time. In this chapter we will explore how algorithmic thinking can help you prevent problems and discover answers.

Algorithms are useful partly because of the inherent predictability of their process. That's why we like them. They are a series of if-then statements that are completely unambiguous. In *Intuition Pumps and Other Tools for Thinking,* Daniel Dennett defines an algorithm as "a certain sort of formal process that can be counted on—logically—to yield a certain sort of result whenever it is 'run' or instantiated."[2] The reliability of a well-designed algorithm in terms of producing consistently logical results is its most attractive feature. Mix flour, water, eggs, and other ingredients in a certain way, and voilà! A scrumptious cake results.

Dennett includes the three defining characteristics of algorithms:

1. Substrate neutrality: "The power of the procedure is due to its logical structure, not the causal powers of the materials used in the instantiation."[3] It doesn't matter whether you read your recipe on a phone or from a book; neither has an impact on the logic of the algorithm.
2. Underlying mindlessness: "Each constituent step, and the transition between steps, is utterly simple."[4] For a recipe to be an algorithm, it must tell you the amounts of each ingredient you need as well as walk you through the process in steps so clear that there is no room for interpretation or misunderstanding.
3. Guaranteed results: "Whatever it is that an algorithm does, it always does it, if it is executed without misstep. An algorithm is a foolproof recipe."[5] Using a good algorithm, the cake will look and taste the same every time.

Algorithms can be simple, like a recipe containing a clear set of instructions that do not vary over time. They can also be complicated, like computer algorithms that try to predict future locations of crime. Furthermore, if we extrapolate our ideas about algorithms beyond humans and our technology, it's possible to consider something like the execution of DNA code as an algorithm, or human learning as being the product of biological algorithms.

Some algorithms can evolve and learn over time. Others stay static. Depending on the requirements of a system, different types of algorithms are more useful for obtaining the information necessary to maintain resiliency and proper functioning.

Moving beyond computers, all systems need algorithms to function: sets of instructions for adapting to and solving problems. Increasingly, algorithms are designed to be directionally correct over perfect. They often evolve—or are designed—to get useful and relevant enough outputs to keep the system functioning properly. Neither nature nor humans worry about creating algorithms that produce the most optimal outputs 100 percent of the time. When we look at systems, it's useful to consider the underlying instructions dictating their behavior in order to determine how to intervene to improve them.

Pirate Constitutions

When groups of people work together with a shared goal, they need coherent algorithms for turning their inputs into their desired outputs in a repeatable fashion. For many people to move toward the same aim, they must know how to act, how to resolve problems, and how to make decisions in a consistent and reliable manner.

For people to follow systems of rules, the right incentives need to be in place. Organizations often rely on the threat of force for compliance, especially when people have not chosen to be part of a system or cannot leave it. But when people choose to work together, it's possible for them to evolve systems of rules that benefit them and that avoid pitfalls such as unjust leadership.

A constitution is one means of making that happen. It can be thought of as a high-level algorithm to limit the power and define the responsibilities of those charged with governance.[6] It is a means of increasing the chance that leaders will work for the benefit of the people, not for their own enrichment. It exists on a level higher than law; it determines how the law itself works. Welding politics, literature, and law, a constitution is something to turn to for guidance when leaders face problems, as well as a source of reassurance for the people. For countries, designing a constitution tends to be a meticulous process that takes into account political ideals. However, it's not just countries that have constitutions. The concept can make sense for any group of people with rules to follow and leaders to keep in check. Nor does a constitution need to be about lofty ideals; it can evolve without planning to achieve quite different aims. All it takes is for a group of people to aim for the same outcome and look for the best, most consistent way of achieving it. A constitution will never be perfect, but clear goals and consistent application with the ability to make amendments can increase the chance it will achieve those outcomes.

In popular culture, pirates of the past are often portrayed as lawless, wild rebels. They roamed the high seas, answering to no one and plundering treasure from whatever hapless ships happened to sail into their paths. In reality, this wasn't the case. To be a successful pirate, it has always been necessary to operate like a controlled business. The pirates who survived the longest and became the richest during the heyday of piracy did so by following rigid rules underscored in many cases by something a lot like a constitution, known as articles, as Peter T. Leeson explains in *The Invisible Hook*.[7]

We can think of pirate articles as an algorithm that helped turn physical labor and resources, such as gunpowder, into valuable plundered goods and money. Every detail that went into a ship's articles needed to have a positive contribution to its profits. Pirates opted for whatever rules helped their bottom line without considering factors that were relevant for landed people.

Looking at the way they formed their articles during the golden age of piracy in the early eighteenth century can teach us a great deal about how groups of people use algorithms to ensure collaboration toward shared goals. They also show that algorithms need room for adaptation and change if they cease to work for the people involved, as well as mechanisms for modification if something breaks. By seeking profit above all else, pirates ended up designing a legal system that was far ahead of its time and arguably fairer than that of mainstream society in that era.[8]

When a person joined a pirate fleet, they renounced their connection to mainstream society and became part of a floating society. That meant they could no longer rely on mainstream law to protect and govern them. As Leeson writes, "Pirates had no government. . . . Pirates had no prisons, no police, and no parliament. They had no barristers, no bailiffs, and no royal bench." With an average crew comprising eighty members,[9] usually from different countries, they couldn't rely on standard social bonds.[10] At the same time, pirates needed to be able to cooperate seamlessly, to ensure everyone put in their full effort, and to ensure adequate leadership without abuse of power. If they could overcome all these hurdles, the rewards could be enormous. A pirate could earn a hundred or even a thousand times as much per year as a merchant seaman.[11] As a result they had a strong incentive to come up with articles that helped them attain the level of organization needed for dangerous attacks.[12] Articles were designed to produce a set of repeatable behaviors in the pirates who followed them and thereby tame uncertainty in the high-stakes situation of raiding another ship. They couldn't control external factors, like the weather or the behavior of the crew of a captured ship, but they could ensure their fellow crew members behaved in predictable ways best suited to profiting.

A typical set of articles required a crew to keep their weapons in good shape, not gamble with one another aboard the ship, not drink belowdecks after eight p.m., and resolve any disagreements on the shore.[13] All had obvious benefits. A pirate with poorly maintained weapons would not be able to fight as well when taking control of another ship. Gambling could lead to conflict and reduce cooperation. Drinking belowdecks would disrupt the sleep of other pirates. Resolving disagreements on the shore meant that fights couldn't injure other crew members or harm the ship. Articles covered the allocation of plunder (which was equal, aside from leaders receiving a bit more), bonuses for anyone who showed unusual bravery (to compensate for the added risk involved), and what we could consider a prototype of disability benefits for anyone injured in battles.[14] Plus they stipulated punishments for wrongdoing, what leaders could and couldn't do, and requirements for any new rules.[15]

This is all very impressive, but why would a bunch of violent criminals want to follow a set of rules imposed upon them? Because pirate society was democratic at a time when mainstream society was not.[16] Implementing a set of articles required unanimous agreement from everyone aboard. This ensured pirates joined a ship only if they were willing to follow its rules.

What if a tyrannical captain decided to abuse his power? Pirates had a solution for that too. They voted their captains and quartermasters into power by majority and could remove them from office at any time, for any reason.[17] Everyone had weapons, and if a captain didn't want to respect the results of a vote, they didn't have much choice once the crew turned on them. Dividing leadership between two people provided an additional check. Captains led during battles, and quartermasters handled the day-to-day matters.[18]

Ching Shih is a pertinent example of how tight systems of rules helped pirates succeed. Born in China in 1775, Ching Shih may have been the most successful pirate ever to live. She began her career as a sex worker in Canton, where she met the pirate Zheng Yi. He proposed to her, and she agreed—provided she had equal share in his wealth and power aboard his Red Flag fleet. When her husband died, she took full control, becoming one of few female pirates.[19] At one point, she oversaw 70,000 to 80,000 pirates and up to 2,000 ships, a fleet of unusual size.[20] To give context, the most famous pirate of all, Blackbeard, probably never led more than 700 individuals, with his crew typically numbering a few hundred.[21] Ching Shih was essentially leading a floating city that needed to be able to control itself without the help of the standard legal system. After all, a pirate who discovered that a crewmate had stolen his already-stolen plunder couldn't report them to the police.

Ching Shih laid out a strict set of rules for all her pirates that was designed to ensure both her power and their success. When they attacked other ships, she ordered her crew not to harm anyone unless they failed to surrender. They could not step onto land without permission—the penalty for doing so twice was death. After the looting of a ship, they had to report all goods and not keep more than a fifth. Deserters were mutilated. It was the death penalty for anyone who gave unsanctioned orders, harmed land people without provocation, or raped a female captive.

Ching Shih's might was so great that, unlike most pirates, she was able to peacefully retire in great wealth, having negotiated terms with the Chinese government.[22]

The existence of pirate laws might be surprising at first glance, but when we consider the context in which pirates worked, they were necessary for success and survival. Looking at how pirate leaders like Ching Shih managed to lead large numbers of pirates in high-stakes situations teaches us how algorithms can ensure cohesion within systems. For a system to produce its intended output, the goals of its parts need to be aligned in the same direction. This increases the chances of consistently achieving a predictable outcome.

Controlling so many pirates was a major challenge, but Ching Shih managed it by enforcing a strict system of rules. Her enforcement is the critical component for understanding her actions through the lens of algorithms. Part of the definition of an algorithm is that it uses the same input every time and produces the same output every time. By all accounts, Ching Shih was invariant in her application of the rules. There were no exceptions. Of course, pirates operated in a complex world where conditions were always changing, and even the tightest system of rules couldn't ensure the same outcomes each time they raided a ship. But her strict enforcement gave Ching Shih the best opportunity to produce consistent and reliable outputs.

New Numbers

Where algorithms can become really interesting is when seemingly innocuous, standard inputs create entirely brand-new outputs.

Algorithms seem to be a natural consequence of repetitive actions. For most humans, doing the same thing in the same way over and over gets boring. We thus wonder if there is a way to codify those repetitive actions to streamline the process. A lot of modern math seems to be a result of the codification of the processes used to manipulate numbers. When you multiply 157 by 2693, you probably don't count the individual units in each group in sequence. You likely use a calculator (programmed with algorithms) or a pencil-and-paper method that has you starting with 7 × 3.

One interpretation of the history of numbers is that certain numbers didn't exist until they were produced by an algorithm. Think of negative numbers. They are common enough now, especially for those of us who live in cold climates, but if you think about it, they aren't intuitive. It's hard to imagine ancient humans looking at a bunch of mammoths and thinking there might one day be a negative amount of them. There could be ten mammoths on the plain, two mammoths, or no mammoths, but negative five mammoths? Not likely.

In the book *Arithmetic*, Paul Lockhart suggests that negative numbers are the result of subtraction. Imagine you are in agriculture three thousand years ago. The addition algorithm says that when you have three bags of grain, and you trade for two more, you will have five bags of grain. But then you decide to give one to your poor cousin. Now you have to "un-add," or subtract. The act of subtracting is really the acknowledgment of the negative. You have five bags of grain and negative one bag of grain. And if you are interested in the processes you've just exposed your numbers to, you've got an interesting problem.

Lockhart says, "The issue here is symmetry—or rather, the lack thereof. With addition, no matter what number I have and no matter what number I add to it, their sum is a perfectly valid entity, already extant in the realm of numbers. With the subtraction operation, however, we have an unpleasant restriction: the number we are taking away cannot exceed the number we have. There definitely already is a number that when added to three makes five, but (at the moment) none of our numbers play the role of 'the thing that when added to five makes three.'"[23] Use of subtraction quite likely prompted the idea of negative numbers, which aren't obvious in the physical representations of amounts we encounter in everyday life.

Essentially our process might have gone something like this. Let's say our ancient subtraction algorithm for two values is something along the lines of: Input two distinct, countable whole quantities. Remove the quantity of the second value from the quantity of the first value. So five bags of grain minus one bag of grain becomes four bags of grain. But because our algorithm doesn't say anything about the minimum value of the quantities, we could easily input six and then nine. Which leaves us with what? The nonintuitive concept of a number representing negative three.

The same thinking gives us an understanding of how we got irrational numbers. After some playing around with numbers and their properties, a process was invented called "square root." The square root of a number is another number that, when multiplied by itself, gives you the original number. So the square root of 9 is 3, and the square root of 64 is 8. We can have a lot of fun plugging various number inputs into the algorithm that calculates a square root. Some numbers don't get such pretty results, and their square root is a fraction. But they are still rational numbers. However, use the algorithm to calculate the square root of 2 (and why wouldn't you, it's such an accessible little number) and you get something entirely different: the world's first irrational number.

Finding Quality Inputs

Algorithms are developed to generate an output. As we've discussed, you start with inputs, you follow a process, and you end up with expected outputs. However, sometimes it's not obvious which inputs will result in the desired outputs. So one use for this model is helping you determine and refine what kind of inputs to feed into it in the first place. You can consider it "algorithmic thinking." You may not have the luxury of a completely closed system in which you can implement complete end-to-end automation, but the lens of algorithms can show you how to organize your system to leave as little to chance as possible.

In the late 1920s, one company developed a repeatable process to try to create the world's first broad-spectrum antibiotic. After World War I, scientists had a good understanding of bacterial infection. They were able to identify some of the primary bacteria, such as streptococcus, that caused incurable infections. They also understood how and why bacterial infection often occurred, such as from exposure to contaminated tools and instruments. But once infection took hold in the body, there was no way to stop it. What was missing was an understanding of bacteria—how it worked and where it was vulnerable.

Bayer, a giant German pharmaceutical company whose origins lay in dye-making, decided there was money to be made if they could find a cure for bacterial infections inside the body. There was some indication that a substance with bacteria-fighting properties could be created; earlier research had produced a treatment for syphilis called salvarsan, but nothing else had been found in the subsequent fifteen years.[24]

In charge of pharmaceutical research for Bayer was Heinrich Hörlein. He thought the research to find bacteria-killing drugs was lacking scale and therefore too much was dependent on individual scientists. So at Bayer, he created an industrial system to identify possible antibacterial compounds and hired dozens of people to put each antibiotic candidate through the same algorithmic-like process.

In *The Demon under the Microscope,* Thomas Hager explains that Hörlein knew the search would take years but also knew that success would result in enormous profits. Thus he aimed "to expand drug research from the lab of a single scientist to an efficiently organized industrial process with carefully chosen specialists guided by a coordinated strategy." Hörlein hired Gerhard Domagk to run the "recipe," putting each compound created by the chemists through an identical testing and evaluation process to see if the result would be an antibiotic that was safe for humans.[25]

Domagk and his team tested the chemicals given to them by Bayer's chemists. One of the most prolific chemists was Josef Klarer. He produced hundreds of new chemicals that were systematically tested by Domagk and his assistants. Each chemical compound was tested against a panel of "the most common and deadly bacteria: tuberculosis, pneumonia, *Staphylococcus, E. coli,* and *Streptococcus pyogenes.*" After a bit of initial refining, Hörlein and Domagk created "a smooth-functioning, reliable machine for discovery." The chemicals were tested both in test tubes and in living animals. In the animals, each chemical was "delivered three different ways (intravenously, subcutaneously, and by mouth)." Every chemical was tested the same way in mice, and meticulous records were kept of each test.[26]

Time went by. Thousands of mice died. But the researchers did not give up on their process. As the years went on, "despite the repeated negative results, Domagk changed neither his methods nor his approach."[27] The team knew their recipe for testing was correct, and one day it would produce a result that would allow them to refine their inputs.

In the fall of 1932, their methodology and patience paid off. Klarer decided to attach sulfur to an azo compound. Chemical KL 695 was put through the testing process that thousands of other chemicals had been put through in the previous years. For the first time, the process produced the desired result: mice that recovered from bacterial infection with no apparent toxicity. Domagk didn't yet know how it worked, only that it did. "Strangely, it did not kill strep in a test tube, only in living animals. And it worked only on strep, none of the other disease-causing bacteria. But, given the number and deadliness of strep diseases, it worked where it counted." Funny enough, Domagk was on vacation during the first round of testing of KL 695 and so missed witnessing the initial breakthrough.[28] But the process by then was so entrenched, any one of the dozens of people on the team could run it.

The discovery of chemical KL 695 allowed the team at Bayer to refine the inputs they used for their testing algorithm. "Klarer now made variations on KL 695, finding that as long as sulfa was attached to the azo-dye frame in the correct position, the drug worked against strep. Attaching sulfa to an azo dye—any azo dye—somehow transformed it from an erratic, ineffective chemical into an efficient anti-strep medication."[29] They kept refining their inputs so that more effective azo-sulfa compounds were discovered, including KL 730.

What the Bayer scientists didn't realize was that it wasn't the azo-sulfa combination that was the key, but rather the sulfa itself. Later research demonstrated the efficacy of sulfa in treating strep infections. Structurally sulfa looks a lot like PABA, a key nutrient for some disease-causing bacteria, like strep. Mistaking it for PABA, the bacteria bind to sulfa but cannot metabolize it, which effectively kills them. Sulfa is cheap and widely available, so once Bayer's sulfa antibiotic was on the market, many companies began to make their own.[30]

Bayer's algorithmic-like approach that led to the discovery of the antibiotic properties of sulfa had far-reaching effects. "Sulfa also changed the way drug research was done. Before sulfa, small laboratories followed investigators' hunches and patent-medicine makers cobbled together remedies without testing the results. After sulfa, industrial-scale chemical investigation guided by specific therapeutic goals—the system for finding new medicines pioneered by Hörlein and his Bayer team—became the standard. Successful drugmakers were those who followed the Bayer model."[31] Bayer continued to discover many useful antibiotics using a system that codified the process as much as possible.

Having the correct algorithm can help you even if you aren't sure about the best inputs to get you the results you want. By testing various inputs in a repeatable process, you can use the results to refine what you feed into the algorithm. You don't always need to be good at knowing the answers, you just need to have a good algorithm for finding them.

AI

In the thick of World War II, Alan Turing was not just breaking codes; he was deciphering the very notion of thinking machines. The German Enigma machine's complex encryption was a formidable wall, and Turing, with relentless logic, not only scaled this wall but also envisioned a world where machines could think—a foundation for what we now call artificial intelligence.

Today's reality of AI stretches that logic into realms beyond what Turing likely could have imagined. Algorithms, those precise step-by-step instructions Turing was so fond of, have grown into a vast labyrinth of decision-making paths. They've become our modern-day sorcerers, capable of wielding scalpels in surgeries with inhuman precision, orchestrating military symphonies of strategy and execution, and propelling scientific inquiry at a pace humans have never reached.

But here's the twist in the tale: AI is not just about cold, hard logic; it's about learning, adapting, and evolving. Algorithms are more than just a set of rules; they're a mental model, a framework through which we're learning to see not just the future of machines, but the future of our own decision making, creativity, and problem solving. In a sense, we're all living in Turing's world, a world where "What if?" is not just a question, but a doorway to possibilities we're just beginning to explore.

Conclusion

Algorithms are recipes. A list of crisp, unambiguous steps that tell you how to get from point A to point B. But they're more than just directions. Algorithms are if-then machines for tuning out the noise and zeroing in on the signal. Have the specs been met? Follow the algorithm and find out. Thinking algorithmically means searching for processes that reliably spit out the results you want, like a vending machine dispensing the same candy bar every time someone punches in E4.

SUPPORTING IDEA:

Complex Adaptive Systems

> Often, scholars distinguish between *complex systems*—systems in which the entities follow fixed rules—and *complex adaptive systems*—systems in which the entities adapt. If the entities adapt, then the system has a greater capacity to respond to changes in the environment.
>
> —SCOTT E. PAGE[32]

SOME SYSTEMS ARE SIMPLE AND NONADAPTIVE. YOU CAN LEARN HOW they work by learning about their parts. They don't change based on their environments. For instance, imagine a basic pocket watch. You can take it apart to figure out how it works, and it keeps working the same regardless of what goes on around it—within limits.

Complex adaptive systems have properties that are greater than the sum of their parts. You cannot understand them by studying their individual components, which may be simple but which interact in unpredictable, nonlinear ways. A few, often basic rules enable the parts to self-organize without centralized control. The way the various components interact and pass information between themselves creates complexity. The ability to change in response to its environment and in pursuit of a goal makes a system adaptive.[33] Complex adaptive systems have "memories"—they are impacted by what has happened to them before.

One example of a complex adaptive system is the traffic within a city. While cars are simple systems in the sense that the way they work is a logical outcome of all their parts working together, when we look at the combined interactions of cars, we see remarkable self-organization. Traffic changes its behavior based on information from its environment. Focusing on one car won't teach you about the entire system because what matters is the interactions between them.

In *Complexity: A Guided Tour*, Melanie Mitchell defines a complex system as one "in which large networks of components with no central control and simple rules of operation give rise to complex collective behavior, sophisticated information processing, and adaptation via learning or evolution."[34]

Within complex adaptive systems, components are all interdependent. They can directly or indirectly influence the behavior of the entire system. If one car breaks down on a main street, it can have a domino effect for the traffic in the rest of the city. Interactions between parts amplify the impact of tiny changes.

In a complex adaptive system, we can never do just one thing.[35] Anytime we intervene, unintended consequences are almost inevitable. Often when we try to improve a complex adaptive system, we end up making things worse because we overestimate our degree of control.

We cannot expect complex adaptive systems to be governed by predictable rules. Nor can we expect to understand the macro by examining the micro. To handle complex adaptive systems, we need to be comfortable with the nonlinear and the unexpected.

Another aspect of complex adaptive systems that can derail us is their ability to learn and change in response to new information. Consider a model that predicts the spread of the flu among a population. It will need to anticipate that people can change their behavior. If people hear warnings of an epidemic or see others getting sick, they may take measures to prevent catching the flu.[36]

> No gluing together of partial studies of a complex nonlinear system can give a good idea of the behavior of the whole.
>
> —MURRAY GELL-MANN[37]

We can still learn from complex systems; we just need to be humble and use the scientific method. We must not mistake correlation for causation, and we should always be open to learning more about the system and accepting that it will change. What we learned yesterday may guide us, but it can change tomorrow. We shouldn't give up just because a system is complex.

From the outside, complex adaptive systems can look chaotic, but they tend to work best when slightly disorganized, as this allows for mutations and experimentation. In the long run, deviations tend to cancel out into more coherent patterns of functioning.

Critical Mass

Going critical.

A system becomes *critical* when it is on the verge of changing from one state to another. The unit of input that causes the change is like all the ones that came before it, yet it has a disproportionate impact. For example, consider the proverbial straw that breaks the camel's back. Before a critical mass is reached, the camel can support the amount of weight it's required to carry. Then the weight passes a threshold at which any additional amount is disastrous, and the final straw tips the camel into another state. Once a system passes a certain threshold and enters a critical state, it takes only a tiny nudge to change it.

When a system changes from one state to another, we say it has achieved critical mass, also known as reaching the tipping point. In social systems, critical mass tends to mean the point when enough people have adopted something, such as a belief or product, that its growth can sustain itself. In his 1978 book, *Micromotives and Macrobehavior*, game theorist Thomas Schelling wrote, "The generic name for behaviors of this sort is *critical mass*. Social scientists have adopted the term from nuclear engineering, where it is common currency in connection with atomic bombs."[1]

The amount of energy required for a system to achieve critical mass is variable. Different systems have different properties and thus require varying amounts of inputs to tip from one state to another.

Heated water is at critical mass when it is hot enough to change from liquid to gas. There is a massive difference between 212 and 211 degrees Fahrenheit. One is the boiling point; the other is not. In business, critical mass is the point where a business makes enough money to no longer need outside investment or the point where the financial growth of a company becomes self-perpetuating. In epidemiology, critical mass can refer to the point where enough people are vaccinated in a population to prevent an infectious disease from spreading to vulnerable people who cannot be immunized.

Using critical mass as a model helps us understand the effort required to achieve sustained change. Systems have certain inflection points where they change from one state to another. It doesn't help us to focus solely on the tipping point and ignore the work required to bring a system there. It's easy to be dazzled by the final input that pushes a system from one state to the next, because it seems to make everything happen all at once. But the straw breaks the camel's back only when there is already a lot of weight on it. The last piece matters only because of all the pieces that came before it.

The critical mass lens also helps us identify the parts of a system we can target to advance change. In social systems, for example, we don't need to spend equal effort changing everyone's mind. We can instead focus our efforts on changing the minds of opinion leaders to more quickly advance change.

Systems in a critical state tend to be precarious, but they don't stay that way for long because they're so easily tipped.[2] Getting insight into what could be the straw is valuable, as is recognizing when a system is poised on the edge of instability. A pencil balanced on its end may appear at equilibrium as it remains upright. But it could topple at the slightest disruption, so it is not stable.[3]

The Overton Window

Day by day, people's minds don't change that much. It's unusual for someone to wake up one day and decide to completely change their tack on a pertinent issue. But in the long run, over decades, the ideas in the mainstream alter drastically. Fringe ideas become mainstream, and mainstream ideas become fringe. One way to understand this phenomenon is by considering the Overton window, a concept developed by Joseph P. Overton in the 1990s as part of his work for the Mackinac Center for Public Policy.

The Overton window is the range of ideas considered acceptable for politicians to propose as policy. Ideas outside of that, no matter how good, cannot gain widespread support. They're too extreme for the current climate and are best avoided lest they harm one's chances of reelection. Over time, the Overton window shifts. Some politicians may advance far-out ideas in a deliberate attempt to move the window further from the norm and make more moderate ideas more palatable.

Ideas move in a progression: unthinkable → radical → acceptable → sensible → popular → policy.[4] For instance, the suffrage movement shifted the Overton window to make the idea of women being able to vote move from unthinkable to policy. Now to suggest otherwise would be unthinkable.

Politicians must prioritize the Overton window over their personal beliefs.[5] It's important to recognize this window isn't universal. The conservative political positions of one country may be considered liberal in another.

The value of the Overton window as a concept is that it encourages us to recognize that attitudes and opinions are not static. What we consider acceptable today may one day be unacceptable. Ideas that are fringe and wacky now may one day be mainstream.

The Work Required for Change

We like to tell stories about tipping points. We look at the landmark cases or individual actions that sparked a cascade of change in the past and wonder how we can re-create them to push our current system into a new state. Using the mental model of critical mass, however, reminds us that it is equally important to pay attention to the effort involved in the buildup.

In September 1893, New Zealand became the first self-governing country to give most adult women the right to vote in parliamentary elections. American women would not earn this right for another twenty-seven years and British women for twenty-five. An important thing to understand about women's suffrage in New Zealand is that it was far from a sudden change, even if it may have appeared as such from afar. Through the efforts of many people over many years, there was a slow shift of the Overton window to the point where women being able to vote became reasonable in the minds of enough people to move the voting system into a new state.

Certain unusual aspects of New Zealand's society and events in its history helped lay the groundwork for changes in the voting system even before the official suffrage movement began.[6] Many of the people living in the country had settled there in recent decades and desired to create a fairer society than the European one they had left behind.[7] Seeing as the population was small (under 750,000 in 1893, including 40,000 Maori),[8] fewer minds needed changing to create a critical mass. The movement received support from prominent male politicians early on, which aided in getting a foothold in Parliament.

Women receiving equal access to education in New Zealand was another key factor in the buildup of opinion change to critical mass. Due to the campaigning of educationalist Learmonth Dalrymple, girls received the same secondary education as boys, with the first school for girls opening in 1871.[9] Dalrymple also successfully ensured women were able to attend university, where they made up half the student body by 1893.[10] Greater education led to improved employment prospects outside the home, beyond the customary option of domestic labor. More and more women entered the workforce once they had better education, gaining social influence in areas such as teaching, journalism, medicine, and the arts.[11] When they faced worse working conditions than men, New Zealander women began to unionize.[12]

In many ways, the New Zealander suffrage movement was entwined with the temperance movement, which sought to restrict or prohibit the consumption of alcohol. Throughout the nineteenth century, alcohol became a growing problem in many countries, leading to poverty, violence, crime, and harm to family life. For New Zealanders, it was particularly harmful among men working in the agricultural, maritime, and industrial industries.[13] As in many other countries, it was reported that many men drank away their wages before even making it home on the weekend, leaving their wives and children bereft. Because women tended to suffer the most as a result of widespread heavy drinking, they were influential in the movement.

Although the temperance movement never achieved the aim of total prohibition in New Zealand, it constructed a framework for women to politically organize. Alongside unionization, it gave women the confidence that they could have influence if they worked together in sufficient numbers with clear goals and a sense of focus. As Patricia Grimshaw writes in *Women's Suffrage in New Zealand*, "Women, on the practical side, learned the arts of organization, administration, and leadership which could be turned to use in later years in their own cause. Women, on the ideological side, entered a sphere in which a new outlook on their basic rights developed rapidly, spurring them to aim at the realization of their full rights as women."[14]

All this work culminated in the suffrage movement, led by Kate Sheppard, which built upon the social change that had been growing since the country's founding. In the early 1890s, Sheppard organized several petitions in favor of women being able to vote, which she presented to Parliament. Despite initial failures, the movement kept trying, gaining more and more support each year. By 1893, her petition had amassed thirty-two thousand signatures, a number all the more impressive considering the tiny population of the country at the time. After numerous attempts, the bill passed by a whisker. The changes in opinion had reached critical mass.

In turn, women earning the right to vote in New Zealand helped motivate and inspire similar movements elsewhere because it showed wider suffrage was possible. After World War II, women's political emancipation spread around the globe, a visible symbol of wider improvements.[15] Once you pass a tipping point, the whole nature of a system changes. It develops new properties, and new things are possible. New Zealand was that tipping point for women's suffrage in many other countries.

When we look back at significant social changes, it's important to recognize the work involved in building a critical mass. Women getting the vote in New Zealand was the result of years of effort on many different fronts to build the capabilities needed to change opinions. As social norms regarding women voting started to change, the movement gained the critical mass necessary for petitions in Parliament to be the final straw that resulted in a new state.

We can learn from the mental model of critical mass that

changing a system doesn't require changing everything about it. Changing a small percentage of its parts can shift the whole thing into a new state. Getting people to alter their beliefs doesn't mean convincing everyone; once you pass a threshold, the change perpetuates itself.

Minority Opinions

Sometimes, people change their minds a lot in a short time. Although it can seem as though this shift occurs overnight, what really happens is that things change slowly until a critical mass of people hold a viewpoint. Interestingly, a majority is not required for things to tip and result in almost everyone changing their minds. Once opinion leaders hold a viewpoint, it spreads easier because people who don't hold this same viewpoint face negative consequences. Targeting opinion leaders can accelerate reaching the tipping point.

Researchers at Rensselaer Polytechnic Institute identified the percentage of a population necessary for social change as 10 percent. They stated that this holds true regardless of the type of network.[16] However, other research suggests the number is much higher, with around 25 percent of a population being the tipping point. Past this point, a minority view can replace the status quo.

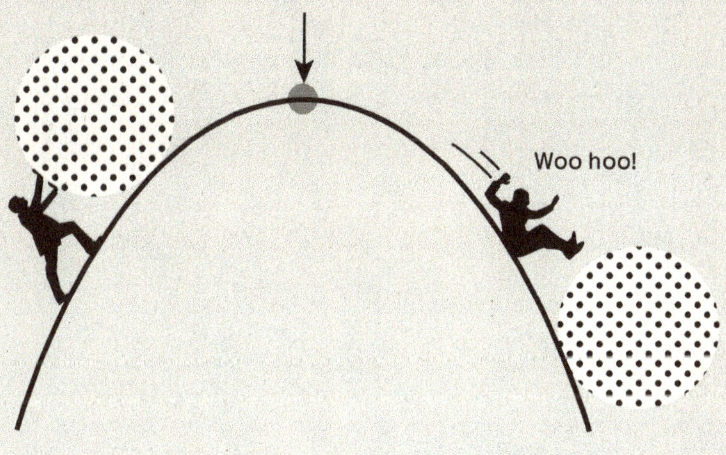

The researchers attribute this to most people not being as committed to their opinions as they imagine, meaning they're liable to change their mind as those around them do. The 25 percent figure is likely to vary depending on the extent of the stake people have in their viewpoints and the social clout of the minority seeking to change things.[17]

Organic Cities

In nuclear physics, critical mass is the minimum amount of fissile material needed to start a self-sustaining reaction. You can pile up the uranium, and nothing will happen until a high enough density is reached. To focus on what prompts the change from inert to active in a nuclear reaction isn't all that interesting. It's just one more bit of uranium. The more interesting question is, how much is needed to kick-start the reaction so that it can continue without further inputs? The lens of critical mass is thus a useful one to apply to other situations in which we'd like to produce self-sustaining reactions, such as cities.

Cities are complex systems where planners have often misidentified the elements required to create enough density to produce self-sustaining interactions.[18] In cities, it's not the amount of infrastructure that produces interactions, it's how that infrastructure is laid out. A certain number of interactions are required for a city to function well and adapt to meet the needs of those living in it. What makes a city safe, interesting, prosperous, and creative isn't the buildings or streets. It's how the infrastructure fosters interactions and relationships between people.

Jane Jacobs wrote extensively in *The Death and Life of Great American Cities* about how to achieve self-sustaining interactions in cities and why they are important. She argued that when we isolate parts of cities, we miss the many interconnected functions they perform. For example, "A city sidewalk by itself is nothing. It is an abstraction. It means something only in conjunction with the buildings and other uses that border it, or border other sidewalks very near it."[19]

The system formed by a sidewalk and its users is what makes an area both safe and interesting. When the area around a sidewalk is subject to active mixed uses—homes, cafés, shops, and so on—there are always eyes upon it and people passing through. These people do not need to know one another or even to talk to one another. It is enough that they see one another are aware they are watching and being watched, and observe one another's behavior. Jacobs writes, "The basic requisite for such surveillance is a substantial quantity of stores and other public places sprinkled along the sidewalks of a district; enterprises and public places that are used by evening and night must be among them especially."[20]

It is the interplay of people that ensures a sidewalk is safe and places limits on antisocial behavior. People moderate how they act knowing someone is or might be watching. Any antisocial behavior that does break out is likely to be swiftly halted by the interventions of bystanders. An organic, unorganized system of control enforced by social norms is more immediate and effective than the use of police, although the threat of them being called plays a role.[21]

To understand why neighborhood safety breaks down in certain situations, we need to consider a sidewalk as needing a minimum number of interactions in order to function as part of a city system instead of just a piece of concrete. You'd feel safer at night walking along a street lined with bars open late than one with stores that close at five p.m. You'd feel safer walking along a main street passing the fronts of houses than an alleyway only visible from a couple of windows. You would feel safer on a crowded street than an empty one with a police officer present. You feel safer on a sidewalk that is part of a whole system of self-sustaining interactions.[22] The more people who are using a sidewalk, at different times and for varied purposes, the better it functions as a safe space. This is true outside cities, but other factors are likely to be relevant for safety in towns or rural areas.

It is this "intricacy of sidewalk use, bringing with it a constant succession of eyes" that also makes an area lively and interesting, and therefore a desirable destination.[23] Activity attracts more activity. Many people using an area brings economic benefits, which further attracts more businesses, especially more unusual and specialized ones, which in turn attracts more people.

Visual activity is appealing to the eye. We like to watch things happening and other people going about their days, so crowds attract more crowds. People who *watch* attract more people who *do* by making an area safer, and people who *do* attract more people who *watch* by making an area interesting.[24] It is a feedback loop that is dependent on a myriad of uses and interactions.

Our experience of a city also has to do with the relationships it fosters with other people. Again, interactions are paramount. Both social isolation and a lack of privacy are risks in cities. An individual may contend with both throughout the course of a day in a poorly designed city. Ideally we gravitate toward spaces where we can have controllable levels of interaction with others. In *Happy City,* Charles Montgomery says, "The richest social environments are those in which we feel free to edge closer together or move apart as we wish. They scale not abruptly but gradually, from private realm to semi-private, to public; from boardroom to living room to porch to neighborhood to city."[25]

One instance of an environment that allows individuals to regulate their level of interaction but also accommodates a wide variety of users is a plaza or square. Present at varying scales as a standard feature of the city, squares are mixed-use areas in which one could, among other things, meet a friend or a date, enjoy a coffee at a sidewalk café, watch a street performer, exercise a dog or child, attend a protest, or strike up a conversation with a stranger. The surrounding bustle allows for both safety and interest. You feel safe meeting a date or talking to a stranger because there are enough people around to take note if something goes wrong. But you also feel comfortable having a private conversation with a friend or writing in a notebook because no one is likely to pay much attention to you in particular with so much going on.

Space alone does not create this environment. An overly large square can actively repel people, as it feels overexposed and empty. A popular one must have enough activity and reasons to visit in a small enough space to create the density needed for spontaneous and ongoing interactions to occur.

Strøget is a network of pedestrianized streets in Copenhagen, Denmark, created in the 1960s as part of an effort to switch the city's focus from cars to pedestrians and cyclists. Closing off the area to cars was a controversial move. People didn't believe Danes would simply want to mingle in a public space, considering the country's typically cold weather and lack of a preexisting café culture.

But today, Strøget is a lively area with an annual peak of 120,000 visitors braving the icy Danish winter on the last Sunday before Christmas.

Strøget works because it manages to combine many possible uses in one area, making it a busy and engaging place to visit. It facilitates the interactions necessary for a city to function in a way that promotes needs like psychological safety and controllable social engagement. Pedestrians and cyclists pass through on their way to somewhere else. Shoppers visit both luxury boutiques and chain stores. Others visit the theater or church. Street performers attract audiences, as do peaceful demonstrations. People sit at pavement cafés or wander along eating inexpensive street food. Tourists visit museums and art galleries.[26] People are willing to brave the cold because the area has so much to offer.

Architect Jan Gehl has since applied the principles of Strøget to other parts of Copenhagen and cities around the world. The city was able to promote a new sort of street culture by recognizing that a bustling public space is the product of several factors coming together at a certain density.[27] Street culture is not specific to certain cultures; it is about having the right kind of spaces for it. These spaces recognize that a minimum of interactions must be maintained in order for them to function in a self-sustained way. The actual architecture should be invisible because the focus is on the people and on bringing out their best qualities.

The idea that infrastructure needs to promote and facilitate a certain number of interactions and not just look good explains why some attempts to design and build cities from scratch have been riddled with problems. If you focus on the infrastructure first and just build a list of requirements—like houses, stores, and streets—you increase the chance that your city won't function well. Rather, the infrastructure needs to be designed to facilitate a critical mass of interactions—something that planned cities often miss. Planned cities may try to design out those interactions because designers see them as a waste of time, or they may even want to discourage any type of organized action.

Planned cities often segregate different functions, like workplaces and homes, ignoring the benefits of mixed-use areas, which are the standard in natural cities. Visually this segregation looks ordered and pleasing, but it doesn't promote the interactions cities require. It's useful for people to be able to access resources close to where they live. It cuts down on commuting and increases time people can spend on relationships.

Mixed-use areas combining residential and commercial elements create more interactions than those segregated for one function. Planned cities may segregate roads and sidewalks for pedestrians, viewing driving and walking as distinct activities. But this prevents people from being able to hail a taxi and combine the two functions.[28]

Brasília, the federal capital of Brazil, was designed in the 1950s and '60s to replace Rio de Janeiro as the capital. Architect Oscar Niemeyer and urban planner Lucio Costa crafted a vision of a utopian city from scratch. In the visual sense, Brasília is a stunning World Heritage site. From the air, it has a beautiful birdlike form. As a place to live, it functions less well.

Areas of Brasília have specific uses: people live in one part, work in another, and shop in another. Without mixed-use areas or much catering to pedestrians, the city cannot form a street culture. Communities cannot cohere due to a lack of areas where people can mingle. Visual order—Brasília is laid out in a grid—does not translate into good function.

Everything in Brasília was built new and modern, to similar specifications. Yet cities need buildings of varying age and quality to allow for people at different income levels. The architects and designers never planned for low-income housing, despite Brasília needing inexpensive labor as much as any other city.[29] As a result, unofficial areas have sprung up around the city that house its poorer residents. Only by deviating from the plan can it function at all.[30]

So although Brasília contains the same parts as a typical city, those parts do not facilitate much interaction. It seems as if its designers believed that the arrangement of the infrastructure is irrelevant to city functioning. But how the infrastructure is laid out is crucial because it facilitates the critical mass of interactions cities need to be able to adapt and grow to meet the needs of those living in them.

Conclusion

Critical mass isn't just a science term; it's a guide for understanding that often things happen slowly and then all at once. It's the moment when a system goes from sputtering along to explosive growth. Like a nuclear chain reaction, once you hit critical mass, the reaction becomes self-sustaining.

Through this lens we gain insight into the amount of material needed for a system to change from one state to another. Material can be anything from people and effort to raw material. When enough material builds up, systems reach their tipping point. When we keep going, we get sustainable change.

Using critical mass as a lens for situations in which you want different outcomes helps you identify both the design elements you need to change and the work you need to put in.

Emergence

Organization without an organizer.

You look at where you're going and where you are and it never makes much sense, but then you look back at where you've been and a pattern seems to emerge. And if you project forward from that pattern, then sometimes you can come up with something.

—ROBERT M. PIRSIG[1]

When we look at systems on the macro scale, they sometimes exhibit capabilities that aren't present on the micro scale. This is known as "emergence," when systems as a whole function in ways we can't predict by looking at their parts. As Aristotle put it thousands of years ago, "The whole is something over and above its parts, and not just the sum of them all."[2] The mental model of emergence reminds us that new capabilities are often produced from seemingly innocuous elements.

Emergence is like watching a flock of birds suddenly move together to form a pattern in the sky; it's the surprise of seeing a whole new thing appear from just simple parts coming together. It's when all the separate pieces, following their own simple rules, create a complex and unexpected dance you could never predict just by looking at the pieces alone.

We cannot understand systems with emergent properties by reducing them to their individual components. Termite mounds exhibit emergent properties. A single termite is powerless, but a million or two working together can build a complex mound up to seventeen feet tall, requiring the movement of a ton of soil and several tons of water each year.[3] Without a leader orchestrating their movements, termites build ventilation and cooling systems, storage chambers, fungus gardens, and specialized housing for the queen.[4]

Emergence is either strong or weak. Weak emergence occurs in systems in which functions are based on identifiable rules. We can model weak emergence by identifying the underlying rules. Strong emergence does not have identifiable rules behind it, so we cannot model it. So it's possible to construct a computer simulation of the flocking behavior of a group of birds (weak emergence) but not of the interplay of cells in our brains that creates consciousness (strong emergence).[5]

One of the primary features of emergence is self-organization. The parts of a system may appear to interact in chaotic ways, but the whole can seem orderly. This occurs without centralized control—the parts organize themselves from the bottom up. For instance, flocks of birds tend to fly in a coherent shape. They don't manage this by following the instructions of a leader; instead, each bird instinctively follows certain rules, like keeping an even distance between themselves and their neighbors.

Emergence and Complexity

Emergence is not synonymous with complexity. Some complex systems exhibit emergent properties, some only resultant properties. Some simple systems have complex emergent properties.

For example, a nuclear power plant is a complex system with numerous parts all working together. But it does not display emergence: the parts work together as expected. Meanwhile, a much simpler game of chess can show emergence, as there are novel outcomes originating from simple rules. The rules governing how pieces can move are basic, but they lead to complex, high-level strategies, and the outcomes of games are unpredictable. The rules don't tell you how a game will end.

The Mothers of the Plaza de Mayo

Emergence is all about understanding that sometimes systems can exhibit capabilities that are beyond the additive properties of their components. Using it as a lens suggests that groupings of people can produce results that are nonintuitive when you consider how the capabilities of any one person should scale. The cumulative actions of groups of people can also result in novel outcomes different from their initial intentions. We can see emergence in protests, in which groups of people with little power can end up having a tremendous influence. Protests can also have unexpected results that organizers and participants never planned.

Every Thursday evening between 1977 and 2006, a group of women, many quite elderly, met in the Plaza de Mayo in Buenos Aires, Argentina. Mostly wearing matching white headscarves, they walked across the square while chanting and holding banners. Though their methods were humble, what they peacefully achieved over the decades is remarkable.[6]

Periods of history form a coherent narrative under a name only in retrospect. We know the period of state terrorism in Argentina between 1976 and 1983 as the Dirty War. The average Argentinian simply experienced it as a period of extreme, random violence. Due to media censorship, many people didn't even know much about the events at the time if no one they knew personally was targeted.

After the Argentine military performed a successful coup against President Juan Domingo Perón, it declared anyone who opposed its policies an enemy of the state. Anyone who came under suspicion, even if they were not an actual threat, risked going missing. Argentinians referred to these people as *los desaparecidos*, meaning "the disappeared." The government did everything possible to erase any proof they ever existed or to obscure their whereabouts. Many were drugged and thrown from airplanes to prevent their bodies from being found. The total death toll is estimated at thirty thousand.[7] In addition, the children of pregnant desaparecidos were put up for adoption or sold, with many never learning their true backgrounds. Even to attempt to trace the whereabouts of a missing friend or family member could be fatal.

Despite the fierce censorship and punishment of dissenters, one group retained power—by virtue of their powerlessness and vulnerability. For the mothers of the many people who disappeared, the grief was unbearable. A handful couldn't contain it any longer, and despite the extreme risk, they decided to challenge the regime. On April 30, 1977, fourteen mothers met in the Plaza de Mayo and marched, demanding to know what had happened to their children. Soon their numbers grew to the hundreds.[8] The mothers wore white headscarves embroidered with the names and dates of birth of their children, which became a symbol of their movement.[9] As the disappearances continued, their tactics grew bolder.

The Argentine government didn't know how to respond. Murdering a visible group of mothers and grandmothers would risk a major backlash. In any case, annoying as they were, a handful of women seemed harmless. They had no power to oppose the government. Officials called them crazy and left it at that.

But they misunderstood the potential for and impact of emergence. As individuals, the Mothers of the Plaza de Mayo had no power or influence over the government. At first they had little support because most people didn't even know about the disappearances.[10] When they worked as a group, repeating the same actions each week for years, the total effect was greater than the sum of its parts. They had a power that was the result of them coming together. Seeing as the regime relied on scaring people into silence, speaking out was the most impactful thing they could do.

As Diana Taylor writes in *Disappearing Acts*, "Only by being visible could they be politically effective. Only by being visible could they stay alive. Visibility was both a refuge and a trap—a trap because the military knew who their opponents were but a refuge insofar as the women were only safe when they were demonstrating."[11]

While the government paid no attention, news of the Mothers of the Plaza de Mayo spread outside Argentina. Countries without media censorship reported on their protests, raising awareness of the brutality of the Dirty War.[12] Human rights groups offered up resources to help the group achieve more.

With increased support came increased pushback. The Argentine government began to target the mothers, and a number became desaparecidos themselves. A policeman fired a machine gun at them during one protest.[13] The founders of the movement were murdered, and the ultimate fate of some members is still unknown. But they refused to back down because they were safer in the public eye, not out of it.

Once the Dirty War came to an end in 1983, the mothers knew their fight was far from over. They still needed to know the fate of their children and wanted those who had murdered them or were responsible for orders that led to deaths to face the consequences. Mothers whose children were pregnant at the time of their disappearances wanted to trace their grandchildren. To date, more than 850 people have been charged with crimes committed during the Dirty War, and more than 120 stolen children[14] have been identified and reunited with relatives.[15] DNA testing has helped to identify bodies from mass graves.

By taking advantage of their power as a peaceful group, the Mothers of the Plaza de Mayo managed to help change things in Argentina. Nothing they did could bring their children back, but they could hope that it prevented others from losing theirs, and it could bring them closure. Their methods inspired similar groups around the world. While their main initial intention was to find out what had happened to their children, their protests had larger effects, such as calling the wider world's attention to the regime's abuse of power. They helped undermine the regime's sense of its ability to control people's thinking.

As a group, the mothers possessed qualities none of them had as individuals. They were visible, and that visibility made them counterintuitively less vulnerable to harm. Oppressive regimes thrive when people are too scared to be seen opposing them. Visible opposition inspires more people to ask questions and to join in fighting oppression. That's why the government at the time went to such lengths to prevent dissent.

What the mothers achieved was not inevitable. Many other similar groups failed to provoke change. The fact that the mothers did was a novel property. Finally, the story can teach us that you don't always need to plan things all the way to the end. If you have a simple starting point on the right trajectory, surprising things can pan out through the power of emergence.

Social Innovation

Knowledge sharing can often produce unexpected results. We start to work together; I bring an understanding of x, and you contribute experience with y. Combining our knowledge means we have x and y covered, but sometimes we are also able to create z. Using the lens of emergence, we can look at learning in humans and highlight that social interaction matters as much as, if not more than, individual smarts if we want to ramp up innovation.

As a species, we can do more than any one human brain is capable of because of cultural learning. We don't need to reinvent the wheel each generation. We have evolved social networks that allow us to learn from our elders and to pass on that knowledge to our children. What is important for humans, though, is that we all don't need to know everything. Look around and you will see many items that you cannot build but that you can use. Cultural learning produces products that are emergent properties of human collective organization.

In describing the role of cultural learning for humans, Joseph Henrich, in *The Secret of Our Success,* explains, "The striking technologies that characterize our species, from the kayaks and compound bows used by hunter-gatherers to the antibiotics and airplanes of the modern world, emerge not from singular geniuses but from the flow and recombination of ideas, practices, lucky errors, and chance insights among interconnected minds and across generations."[16] Basically humans create things as a group that no one person is capable of.

Furthermore, as cultural learning gets passed from generation to generation, "our cultural learning abilities give rise to 'dumb' processes that can, operating over generations, produce practices that are smarter than any individual or even group."[17] Thus it is not just the knowledge that accumulates, but our abilities to learn from and teach others, that grow and give rise to emergent properties.

Think of it this way: Could you build a pyramid or a telephone? Even if you worked with the five or ten smartest people you know? How about survive in a forest? How many people would you have to bring with you to guarantee one of you knew how to start a fire? There is so much knowledge that has accumulated in the history of humanity, it isn't possible to know all of it. Henrich explains that the "practices and beliefs [of cultural learning] are often (implicitly) *much* smarter than we are, as neither individuals nor groups could figure them out in one lifetime."[18] Cultural learning has produced a cultural mind: an emergent property allowing human knowledge to accumulate and grow far beyond the scope of any individual.

How does cultural learning work? In their paper "Culture and the Evolution of Human Cooperation," Robert Boyd and Peter J. Richerson look at living in the Arctic as one example and explain:

> Arctic foragers could make and do all the other things that they needed because they could make use of a vast pool of useful information available in the behavior and teachings of other people in their population. . . . Even if most individuals imitate most of the time, some people will attempt to improve on what they learned. Relatively small improvements are easier than large ones, so most successful innovations will lead to small changes. These modest attempts at improvement give behaviors a nudge in an adaptive direction, on average. Cultural transmission preserves the nudges, and exposes the modified traditions to another round of nudging.[19]

Humans are generally very good at sharing our improvements and insights with those around us. Furthermore, we find it natural to learn from other people. Thus, although innovating is important in terms of adaptability and survival, what makes humans unique is our social networks that encourage the sharing and uptake of innovation.

Cultural evolution is part of the natural selection process.

No one guides cultural learning. It's not prescribed. There is no authority setting out what we will learn every generation. And for most of what we do, we have no idea why it works.

Henrich traces the development of cultural learning in the human line. Compared with our nearest relatives, chimpanzees, we learn from more individuals right from birth. He suggests that "once individuals evolve to learn from one another with sufficient accuracy (fidelity), social groups of individuals develop what might be called *collective brains*."[20] It is these collective brains—products of large, interconnected groups with strong social norms—that have the potential to generate emergent properties and propel a society to increased sophistication in technological complexity.

Language is a great example of the collective brain propelling the development of complexity. When it comes to language development, Henrich says, "No single individual does much at all, and no one is trying to achieve this [development] as a goal. It's an unconscious emergent product of cultural transmission over generations."[21]

Henrich explains how cultural learning has put selection pressures on humans, changing both our bodies and our instincts. Thus, we start out in life not as a total blank slate but with a huge amount of cumulative cultural evolution behind us. In his paper "The Pace of Cultural Evolution," Charles Perreault concludes, "Culture allows us to evolve over time scales that are normally accessible only to short-lived species, while at the same time allowing us to enjoy the benefits of having a long life history, such as a large brain, an extended juvenile period, and long life span."[22]

When explaining the power of cultural learning, Henrich says, "The first thing to realize is that you are much smarter than you would otherwise be because you've tapped into and downloaded an immense repository of mental apps from a vast pool of culturally inherited knowhow and practices."[23] People specialize because no one can know everything. Then they interact. And in that system in which the interaction occurs, something happens that otherwise wouldn't.

He argues that "innovation does not take a genius or a village; it takes a big network of freely interacting minds."[24] Innovation, then, is not the product of one-off smarts but is the result of the emergent property that our cultural learning has produced.

Conclusion

Nearly everything is an emergent effect—a table, a space shuttle, even us—combinations of ingredients that come together in a specific way to create something new. Emergence is the universe's way of reminding us that when we combine different pieces in new ways, we get results that are more than the sum of their parts, often in the most unexpected and thrilling ways.

Using this mental model is not about trying to predict emergent properties but rather acknowledging they are possible. There is no need to stick with what you know; mix it up and see what happens. Learn new skills, interact with new people, read new things.

SUPPORTING IDEA:

Chaos Dynamics

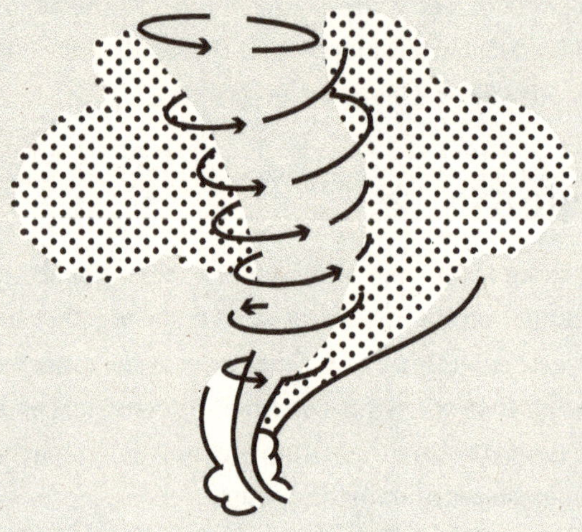

> Most systems behave linearly only when they are close to equilibrium, and only when we don't push them too hard.
>
> —STEVEN STROGATZ[25]

CHAOTIC SYSTEMS ARE SENSITIVE TO INITIAL CONDITIONS. THIS SENsitivity gives rise to a phenomenon known as the butterfly effect, so named for the work of MIT meteorologist and mathematician Edward Lorenz. In the 1950s, Lorenz was working on weather-prediction computer models. One day he entered data into a program and left to get a coffee. When he returned, he found the predictions were completely different than when he'd entered the same data earlier that day. At first he thought there was some sort of technical error. Then Lorenz realized he'd accidentally entered a rounded-up number for one of the variables. The discrepancy was tiny, yet the differences in the results were stark.[26]

From this accident, Lorenz discovered chaos dynamics, or the butterfly effect. He found that it wasn't just weather; other chaotic systems exhibited the same sensitivity to initial conditions. It explained why predicting the weather was such a challenge. In later research and talks, Lorenz compared the difference to the change in air pressure produced by the flap of a butterfly's wings.

Predicting the future behavior of chaotic systems is difficult or impossible because modeling outcomes requires perfect understanding of starting conditions. Any inaccuracies will result in incorrect–perhaps drastically so–predictions. As we progress into the future, the impact of such deviations is magnified further and further, so predictions become exponentially less accurate.[27]

The butterfly effect is significant because it contradicts many of our assumptions about the world. We tend to assume systems are deterministic and tiny differences shouldn't matter too much. In a lot of what we encounter in our day-to-day life, that's true. But it's false for chaotic systems. Without perfect accuracy, we can't make useful, comprehensive predictions about them. It's often only possible to make probability-based predictions, which is why you might hear that there's a 60 percent chance of rain tomorrow.

Since Isaac Newton first codified laws explaining the functioning of the universe at a fundamental level, people have wondered whether it would one day be possible to completely understand the world. Could we one day identify all the relevant laws and be able to predict everything? In 1814, the mathematician Pierre-Simon Laplace declared Newton's laws would enable us, should we know the position and velocity of every particle in the universe, to predict anything, forever. More than a century later, computers made it seem as though we could put Laplace's prediction to the test.[28]

The butterfly effect suggests otherwise. Even when we can identify deterministic rules, we cannot make perfect predictions. In the face of chaos, we should expect to be surprised. We may know the rules governing a chaotic system's behavior, but we cannot know its precise initial conditions. When we look at the behavior of chaotic systems, we are in fact seeing the outcomes of deterministic rules. Even if we cannot predict their future behavior, it still has its own logic.

> For want of a nail the shoe was lost;
> For want of a shoe the horse was lost;
> For want of a horse the battle was lost;
> For the failure of battle the kingdom was lost—
> All for the want of a horseshoe nail.
>
> —ANONYMOUS

> As far as the laws of mathematics refer to reality, they are not certain, and as far as they are certain, they do not refer to reality.
>
> —ALBERT EINSTEIN[29]

What Popular Culture Gets Wrong about the Butterfly Effect

The image of a butterfly flapping its wings and causing a typhoon is a vivid one, and it's no surprise it went on to inspire endless films, books, songs, and motivational quotes. It's unusual for a mathematical idea to become so mainstream. The idea of a tiny thing having a big impact on the world is powerful.

But this is a misreading of the actual meaning of the butterfly effect.[30] It's not that the wing flap *causes* the typhoon; it's that the difference in starting conditions between a world where the butterfly flaps its wings and one where it doesn't is sufficient to mean a typhoon in one and not the other. Chaotic systems are so sensitive to starting conditions that the minutest differences can lead to highly divergent outcomes. We cannot, however, look at an outcome and say that a particular change in conditions caused it. Within chaotic systems, no moment is any more significant than any other. Every single moment changes everything that happens after.

> Some systems . . . are very sensitive to their starting conditions, so that a tiny difference in the initial "push" you give them causes a big difference in where they end up. And there is feedback, so that what a system does affects its own behavior.
>
> –JOHN GRIBBIN[31]

Irreducibility

As simple as possible but no simpler.

It can scarcely be denied that the supreme goal of all theory is to make the irreducible basic elements as simple and as few as possible without having to surrender the adequate representation of a single datum of experience.

—ALBERT EINSTEIN[1]

Albert Einstein's idea was that it is possible to reduce any theory down to a certain level that makes it as understandable as possible to as many people as feasible, but past a certain point, it will lose its meaning. Some things—like feelings, life, or even a game of chess—have to be taken as a whole because the magic lies in how all the parts work together, not just in the pieces themselves. The point at which reducing something further loses usefulness is the point where it is effectively irreducible.

Using irreducibility as a model has an echo of first principles thinking. It's a tool for thinking through to the basics: the minimum amount of time, or components, or structure required to maintain the overall qualities.

What is the minimum amount necessary for a thing to still be that thing? Irreducibility is about finding the point beyond which you will inevitably change the fundamentals so that you can recognize when you are changing the system to something different.

There are certain irreducible limits to any system past which the system ceases to function as intended. One of the challenges is being able to identify those limits and not get sidetracked by what you think ought to be there.

Irreducibility is exemplified in the parable of the goose and the golden eggs. In this story, a farmer finds a goose that lays a solid-gold egg each day. The farmer grows tired of waiting for just one egg each day and cuts the goose open, imagining it will be full of gold. Instead, it dies, and the farmer is left with no more gold because emergence is irreducible. The parts of a system with emergent properties do not display those properties, only their aggregate does. If you disassemble such a system, like the farmer cutting open the goose, it loses its emergent properties.

Loose Lips Sink Ships

In communications, getting to the essence of the thing is important because simple communications are easier to understand. They contain less ambiguity and give fewer options for interpretation. Wartime propaganda posters are an excellent example of using few words and images to convey complicated information. Poster artists sought the minimum number of words and images they needed to depict their message.

Propaganda posters from World War I and World War II often contain simple images with few words that nonetheless convey an incredible amount of information. Just consider the slogan Loose Lips Might Sink Ships. These five words were often paired with a simple image of a boat sinking. Together the words and images impart a lot of meaning. They ask people not to talk about anything that could negatively impact the war effort. They suggest that spies are circulating within the home population. The poster also suggests that the war could be compromised if everyone is not on the same page in terms of offering vocal support.

In addition to the messages implying that the words of civilians can derail the war, the posters convey broader themes. They communicate that everyone is in it together and everyone has a role in the war effort. The posters also serve to condition people to think behavior changes are needed for their side to come out successful. If we imagine being a poster artist, we can understand how difficult it is to convey complex themes and messages like these in simple graphics and slogans.

Poster artists must consider the minimum number of elements to be drawn in order to still communicate their intended message. Posters that read more like novels or that are filled with multiple complicated images are not effective.

Abram Games was a graphic designer and the official war artist for the British during World War II. Many of his posters are visually stunning and are excellent examples of going right to the edge of irreducibility. The British National Army Museum describes his technique: "Always keen to derive maximum meaning from minimum means, his use of clever symbolic devices and simplified forms resulted in some of the most arresting and powerful posters of the era."[2] The images may have been uncomplicated, but the message was clear. His posters were an effective means of communicating complex topics. They were not so simple as to introduce ambiguity or confusion.

Games's posters covered a range of topics, from inspiring patriotism to "instilling desirable habits and behavior in soldiers and civilians alike." The National Army Museum explains, "Among other things, his portraits encourage people to avoid waste, give blood, buy war bonds, handle weapons and ammunition properly, avoid gossip and maintain fighting fitness."[3] To promote this wide spectrum of behavior change, Games not only used few images but often reduced them to simple forms.

Wartime posters make use of common symbols and symbolic representations. These types of symbols are often culturally specific, such as an eagle to represent the United States, or red to represent warning or danger. This is a critical component of being able to simplify the message. The less you have to explain, the more you can communicate in any one poster.

Joseph Kaminski, in the paper "World War I and Propaganda Poster Art," provides an analysis of one recruiting poster for the American Air Service. Two servicemen against a backdrop of a plane mid-flight implore readers to join. The phrase "Give 'em the gun" is centered, and the words "learn" and "earn" are highlighted at the bottom. Kaminski explains that "learn" and "earn" are "meant to appeal to the individual's self-centered interest of learning a useful skill and making money so they can live comfortably after the war."[4] Thus the poster appeals to those who want to belong and those who want to fight, and shows how war experience can be useful later on. None of that messaging is explicit. The poster doesn't spell out what you will learn or how it will help you earn. But the placement of the words on a recruiting poster, in addition to their large size, is the minimum amount needed to still convey the complex message.

Using the lens of irreducibility on wartime posters demonstrates why in communication it can be so effective to find that minimum amount needed without compromising comprehension. Simplicity can convey a powerful meaning. But too much simplicity conveys no meaning at all.

Typography

The mental model of irreducibility also teaches us that when we simplify or change things past a certain point, they cease to work or have meaning. There are limits to how much we can reduce while maintaining the important qualities that make a thing what it is. Being aware of those limits allows for experimentation and creativity.

Designers of all kinds often pay attention to the irreducible components of whatever they're designing. If they want to make things simpler or be creative, they need to consider how they can do so while still being comprehensible. Designers need to identify what makes something what it is so they can ensure the irreducible components are present. If they remove or change into an unfamiliar form something that is essential for users to understand what they're looking at, the result is useless. Recognizing those limits is a key part of good user-friendly design. Subverting the limits can be bad design—but it can sometimes also be an exercise in finding new ways to represent the same thing or in challenging expectations.

Typography is one area we can look at through the lens of irreducibility. Look around you at all the different fonts in your vicinity as well as their variant sizes, spacing, colors, and so on: in this book, on food packaging, on billboards, street signs, clothing labels, newspapers, slogan T-shirts, and so on. They all vary a great deal, yet you can still read them. Whoever designed the font retained the irreducible elements of each letter. Despite the differences in overall design, they figured out what makes each letter recognizable as itself.

Eric Gill's 1931 book, *An Essay on Typography,* is an ideal starting point for considering irreducibility in typography. At their core, Gill explains, "Letters are signs for sounds. . . . Letters are not pictures or representations. They are more or less abstract forms."[5] We have created them as signifiers, and we can modify them to suit new mediums or the social demands. Letters have changed a great deal over time, yet each generation of designers aims to identify the irreducible elements of older forms, to hold on to them, and to ensure their type remains legible.

The letters of the English alphabet do not directly symbolize the sounds of the language. A designer must "take the alphabets we have got, and we must take these alphabets in all essentials as we have inherited them."[6]

There are three core versions of the English alphabet: lowercase, uppercase, and italic. Each forms letters differently, but each is still recognizable because it contains the same irreducible elements. It is possible to change parts of the design without losing these elements. Gill writes, "A Roman capital A does not cease to be a Roman capital A because it is sloped backwards or forwards, because it is made thicker or thinner, or because serifs are added or omitted; and the same applies to lowercase and italics."[7] It is possible to change those elements because they are not irreducible—certain features of the letter's shape are. Looking at a text mixing all three alphabets highlights that each has its own irreducible element. Capitals should be larger than lowercase when used together, and italics should be narrower and sloping.[8] These are irreducible elements of the alphabet, not the letters themselves.

For a designer, identifying and retaining those irreducible ele-

A letter can be stripped of every flourish, and its components manipulated, but there is a point beyond which too much change renders it no longer the symbol it once was. Typography designers must balance creativity and comprehensibility.

ments of each letter is an important, rare skill: "Everybody thinks that he knows an A when he sees it, but only the few extraordinary rational minds can distinguish between a good one and a bad one, or can demonstrate what constitutes A-ness. When is an A not an A? Or when is an R not an R? It is clear that for every letter there is some sort of norm."[9]

Gill explains that the irreducible elements of a letter may be different depending on its context. For example, "A square or oblong with its corners rounded off may, by itself, be more like an O than anything else, but in conjunction with a D made on the same principles there is not much by which to recognize which is which, and from a distance the two are indistinguishable."[10] The irreducible elements of a system are not fixed and depend on the context and goals of that system.

In the book *The Ten Commandments of Typography: Type Heresy*, Paul Felton explores how experienced designers who know the rules can break them while still getting a message across.[11] It comes down to understanding the irreducible elements of that component of type and how they vary between contexts.

The most important feature of a headline, for example, is that it is the first thing a reader notices and therefore reads when they look at the page. Convention states the easiest way to achieve this is to make the headline much larger than the rest of the text and to place it at the top of the page. Felton illustrates that the eye will also naturally go first to the boldest text on the page if everything is the same size, so it is also possible to differentiate a headline by making it bold, in which case it can be positioned anywhere.[12] What might appear to be an irreducible element is in fact not. The irreducible element of a headline is that it is immediately noticeable, not that it is larger than the rest of the text.

Sometimes irreducible components are obvious. As famously

attributed to Warren Buffett, you can't produce a baby in one month by getting nine different women pregnant. Natural selection has resulted in an irreducible pregnancy process. Irreducibility, however, is not always this clear. Typography shows us the importance of identifying irreducible components. Each letter has elements that need to be present for legibility. The same goes for the overall way you lay out text on a page. When we mistake the irreducible components and then jettison the rest, we change the nature of the system, which often results in a new system. Fonts that fail to retain the irreducible elements necessary for readability move into the domain of visual art as opposed to communication.

Gall's Law

Gall's Law, put forward by author and pediatrician John Gall in *The Systems Bible*, states that complex systems that work invariably evolve from simple systems. Attempting to build a complex system from scratch tends to be ineffective. Complex systems emerge from basic components. Although it's not foolproof, we can see examples of Gall's Law everywhere. A convoluted bureaucratic process in an organization probably began with something simple, a single form that served its purpose. Complex organisms like tigers and whales evolved from single-cell bacteria. Sprawling cities started off as small towns with a handful of inhabitants. Complex technologies like airplanes evolved from simpler ones like bicycles. Gall's Law explains we cannot always establish how a complex system works by looking at its parts. It also teaches us to avoid trying to design complex systems from scratch.

Conclusion

Irreducibility is about essence. It's the idea that some things can't be broken down into smaller parts without losing what makes them tick. It's the idea that not everything can be explained by looking at its components. Emergent properties arise from complex systems that can't be predicted by studying the individual parts.

Grappling with irreducibility requires a shift in thinking. Instead of trying to break things down, sometimes you have to zoom out. Look at the big picture. Embrace the complexity. Because some problems don't have neat, modular solutions. They're irreducibly messy.

Using irreducibility as a lens helps you focus on what you can change by understanding what really matters.

The Law of Diminishing Returns

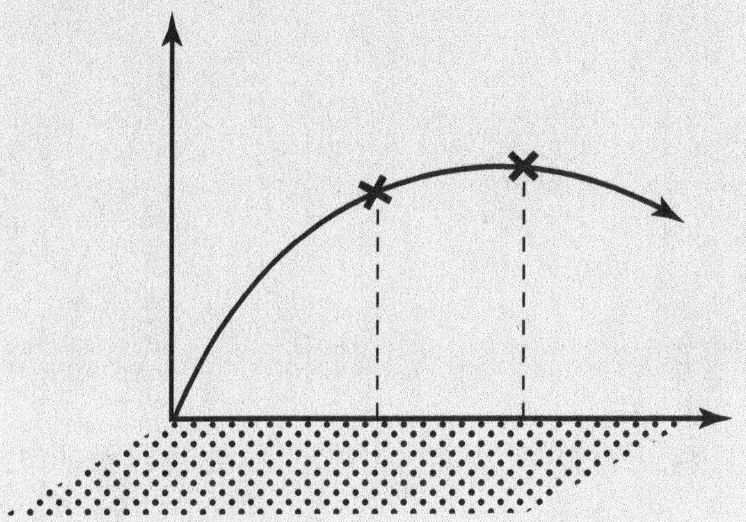

Hard work stops paying off.

When we put more effort or resources into something, we usually expect to get more out of it. Work more hours, be more productive. Exercise more, become fitter. Assign more people to a project, complete it sooner. Using the law of diminishing returns as a model shows us that the relationship between inputs and outputs in systems is not always linear. Past a certain point, diminishing returns almost always set in.

The law of diminishing returns posits that inputs to a system lead to more output, up until a point where each further unit of input will lead to a decreasing amount of output. In other words, at that point more effort leads to less return. Progress even further despite diminishing returns, and more inputs may reduce the amount of total output.

Consider adding sugar to your lemonade; the first scoop sweetens it a lot, but each extra scoop makes it only a bit sweeter than before. If you keep going, more sugar doesn't make it sweeter, it just starts piling up at the bottom, unused.

The concept of diminishing returns applies in almost any system. In economics, it is a specific term for the fact that increasing inputs, like materials and labor in production processes, increases outputs, but not indefinitely. Past a certain level, more inputs will lead to lower increases in outputs, until the inputs start to become a hindrance. A classic example is the number of workers in a factory. Hire more people and production goes up. Hire too many people and the factory gets crowded, people get in one another's way, and there isn't enough equipment to go around. Each additional worker then contributes less to the factory's output.

One early application of the law of diminishing returns was in farming, with the advent of artificial fertilizers in the nineteenth and twentieth centuries.[1] Farmers found that adding more nutrients to their soil increased crop yields at first, making plants grow bigger in less time. But past a particular ratio of fertilizer to soil, adding more meant less corresponding increase in yield. Adding even more meant less yield in total, as the soil became overloaded.[2]

Diminishing returns are everywhere. Working an extra hour might make you more productive; working an extra three might mean more mistakes, so less work gets done per hour.[3] Tweaking the little details of a project might improve it, but doing so for too long might mean the improvements aren't worth the time invested. Receiving enough funding to get off the ground might be a godsend for a new company, but receiving too much might mean decreasing benefits, as proving profitable for investors takes precedence over serving customers. When you're learning a new skill, early practice sessions have a huge impact on your abilities, then subsequent hours of practice lead to diminishing improvements in performance.

The law of diminishing returns teaches us that outcomes are not linear and not all inputs to a system are equal. Often we focus on the trivial at the expense of the meaningful. An extra worker in a factory with ten employees is not equivalent to an extra worker in the same factory with one hundred. An extra hour of work at nine p.m. is not the same as an hour of work at nine a.m. The advantage of understanding the law of diminishing returns is being able to calculate where that point is for different systems so we know how best to interact with them.

The Viking Raids of Paris

Diminishing returns happen because systems adapt. They become accustomed to certain inputs and stop responding to them in the same way. The law of diminishing returns teaches us that a way of interacting with a system that produces desirable results at first can become less and less effective over time. No matter how impressive the initial windfall may be, we should anticipate eventually getting less for our effort.

In 814, the Holy Roman emperor and king of the Franks, Charlemagne, died. The death of the ruler of Francia (now France) left a sudden power void in Europe. Throughout his life, Charlemagne led successful military campaigns against the Saxons and the Vikings. Europe had no other leader of equivalent might to fill his role of keeping them confined to Scandinavia. His successor Louis the Pious didn't inspire the same fear as the leader who once massacred forty-five hundred captive Saxons in one go.[4]

> The Vikings were never defeated; rather they allowed themselves to be assimilated.
>
> —NEIL OLIVER[5]

The first little fleet of Viking ships sailed up the river Seine in 820, looking to test Paris's defenses. Frankish guards beat them back without much trouble. But this was only a pilot raid. The first notable raid occurred in 841, when the Vikings targeted the abbey of Saint-Denis, as churches tended to hold the most wealth at the time. It proved to be a profitable attack. Viking leader Asgeir enriched himself by taking a large number of hostages, returning some for ransom and selling the rest as slaves.[6] After the initial success, the Vikings soon launched more raids.

The Viking leader Reginfred, who conducted the most notorious raid of all in 845, is so shrouded in mystery that historians are unclear if he was a single individual or a composite. He is sometimes also known as Reginherus, Reginhero, or Ragnar Lodbrok. Under his command, 120 ships carrying thousands of Vikings advanced up the river Seine toward Paris.[7] Guessing they would target Saint-Denis, the Frankish leader Charles the Bald, grandson of Charlemagne, placed one half of his army on each side of the river. His plan was misguided. By dividing his force, he allowed the Vikings to concentrate theirs, targeting one half at a time. Any soldiers they didn't slaughter they took as prisoners.[8] Then the Vikings demanded a ransom of seven thousand French pounds of silver and gold.

The 845 raid of Paris was not an attempt to take control of the city—it was about profit. Their pockets full, the Vikings left, ransacking a few villages along the way. Villagers viewed them as some sort of divine punishment for their sins.[9]

Historians remain divided on whether the ransom was a wise choice or not. It was certainly controversial among the people who had to pay for it.[10] Charles the Bald paid it because it got the Vikings to leave without inflicting further damage, saving him the expense of mobilizing an army again. He was also contending with divisions within Francia and was unsure whom to trust.

But in doing so, he set a dangerous precedent. Paying the ransom encouraged more Viking attacks.[11] Between 845 and 926, the

Franks paid an estimated total of 685 pounds of gold and 43,000 pounds of silver to the Vikings.[12] Buoyed by the success of the 845 Paris raid, they continued to besiege any towns that held enough wealth to be of interest.[13]

The Franks did not just sit back and let this happen. Walls went up around Paris to withstand attacks. They built bridges across the Seine to block ships from reaching the city. Towers equipped with hundreds of guards capable of pouring boiling wax and oil on any Vikings below added to the protection.[14] Unable to get close to the city, the Vikings resorted to sitting out lengthy sieges, which taxed them in terms of resources, morale, and human life due to disease. They tried setting fire to boats and pushing them toward the bridges, but they sank without causing damage.[15]

Diminishing returns set in for the Vikings. Raiding Paris resulted in smaller and smaller ransoms at a higher cost. It became difficult and time-consuming relative to the rewards. In 886, a weakened Viking leader requested just sixty pounds of precious metals in exchange for leaving. In 911, the Viking leader Rollo received an enticing offer from the Frankish king, Charles the Simple. Rather than gold, Charles offered to give him land, a title, and his daughter's hand in marriage. There was one condition: Rollo had to protect the area from any further Viking attacks. They shook on it and thus founded Normandy.[16]

The Viking raids of Paris show us that we cannot keep performing the same actions and expecting the same results. Things change. When we first try something new, the returns can be dramatic. We might be tempted to keep repeating ourselves, expecting to reap the same benefits. But we're likely to end up expending more effort for less return. When that happens, it's time to change tack. During the first few attacks on Paris, the Vikings extracted large ransoms because people were unprepared, lacking appropriate defense mechanisms. Over time, they built up their ability to withstand attack.

In addition, the areas simply began to run out of wealth to extract. The Franks stopped reconstructing their holy buildings so the Vikings would have less incentive to attack them. Finding new villages meant going farther afield, which cost more and carried greater risk. Due to the distances traveled, the Vikings began to spend months at a time in Europe to avoid sailing during the winter. Eventually it made sense for them to just settle for good. Once the returns weren't worth the effort, Rollo took the opportunity to benefit from Europe in a different way. His choice teaches us that noticing diminishing returns means it's time to try something new.

> The main body of Vikings were given lands in the Seine basin in exchange for protecting Paris. They settled into northern France and within a century were speaking a dialect of French and became known as the Normans.
>
> —MARK KURLANSKY[17]

Only after the raids stopped did Paris as we know it today begin to take shape, as the Franks found the courage to begin grand construction projects like Notre Dame cathedral. It would take a long time for the memory to fade and the area to recover.[18]

The Diminishing Returns of Mass Incarceration

> New opinions are always suspected, and usually opposed, without any other reason but because they are not already common.
>
> —JOHN LOCKE[19]

Incarcerating people has a long history as a means of punishing criminals and, in theory, making society safer. But incarceration has diminishing returns. Taking the most dangerous, violent individuals in a society off the street makes everyone else much safer.[20] After all, most violent crimes are the work of a tiny minority of the population. However, the more people a society incarcerates, the less everyone benefits. As we punish more minor crimes with prison sentences, the safety gains decrease. If incarceration continues increasing, it may reach the point of diminishing returns, where the benefits are outweighed by the cost to taxpayers and by the inability of incarcerated individuals to contribute to society. Mass incarceration rests on the assumption that locking up people who commit crimes is always a good idea. But that belief has a logical end point.

French sociologist Émile Durkheim argued that a certain amount of crime is inevitable in any society because what is considered criminal is based on the "collective sentiments" of a society. As long as people are divergent and have many different ideas about the correct ways to act and live, in any group there will be individuals whose actions will not follow the norms and who will be labeled as criminal. Durkheim did not condone crime but did argue that it is impossible to conceive a society without it.[21] This is not to say that acts we currently label as criminal are merely divergent behavior, but that divergent behavior that people end up labeling as criminal is inevitable.

Even in a hypothetical world where none of the acts we condemn by law occurred, there would still be variations in behavior that some would consider criminal. Preventing the worst sorts of crimes does not create a perfect society. It just means people attach greater significance to crimes that are more minor. Continue this process and you end up with a world where someone might be, say, put to death for spitting their gum on the ground because it is the worst conceivable infraction.

> What the wise do in the beginning, fools do in the end.
>
> —**WARREN BUFFETT**[22]

Exploitation Films from the 1950s to the 1970s

Our reactions to novel things are subject to diminishing returns. Enjoyable things tend to become less enjoyable if we're exposed to them a few times. The first snowfall of the year is beautiful. By March, you can't remember why you chose to live in a cold climate. The first time you go on a roller coaster, it gives you a thrill. After a dozen rides, you get bored. A new threshold has been set. If you want people to pay attention, you need to keep raising the bar, pushing past their evolving threshold.

One area where this habituation is apparent is in films. A new technique that terrifies millions in a horror movie is a dull trope the dozenth time another director copies it. A film that kept someone awake at night when they were a teenager might end up being something they show their kids on a weeknight. A powerful advertising campaign might seem quaint after it becomes a convention. We can use the mental model of diminishing returns to consider how we become nonchalant about things that used to provoke a reaction, by looking at the history of exploitation films.

An exploitation film is a type of movie that seeks to generate interest by capitalizing on current trends, niche genres, or sensational content. Often, these films are B movies, with low budgets, and tend to feature an unknown cast and crew. Some, like *The Blair Witch Project,* set new trends and gain a cult following.

Exploitation films are higher risk, higher reward. Early on, they pushed the limits of what was acceptable—constantly setting new thresholds a little bit at a time by tackling themes like sex, violence, drug use, and fear. Before the genre gained popularity in the 1960s, these movies were often wrapped in the guise of education to evade censorship.

As soon as the film industry began to take shape in the 1910s, people panicked about the morality of the medium. Some worried the content of films could corrupt viewers and pressed for censorship. In the 1930s, this concern led to the Motion Picture Production Code, which placed restrictions on what Hollywood could include in films. At the time, Hollywood was the film industry. Major studios owned the means of cinematic production, distribution, and exhibition, which gave them full control over the movies the public saw.[23]

In 1948, a landmark US Supreme Court ruling declared that the big Hollywood studios were violating antitrust laws and could no longer remain vertically integrated. Around the same time, network television was taking hold, and theaters were looking for new ways to get audiences through their doors. Into the mix came the rise of youth culture, as entertainment industries began to cater more to the tastes of young people. These three main factors laid the foundation for the exploitation film industry.[24]

As Ric Meyers writes in *For One Week Only,* "Fools and filmmakers rushed in where wise men feared to tread. They pored over the various rules and regulations that controlled the motion picture industry until they fell through a loophole."[25] These types of films began with the "nudist camp" pictures of the 1950s, which claimed to be documentaries. With the rise of grindhouse theaters and drive-ins, exploitation films took off. Low-budget studios churned out films to meet the demand for shocking content.

> Horror is fear of the unknown. Terror is fear of the known.
>
> —**RIC MEYERS**[26]

To look at the history of exploitation films during this era is to see a repeated pattern of audiences responding strongly to one film, then directors and studios hastily copying its distinguishing features—on and on until the impact was lost. Audiences couldn't be as surprised the tenth time they saw a possessed child or a group of campers being picked off one by one. They needed to see more deaths, more graphic gore, more taboo subjects, more nudity. Everything had to turn up a notch each time or diminishing returns set in.

Sometimes titles were copied. The 1962 film *What Ever Happened to Baby Jane?*, an acclaimed Academy Award winner, was eventually followed by *What Ever Happened to Aunt Alice?* (1969), *What's the Matter with Helen?* (1971), and *Who Slew Auntie Roo?* (1971). Similarly, we have *Don't Look in the Basement* (1973), *Don't Open the Window* (1976), *Don't Go in the House* (1979), and *Don't Answer the Phone!* (1980). When making a new film with a copycat title was too much of a stretch, production companies were not averse to rereleasing an old one with a new name and poster. Any successful exploitation film would see its basic premise replicated ad nauseam until the effect wore off.[27]

Advertising materials were fair game too. After *Color Me Blood Red* (1965) used the tagline "You must keep reminding yourself it's just a movie, it's just a movie, it's just a movie," similar sentiments followed for films lacking the clout to warrant it. *The Last House on the Left* (1972) advised viewers, "To avoid fainting keep repeating, it's only a movie . . . only a movie . . . only a movie . . ." Hallmark then reused essentially the same marketing for *Don't Look in the Basement* (1973) and *The Horrible House on the Hill* (1974).[28] Makers of exploitation films had to keep coming up with new ideas to get a response. Any part of a film that got a reaction was fair game for copying, which deadened future responses and made viewers more skeptical of marketing materials. A clever new title structure might be a surprise to audiences at first, but copies wore them out.

Despite occasional later freak successes for low-budget, shocking films like *The Blair Witch Project* (1999), exploitation films as they existed from the 1950s to the 1970s are largely dead.[29] As we mentioned before, their key characteristic was covering content mainstream cinema couldn't or wouldn't touch. But times have changed. Viewers are no longer easily shocked. Fringe themes have been absorbed into the mainstream. Ric Meyers writes, "The major movie studios, who once spit on the very idea of making money off sex and slaughter, now bank on it." It takes much higher budgets to interest audiences, and with less censorship, mainstream films have become less tame and audiences more desensitized.[30]

Meyers explains, "Exploitation films were the price we pay for, essentially, living a lie. Once upon a time, many would like others to think that they were well-adjusted, considerate, intelligent people who would never enjoy—even revel in—the suffering of others." But exploitation films were an extension of the same urges that drove people in the past to watch gladiators slaughter one another or accused witches burn. The films were an unabashed recognition of those urges and thus "allowed one to receive all of the perverted pleasure of looking at a car wreck without the guilt of knowing that the victims are real."[31]

Our reactions to shocking content diminish over time, and we have to seek out something worse to get the same reactions. That's why exposure therapy can be an effective means of overcoming phobias. Exploitation films show that strong reactions cannot continue indefinitely. We return to being unsurprised after we've seen the same thing a few times. Exploitation films may seem an unimportant footnote in cinematic history, yet they reflect the cycles culture goes through as the fringe becomes a banal part of the mainstream.

Exploitation films changed what we considered average in films. To produce content at the far end of the spectrum, films had to respond to continually changing standards. Diminishing returns is an interesting model through which we can explore why we become indifferent to novelty and thus always push the boundaries in trying to find something that causes the rush we experience when we find something new.

Diminishing Returns and Societal Collapse

Why do complex societies, like the Roman Empire, collapse? One theory, advanced by Joseph A. Tainter in *The Collapse of Complex Societies*, is that it comes down to diminishing returns. As societies grow and develop, they become more complex and require more and more "energy flow" to stay intact.[32] With increasingly advanced networks between individuals, "more hierarchical controls are created to regulate these networks, more information is processed, there is more centralization of information flow, there is increasing need to support specialists not directly involved in resource production, and the like." More complex societies extract an exponentially higher amount of energy from individuals just to stay intact than simple ones. At a certain point, the cost may exceed the benefits individuals derive from being part of that society. When this happens, it may begin to disintegrate.[33] Being complex no longer carries benefits, and it makes sense to return to a simpler level of organization.

Conclusion

Diminishing returns is the idea that the easy wins usually come first. The more you optimize a system, the harder it gets to eke out additional improvements. Like squeezing juice from a lemon. The first squeeze is easy. The second takes a bit more work. By the tenth squeeze, you're fighting for every last drop.

When you're a beginner, every bit of effort translates into significant gains. But as you level up, progress becomes more incremental. It takes more and more work to get better and better. That's why going from good to great is often harder than going from bad to good.

Understanding diminishing returns is crucial for allocating resources efficiently. You want to focus on the areas where you can get the biggest bang for your buck. Sometimes, that means knowing when to stop optimizing and move on to something else.

MATHEMATICS

What is mathematics?
It is only a systematic
effort of solving puzzles
posed by nature.

—SHAKUNTALA DEVI[1]

SUPPORTING IDEA:

Distributions

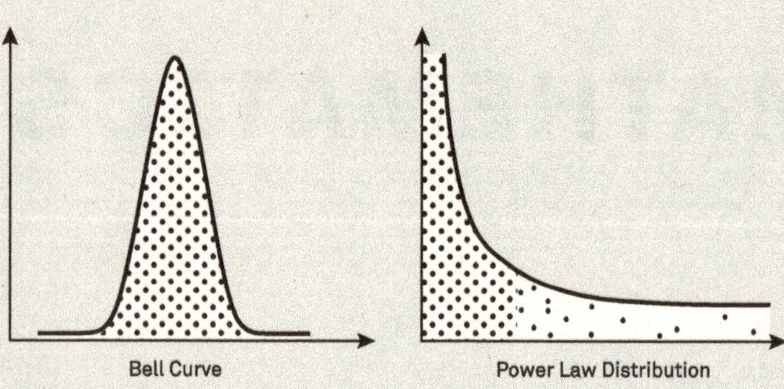

DISTRIBUTIONS ARE DIFFERENT WAYS A GROUP OF SOMETHING—LIKE people's heights, grades on a test, or flavors of ice cream sold—spreads out or bunches up. They tell you how often each item shows up.

Distributions help you contextualize what to expect given a certain data set. They help you make predictions about the probability, frequency, and possibility of future events. There are many different types of distributions. The four characteristics that will most determine the type of distribution you are dealing with for any given data set are:

1. Is the data made up of discrete values, or is it continuous?
2. Are the data points symmetric or asymmetric?

3. Are there upper and lower limits on the data?

4. What is the likelihood of observing extreme values?[2]

Distributions are often idealized (unrealistic) representations of a data set. According to NYU Stern School of Business, "Raw data is almost never as well behaved as we would like it to be. Consequently, fitting a statistical distribution to data is part art and part science, requiring compromises along the way. The key to good data analysis is maintaining a balance between getting a good distributional fit and preserving ease of estimation, keeping in mind that the ultimate objective is that the analysis should lead to better decisions."[3]

The distribution we are all most familiar with is the normal distribution, and it is one of our most important lenses for looking at the world. Its influence is everywhere from education to medicine, even if it is often invisible. But it's also an easy mental model to take too literally and end up trying to fit reality to the model, not vice versa. Reality rarely fits into a neat normal distribution, and we miss a lot of important nuance and variation when we try to make it do so.

A set of data points is normally distributed if the majority of values cluster around a midpoint, with a few falling on either side. The farther from the midpoint, the fewer values show up. The midpoint is simultaneously the mean, mode, and median value. When plotted on a graph, normally distributed data forms a characteristic symmetrical shape known as a bell curve. Leonard Mlodinow, writing in *The Drunkard's Walk*, summarizes it as such: "The normal distribution describes the manner in which many phenomena vary around a central value that represents their most probable outcome."[4]

Many common measurements, such as height, IQ, blood pressure, exam results, and measurement errors, are normally distributed. This tends to be the case for values that are subject to certain physical constraints, such as biological measurements. Normal distributions usually also characterize the price of common household goods. If you have an idea of the average price of toothpaste, you can use an estimation of the distribution to tell you if you are paying too much for the one in front of you or if you are getting a good deal.

In a normal distribution, the more extreme a value is, the less likely it is to occur. However, it's important to note that the tails in most distributions, even normal ones, go on forever. The probabilities of these values get smaller but are not impossible.

We refer to values far from the mean as long-tail values. Seeing as they are highly unlikely, we tend to forget about them. But if we get too caught up in seeing the world as normally distributed, we can forget that long-tail values tend to have an outsize impact. If you commute to work, it probably takes roughly the same time each day with minor variations. Once in a while, though, there might be a major issue like a road closure or broken-down train, which means it takes significantly longer, with the corresponding ripple effects for your day.

Normal distributions can be contrasted with power law, or exponential, distributions. The values in a power law distribution cluster at low or high points. Even though the distribution might cover a large diversity of potential values, the vast majority of points on the curve will represent a comparably small subset.

Wealth follows a typical power law distribution. Although the range of the possible wealth of an individual is quite large, most people cluster around a small range of values at one end of the curve. There are exponentially more people with $1,000 in assets than $1 billion. In our wealth curve, excessive wealth may be rare relative to the entire population, but there is no real cap on the wealth any one person can accumulate. In *Algorithms to Live By*, Brian Christian and Tom Griffiths say that power law distributions are also called "'scale-free distributions' because they characterize quantities that can plausibly range over many scales: a town can have tens, hundreds, thousands, tens of thousands, hundreds of thousands, or millions of residents, so we can't pin down a single value for how big a 'normal' town should be."[5]

> Something normally distributed that's gone on seemingly too long is bound to end shortly; but the longer something in a power law distribution has gone on, the longer you can expect it to keep going.
>
> —BRIAN CHRISTIAN AND TOM GRIFFITHS[6]

Being able to identify when you are in a power law distribution situation can help you be realistic about the effort required to break out of the end cluster. It also forces you to consider the diverse range of potential values you have to contend with. When imagining future wealth, a diversity of possible data points can be motivational, but the opposite is true if your power law distribution is about potential calamities.

There are other distributions. Geometric distributions give you intuition as to when a particular success might happen, and binomial distributions can suggest how long it will take to get particular numbers of successes. The Poisson distribution can give you an idea of the distribution of rare events in a large population. And understanding memoryless distributions, where the probability of an event occurring in the future is independent of how long it has been since the last event occurred, can make you feel better when you have to wait awhile for the next bus.

You never really know if you have the right distribution for your data. You can test your distribution against the ideal and conclude that they are similar with a high degree of confidence, but future data points may change the distribution.

The Good Life

One philosophy that has been misunderstood since it was first articulated is that of Epicurus. Writing around 300 BCE, he came to prominence after Plato and Aristotle and was a contemporary of the early Stoics. One of his core ideas centered around the value of pleasure. Epicurus argued that pleasure is the only realistic measure we have of evaluating our lives. When we experience pleasure, things are good, and thus the pursuit of pleasure ought to be the driving force behind our choices.

At first glance, his philosophy seems to advocate a life of selfish indulgence. Criticized for promoting a hedonism that would lead to the breakdown of society, Epicurean philosophy has endured much maligning over the millennia. However, a complete read of his philosophy reveals how pursuing the Epicurean ideal of pleasure actually leads to a very sedate, mindful life. Using the lens of a normal distribution curve helps us understand why and thus suggests modern uses for this ancient philosophy.

In his "Letter to Menoeceus", Epicurus writes, "No pleasure is a bad thing in itself. But the things which produce certain pleasures bring troubles many times greater than the pleasures."[7] These latter types of pleasures are the ones we should avoid, because what positive feeling we gain in the short term is outweighed by the ensuing negative experience.

An excellent way to thus capture Epicurus's idea of pleasure is the bell curve. If we imagine those things that cause us great pain being the values on the far left and those things that cause us great pleasure being on the far right, where we want to be is in the middle. The ideal state is one of neither pleasure nor pain. As Daniel Klein writes, for Epicurus, "Happiness is tranquility."[8] The state we should aim to be in is at the top of a normal distribution curve—a life free from pain and also free from the negative consequences of excess pleasure.

Far from promoting the pursuit of indulgence in all things pleasurable, Epicurus writes, "For we are in need of pleasure only when we are in pain because of the absence of pleasure, and when we are not in pain, then we no longer need pleasure."[9] For Epicurus, "'Pleasure' is the logical opposite of 'pain.' In other words, for him pleasure meant non-pain."[10] His conceptualizing of pleasure lends itself well to imagining life events plotted along a normal distribution curve. There are extremes at either end that are possible, but the most rewarding life is one that hovers around the middle, experiencing neither too much pain nor too much pleasure.

How does one achieve this midpoint, and what does life look like there? Epicurus said, "Therefore, becoming accustomed to simple, not extravagant, ways of life makes one completely healthy, makes man unhesitant in the face of life's necessary duties, puts us in a better condition for the times of extravagance which occasionally come along, and makes us fearless in the face of chance."[11] He believed that living a simple life was the best way to avoid pain, which is a pleasure in itself. Albeit a very sedate, mindful one.

It is the focus on pain reduction that gives us indicators of the value of aiming for the median of the normal distribution curve of life. As Catherine Wilson explains in *How to Be an Epicurean*, Epicurus "stated clearly that the best life is one free of deprivations, starting with freedom from hunger, thirst, and cold, and freedom from persistent fears and anxieties."[12] Thus conceptualizing pleasure as a life free from pain demonstrates why the extreme pleasure end of the curve would be well worth avoiding. Excess pleasure of the indulgent kind results often in pain. From the more visceral experiences of pain, such as a stomachache from too much rich food, to the painful psychological consequences of always choosing what feels right now at the expense of future satisfaction, when we focus on immediate gratification, we often sacrifice the happiness and contentment of our future selves.

For Epicurus, paying attention to the knowledge we gain from our experiences is critical for achieving a pain-free life. We need to be in tune with ourselves, noticing how our actions impact our bodies and psychological states. We also need to actively perform second-order thinking, considering the effects of our actions.

Epicurean philosophy thus invites us to reconceptualize what we consider pleasure in order to attain that pain-free median at the top of the curve. Wilson explains, "Regardless of the trouble other people can cause for us, Epicurus believed close human relationships to be the greatest source of pleasure in life."[13] Pleasure is not, then, about the attainment of things, status, and stuff, but about the interactions we have and the knowledge we gain from them. It is a philosophy of experience rather than consumption.

Compounding

Play the long game.

Play iterated games. All the returns in life, whether in wealth, relationships, or knowledge, come from compound interest.

—NAVAL RAVIKANT[1]

Compounding is like a snowball rolling downhill: the longer it rolls, the bigger it gets because it's not just the original snow but also the fresh snow it picks up along the way.

Compounding follows a power law, and power laws are magical things. Knowledge, experience, and relationships compound. When it comes to our personal capabilities, there are few limits to the possibilities suggested by this model.

One of the key things to understand about compounding is that most of the gains come at the end, not at the beginning. You have to keep reinvesting your returns to experience the exponential growth that is compounding.

Albert Einstein supposedly described compounding as the eighth wonder of the world. While he probably didn't, whoever did wasn't far off the mark. Compounding is an immensely powerful and often misunderstood force.

The most visible form of compounding is compound interest, in which the interest on a sum of money, if reinvested and untouched, goes on to itself earn interest. This means the total sum of money grows faster and faster, like a snowball rolling down a hill. Even a small amount of money can compound into a fortune over a long enough time span.

In the same way that money compounds and grows by earning

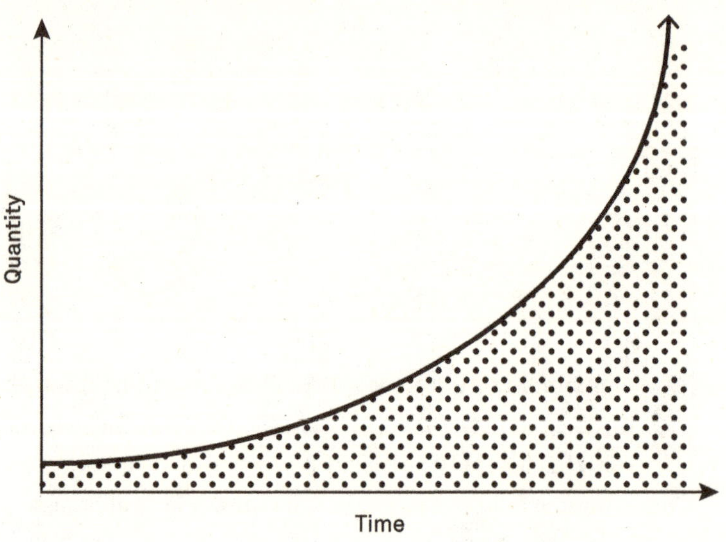

Exponential gains increase more dramatically the longer we leave them to compound.

interest, debt can compound too, even to the point where it becomes essentially impossible to pay off. This is called a debt spiral. Many people (and governments) who get into debt fail to realize just how powerful compounding can be over time. As Debt.org[2] puts it, "Compound interest is a powerful tool for building wealth. It's also a devastating tool that can destroy wealth. It just depends on which side of the financial equation you use it."

Compounding is a crucial, versatile mental model to understand because it shows us that we can realize enormous gains through incremental efforts over time. It forces us to start thinking long-term because the effects of compounding are remarkable only on a long timeline and most of the gains are realized near the end.

Money isn't the only thing that compounds. Everything from knowledge to relationships can grow exponentially if we keep adding to it and reinvesting the returns. All that matters is making continuous progress, no matter how small.

Exponential functions are hard to envision, so it's no wonder we tend to underestimate the power of compounding. We're used to thinking in terms of linear dynamics, but compounding is nonlinear. Of course, other forms of compounding are not literal, and it's not like we can use a formula to calculate how something like knowledge builds upon itself. But we can use the concept as a metaphorical lens for thinking about how things grow.

> An apparently trivial indulgence in lust or anger today is the loss of a ridge or railway line or bridgehead from which the enemy may launch an attack otherwise impossible.
>
> —C. S. LEWIS[3]

In a process similar to compound interest, the impact of decisions we make early on in any endeavor grows over time. These early decisions can have a greater impact than decisions made later on because their consequences compound. For instance, imagine a new graduate who takes a job that is disconnected from their true interests. It might seem like a temporary, harmless choice, but it increases the chances the next job they get will be in the same area. The more experience they accrue, the better they're likely to be, and before they know it, switching is a challenge. It's important to consider how the consequences of our choices can multiply over time.

You Don't Always Know the Payoff

When we invest in things that compound, we don't always know how we will be able to leverage our compounding interest. Think of investing your money. If you know how much you will put into an account and the interest rate under which it will accrue, you can estimate how much money will be in your account in twenty years. What you cannot predict is what you will be able to do with that money. At the outset, you may imagine you'll buy yourself your dream home. But twenty years from now, you might leverage the money to make a different career choice. The security of having it in the bank might mean that you can take bigger risks to pursue your dreams.

Small investments over time in areas like relationships and learning have immediate benefit, which is usually what prompts us to undertake the initial commitment. But one of the most fascinating properties of using compounding as a lens is that it illuminates how investments now can give us opportunities later that we can't even imagine now.

One example of how compounding knowledge creates options is the long-term effects of Jewish education norms. In *The Chosen Few,* Maristella Botticini and Zvi Eckstein trace the role of education in the Jewish religion and show how it was an investment that gave the Jewish people incredible opportunities.

In the first century of the Common Era, Jewish scholars and religious leaders "issued a religious ordinance requiring all Jewish fathers to send their sons from the age of six or seven to primary school to learn to read and study the Torah in Hebrew. Throughout the first millennium, no people other than the Jews had a norm requiring fathers to educate their sons."[4]

Botticini and Eckstein make it clear that there was no plan in the early days of Jewish education that this practice would offer advantages down the road. As they explain, in the beginning "sending children to school to learn to read and study the Torah was a sacrifice with no economic returns in the agrarian economies in which the Jews lived." Following the rule to educate was costly in terms of both maintaining the educational infrastructure and productive time lost. Initially the only tangible benefit of following the rule was probably something like spiritual satisfaction.[5]

When the norm of education was instituted, Jewish people were primarily farmers. Within a few centuries, they had given up farming for more lucrative professions as craftsmen, merchants, and moneylenders. Botticini and Eckstein demonstrate that "the direction of causality thus runs from investment in literacy and human capital to voluntarily giving up investing in land and being farmers to entering urban occupations to becoming mobile and migrating."[6]

The authors argue, "Learning to read helps people learn to write. It also helps develop numeracy and the ability to compute prices, costs, interest rates, and exchange rates, and thus to keep account books." Therefore, literacy creates opportunities. Jewish people did not have to be farmers, a profession with less earning potential than those options available in the growing urban centers. Not only does literacy give you a competitive edge to be, say, a moneylender or merchant, but it also "raises productivity and earnings in these professions."[7]

First in the Muslim caliphates and then in medieval Europe, Jewish people were consistently able to move into more financially rewarding professions at a significantly higher rate than non-Jewish people. "The literacy of the Jewish people, coupled with a set of contract-enforcement institutions developed during the five centuries after the destruction of the Second Temple, gave the Jews a comparative advantage in occupations such as crafts, trade, and moneylending." So while "most of the population in medieval Europe consisted mainly of illiterate peasants, sharecroppers, and agricultural laborers," Jewish people were able to leverage their literacy (and other aspects of their culture) to specialize in lucrative professions.[8] They took advantage of the opportunity their education gave them by moving into professions that paid well.

Just because you don't anticipate all the opportunities an investment will give you down the road doesn't mean you don't take advantage of them when they arise. From very early days, Jewish people invested in education. At first, likely for spiritual reasons, the investment nonetheless allowed them to capitalize on changes in the world economy. Their literacy allowed them to be first movers when new professions arose that required and thrived on an understanding of words and numbers. Botticini and Eckstein explain, "The Jewish community reaped the benefits of their investment in literacy by selecting into urban skilled occupations."[9]

We cannot know all the opportunities that will arise because of the investments we make today. Botticini and Eckstein conclude that "high levels of literacy and the existence of contract-enforcement institutions became the levers of the Jewish people." And they used these levers to "continue to search for opportunities to reap return from their investment."[10]

The lesson of applying the lens of compounding to Jewish education norms is to invest in things that provide you with benefit. The early Jewish people received from their investment in literacy a benefit in terms of their religious commitment. As time continued, the knowledge they accrued compounded, giving later generations exceptional opportunities.

Reinvesting Experience

Experience can also compound. If we choose to build on the skills we've developed by using them in new situations, we are significantly more capable later in life. Using compounding as a lens to look at personal experience isn't about proving an equation. Rather, this model can give us insight into what it means to reinvest what we learn through experience.

In 2008 Mireya Mayor, a scientist and explorer for National Geographic, participated in an expedition to retrace the path of Henry Morton Stanley, the man sent to find Dr. David Livingstone in Tanzania. Livingstone, the nineteenth-century rock star explorer of his generation, had gone missing, and Stanley was sent by an American newspaper to try to locate him. Mayor was part of a team of four who were filmed trying to complete the treacherous journey with the same equipment Stanley would have had in 1865. Despite challenging terrain, illness, and a variety of dangerous animals, she and the rest of the group completed the challenge. How Mayor was able to do things like trek for hours in incredibly hot, humid temperatures while battling dysentery can be illuminated through the lens of compounding.

One of the key components of financial compounding is the reinvestment. When the money you have invested earns interest, you can't take it out and go buy a new pair of shoes. You have to reinvest that interest into the original investment, so you increase the amount of funds earning interest.

We can think of using what we've learned in a similar way. The insights we get from experiences will pay off more if we reinvest them into further experiences.

Exponential gains from what we've learned aren't standard. Not everyone who has a degree in journalism wins the Pulitzer.

Not everyone who has a lemonade stand as a kid ends up running a national juice chain.

Humans have evolved to be pretty good at using past experience to guide future decisions, so a lot of knowledge compounding happens naturally over time, especially when we are young. But sometimes we get stale. We stop reinvesting that interest because we stop challenging ourselves. We stop compounding our learning. Twenty years of living becomes the same year repeated twenty times.

To gain insight and eventually wisdom, we need to reinvest our knowledge and let it compound. One way to do that is to be more deliberate about identifying how our past experiences can improve our chances of success in future ones.

Getting back to Mireya Mayor, it's unlikely she would have been successful on her Tanzanian expedition if it had been her first. It was tough. The conditions and the team dynamics were brutal. But she had years of insights from previous expeditions to draw on and apply.

Her first expedition was to Guyana in 1996, where she started doing the field research necessary to become a primatologist. She recounts how she packed for this expedition to study a rare species of monkey: "I purchased my plane tickets, the impractical teddy-bear backpack, and a pair of trendy hiking boots."[11] Her luggage also included a sleeping bag, tweezers, and a little black dress. She learned that the sleeping bag was unusable due to the deadly creatures that crawled around the forest floor and that hiking boots need to do more than look good. But she also learned that tweezers are invaluable on field expeditions because they can be used to remove a variety of small organisms that like to lodge in the skin.

In reflecting on her knowledge about packing gained from fieldwork, she writes, "By the time I had a few other trips to remote places under my belt, I had become an expert at packing minimalist." This expertise was gained through experience and included insights on the value of packing mirrors (for signaling and tick checks), tampons (for starting fires), and Windex (for neutralizing flesh-eating bacteria).[12]

Beyond what to pack for survival in the jungle, Mayor's story suggests further reinvestment of experiences compounding into her eventual success. Granted, she doesn't use the words "deliberate reinvestment," but the stories she shares demonstrate a conscious reflection on how to use past knowledge. For example, before she was an explorer and primatologist, she was a cheerleader for the Miami Dolphins American football team. At first glance one might think there was no useful knowledge that could be applied from one job to the other, but Mayor writes, "Working under pressure is nothing new to me. Even when I was an NFL cheerleader, I had to perform under the gun. Dancing in front of more than 75,000 screaming fans, remembering to smile, and making sure my hair remained in place in scorching heat after twisting an ankle—that's pressure."[13]

Mayor made numerous trips to Madagascar to study small primates that are unique to the island, like Perrier's sifaka. Over time she built relationships with everyone from other primatologists to organizations with grant money to the locals she relied on to navigate the island and support the expeditions. After years of fieldwork, she became a wildlife correspondent for National Geographic. She says, "Years before I appeared on television pointing out little-known facts about snakes or describing the mating behaviors of gorillas, I was putting in the legwork."[14]

This legwork gave her the knowledge to take on a vast array of assignments for National Geographic, from diving with sharks and giant squid off the coast of Mexico to working with leopards and giraffes in Namibia. Following Mayor through the journey of her career, from cheerleader and graduate student to television host, explorer, and primatologist, it's clear that her early experiences allowed her to take on increasingly complicated and dangerous challenges.

Which brings us back to Tanzania and the expedition to recreate the journey of Stanley's ultimately successful search for Livingstone. The journey was dangerous right to the final day. This is her description of the end:

> Back in canoes, we paddled up a tributary that ran through a swamp; it was slow going. A blood-red torrent of unknown origin came out of the swamp and reminded me of descriptions in Stanley's journals. When we couldn't go any farther, we stepped out into the swamp. There were snakes and crocs everywhere. We were treading through mud up to our waists when suddenly my bad cheerleading ankle gave out on me. I tore a toenail off as I landed face first in the mud. This was no spa treatment. In the process I lost my shoe and would have to walk through the swamp barefoot, getting slashed by razor-sharp grasses while being sucked into the mud. Tanzania had already kicked my ass, but it was nothing compared to these last few miles.[15]

Mayor's success at completing the arduous expedition is testament to her ability to reinvest the knowledge accrued from past experiences and capitalize on the resulting growth. A career like Mayor's reveals the power of using the lens of compounding to shape how we use our hard-won insights to allow us to take on exponentially greater challenges.

Compounding Relationships

Relationships are another thing that compound, becoming stronger over time if we keep investing in win-win dynamics. Imagine a network of nodes that connect to one another at random. The likelihood of any given node receiving an additional connection is proportional to the number of connections it already has. Through randomness, a small number of nodes will end up receiving most of the connections—a phenomenon called "preferential attachment."

Preferential attachment is a type of compounding that occurs when a certain thing (such as money or friends) is more likely to accrue to individuals or entities that already have more of it. For instance, people who have many friends tend to keep making more and more. They have more opportunities to meet new people through the ones they already know.

For someone to gain a serious cumulative advantage, it's not even necessary for them to have dramatically different starting conditions than their peers. Michael J. Mauboussin writes in *The Success Equation* that small differences in the economic climate when someone graduates from college can compound. For each additional percentage point higher the unemployment rate is when someone graduates, they can expect to earn 6 percent to 7 percent less in their career.[16] To graduate during a recession means having a serious disadvantage, regardless of how smart someone is or how hard they work.

Thus where you start in life may have a huge impact on where you end up, but it doesn't have to define it. Some people can achieve extraordinary things against the odds by understanding and leveraging the concept of cumulative advantage. Such people grab hold of one tiny advantage and get every additional possible benefit out of it. Then they keep repeating that process until they get where they want to be. One way of doing this is through networking. Each person you know has the potential to lead you to additional people. The stronger your network, the more influential or interesting the people you could get introduced to. Professional and social networks build upon themselves. Some people have an uncanny ability to take a connection with one person and use it to accelerate their careers.

Sidney James Weinberg was not your typical Wall Street banker—not by today's standards, nor even by the standards of the early twentieth century, when he rose to the pinnacle of the banking world. For a start, there was his background. Weinberg didn't come from an illustrious family. He didn't have a top-tier education or a long list of credentials. He didn't get a leg up from well-positioned Wall Street contacts either. Instead, he was the son of a Polish liquor dealer and one of eleven children. His education didn't stretch beyond his thirteenth year, when a teacher deemed him ready to enter the workforce. By that point, he'd already been working for several years selling newspapers and doing other menial jobs.[17]

Nor did he particularly look or sound the part of a Wall Street success story. Weinberg was just five feet, four inches tall and was usually dwarfed by the other bankers around him. His back was marked with knife scars from childhood street fights.[18] He never made any effort to disguise his distinctive Brooklyn accent or lie about his background, even going so far as to proudly keep the spittoon he'd polished when he first got his start doing low-level work at Goldman Sachs.[19] He was famously outspoken and always willing to make jokes at his own expense.[20]

Yet despite his unorthodox background, Sidney Weinberg became one of the most powerful people on Wall Street, holding the position of Goldman Sachs CEO for thirty-nine years. What set him apart was his understanding of cumulative advantage. His greatest assets were the relationships he carefully built and then continued to build upon to form more relationships. He understood that the more people he knew, the more people he could meet. By focusing on strengthening and then leveraging his relationships, Weinberg achieved remarkable success.

He started off on Wall Street at about age fifteen. These being the days before security was a thing, he picked a skyscraper and went from office to office, looking for any available work. Eventually he earned a menial job as a janitor's assistant at Goldman Sachs for a few dollars a week.[21]

One day Weinberg was tasked with taking a delivery to Paul Sachs, the founder's son. Sachs was charmed by him and had him promoted to the mailroom. Having a sudden opportunity to prove himself, Weinberg made an impression by reorganizing the mailroom to be more efficient, convincing Sachs he had potential in a banking role within the company. Sachs paid for Weinberg to take his first banking course and mentored him through university. When Weinberg returned to Wall Street after serving in World War I, his hard work paid off: he was now a salesperson. Eight years later, he was a securities trader. Another three years after that, Weinberg was the CEO. While we don't know exactly what happened during those years, everything began with that lucky meeting with Paul Sachs, which gave Weinberg a chance to prove himself. From there, he was able to get a better role in the company, which gave him access to even more people and more opportunities for promotion.

We can understand Weinberg's phenomenal rise if we consider the ways in which he worked to build beneficial relationships that offered him accruing influence and opportunities throughout his entire career. We can see clues as to how he managed this further on in his career. One way that Weinberg built relationships was by serving on the boards of corporations—at one point over thirty, for which he attended more than 250 meetings per year. He befriended every CEO he could by being as helpful as possible. Board meetings weren't a distraction from his main job, they were a way to further it.

When Franklin D. Roosevelt ran for president, he was an unpopular candidate on Wall Street. Weinberg saw a chance to stand out by supporting him and raising campaign funds, bridging business and politics. He already had influence on Wall Street, which he was able to convert into political influence. After Roosevelt won the election, Weinberg organized an advisory board of corporate executives, all carefully chosen to align with his own business interests.[22] He knew that giving the executives such a high-status position would ensure their patronage later on. Many indeed became clients of Goldman Sachs.

It's worth noting that Goldman Sachs was not the giant it is today, meaning Weinberg's political influence was unusual and likely the result of his relationship-building.[23] He always declined offers of political roles; Wall Street was his world, and politics served simply as means of building relationships. Throughout his career, he advised a total of five US presidents, using the entry point of Roosevelt's campaign.

Building lasting relationships with Goldman Sachs clients was also an important part of Weinberg's work. But he didn't just help people who were of direct use to him. One story tells of him sending a hundred dollars a week to a business rival who fell on hard times. As he told others, friendship should always come before business.[24]

Weinberg saw both the number of his relationships and their

durability compound over time. His conscientious approach to his interactions with people suggests he invested in his relationships. When we aim to make our relationships reciprocal, seeking to give as much as possible before we take, we can reap the benefits of compounding. The more we strengthen and deepen relationships, the more they build on themselves. The Wall Street of Weinberg's heyday was built on relationships. These days, we're not likely to see another Sidney Weinberg because the old system of reciprocity is no longer sufficient. When we create societies in which starting conditions matter more than capacity and effort, we narrow the range of who can reap the benefits of compounding even if they start from nothing. That initial foot in the door upon which relationships build can be the hardest part.

Conclusion

Compounding is the magic of exponential growth. It's the idea that small, consistent gains can snowball into massive results over time. Like a tiny snowball rolling down a hill, picking up more and more snow until it's an avalanche.

Compounding requires us to think long-term about our knowledge, experiences, and relationships. It tells us that the small stuff we learn, the people we meet, and the connections we deepen, when reinvested into our lives, build up our fortunes in wisdom and relationships, not by chance, but by the steady, patient accumulation of efforts. The majority of success doesn't happen by accident, and the lens of compounding illuminates the investments we need to make to get there.

Compounding is how you turn ordinary into extraordinary, one tiny gain at a time.

SUPPORTING IDEA:

Network Effects

NETWORK EFFECTS OCCUR WHEN THE UTILITY OF A PRODUCT OR SERvice increases as more people use it. More users means more value for all users. An obvious example is the telephone. If you own one but none of your friends do, it's not much use. But with each additional friend who gets one, the utility increases.

Network effects may also be indirect, as when a group of people using something for one purpose generates value for a group using it for a different purpose. For instance, more drivers joining a ride-sharing app means more utility for riders.

Network effects set off a reinforcing feedback loop wherein the added value attracts new users, who in turn create new users. Getting network effects started can be difficult, as certain types of products and services have little use until they reach a critical mass of users. But once this occurs, it creates a strong competitive advantage over new entrants to the market, even if they have a better product.

However, first movers are not always the most successful in a market, as later movers can learn from the early mistakes. Ultimately network effects can lead to a winner-takes-all market, in which one product or service captures most of the users. Competitors can secure only a negligible share. Users become reluctant to switch to an alternative because of the advantages created by network effects. Once network effects take hold, a product or service will continue to grow in popularity even without additional marketing.

The single most important factor behind the rise of many of the most significant technologies over the past two centuries is network effects. It not only contributes to the success of new technologies, it also secures it long-term. For this reason, companies put a lot of effort into attracting early users in hopes of reaching the critical mass requisite for network effects to take hold. Often, it is a matter of luck.

Network effects don't just occur for technology. We can apply the concept to any situation in which the value of something increases the more people use it. If a large number of skilled workers live in an area, it will attract companies offering well-paid jobs that use their skills, attracting yet more workers. Stores of value like gold are subject to network effects. The more people hold them as a long-term store of value, the more stable their prices become and the more appealing they are to future investors.

But network effects cannot continue forever. More users build more value only up to a certain point, past which negative network effects set in. This occurs when user base growth results in less, not more, value. Negative network effects can take several forms. A product or service may become overloaded and unable to serve its users as before. For instance, a public train network may benefit from a growing user base. More users means more investment in infrastructure, more frequent service, and possibly lower cost. However, if too many people use it, the trains may become overcrowded and dangerous. If there isn't space to build more train lines, this may reduce value for users.

Negative network effects can also occur when too many users

change the fundamental nature of something. A small online forum may have a tight-knit user base with high standards for posting. If there is an influx of new users, they may change the forum's norms and dilute its value, destroying what attracted them in the first place.

Sampling

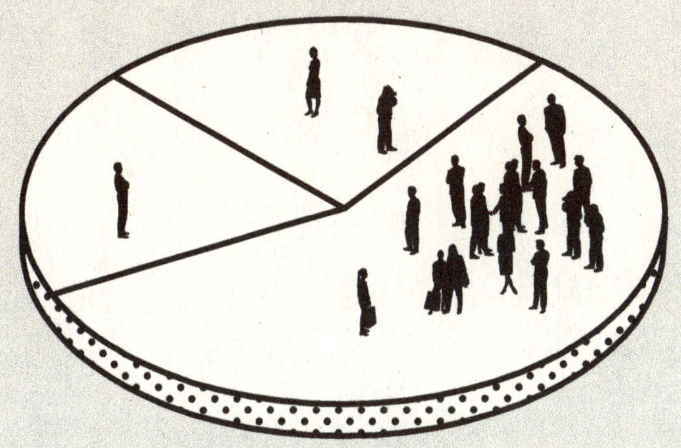

Your samples become your reality.

Numbers are intellectual witnesses that belong only to mankind.

—HONORÉ DE BALZAC[1]

Sampling is like taking a few sips to judge a bottle of wine. In math, it means picking a small, manageable bunch from a huge group to learn something about the whole. It's a shortcut that when done correctly gets you pretty close to the full picture and when done poorly leads you to the wrong conclusions. Understanding the influence and importance of sampling is a fundamental key to understanding the world better.

The mental model of sampling is a first principle for a number of concepts in mathematics, especially in statistics. Seeing as we often use statistics to gain a picture of reality, taking sampling into account will broaden your knowledge of other areas involving measurement, such as psychology. It will also help you think about risk and reward while disentangling luck from skill.

> Your personal experiences with money make up maybe 0.00000001 % of what's happened in the world, but maybe 80 % of how you think the world works.
>
> —MORGAN HOUSEL[2]

When we want to get information about a population (meaning a set of alike people, things, or events), we typically need to look at a sample (meaning a part of the population). It is usually not possible or even desirable to consider the entire population, so we aim for a sample that represents the whole.[3] We use samples to tell us about the world. The exception is a census, which aims to include everyone, not just a sample.

Sample size refers to the number of people, things, or events we look at from a population. It can have an enormous influence on the results we get. According to the law of large numbers, the larger the sample size, the more the result obtained will converge with the true value. For instance, the likelihood of getting any of the numbers from one to six when you roll a fair die is 1 in 6. If you roll a die 6 times, it would be unusual for each number to show up once. If you roll it 600 times, the frequency of each number would be closer to 1 in 6, and even closer if you roll it 6,000 times or 60,000 times.

Sampling gives you an idea of the possible values in your data set. The law of large numbers helps identify the probability of any of those values occurring.

As a rule of thumb, more measurements mean more accurate results, all else being equal. Small sample sizes can produce skewed results. If your sample for assessing the color of swans is the white birds in your neighborhood pond, you might deduce all swans are white. But if you looked at a larger sample of swans from different places, you'd discover some are black. Even if you took a small sample from your local pond dozens of times, it might not be representative and would always mislead you. Small sample sizes can fail to include rare or outlier results, making it seem like these don't exist. If you are once again just looking at the birds in a particular pond, you might ascertain that all swans have two legs. But if you took a much larger sample (or visited a wildlife sanctuary), you could well discover a swan that has had an accident and has only one leg.

One area where sampling is especially salient is in scientific studies of people, in which case the sample size is the number of participants. The larger the sample, the lower the margin of error and the higher the sampling confidence level, meaning the more probable it is the results will generalize to the whole population.[4]

But we have to make trade-offs. Studies with small sample sizes are not useless. Managing the funding and logistics for a larger study might be impractical, so a small one can provide evidence that further research is worthwhile. Researchers can combine a number of small studies in a meta-analysis to get a broader overview. If the costs of a study are high, such as a psychological study in which participants are subjected to a great deal of distress, a small sample may be more ethical. Researchers have to consider a range of factors to establish the right sample size, including the expected effect size and the expected dropout ratio.

In addition to being an appropriate size, samples need to be random to be representative of a varied population. This means every person, thing, or event within the population has an equal chance of ending up in the sample.[5] George Gallup, who could be called the inventor of the opinion poll, once gave a useful analogy for the necessity of a random sample. He said you can decide if a pot of soup needs more seasoning by tasting a single spoonful—provided you've stirred it well first.[6]

A large sample size is certain to be more accurate only if it is representative, which means it's important to be aware of sampling biases. For instance, the healthy worker effect refers to the fact that people who are unwell are less likely to be employed, meaning that workers within a field or for a company will be, on average, healthier than the general population. If you're trying to measure the impact of a dangerous chemical on factory workers who handle it, a sample of those currently employed in that type of factory will not be representative—no matter how large. You'll need to factor in those whose health has been damaged so much they no longer work or have moved to another field.[7]

Thinking about sampling can help us overcome some forms of bias. For example, we tend to place too much emphasis on anecdotes, in particular those coming from people close to us or that make good stories. We're all the more inclined to respect anecdotes if they confirm what we already believe. An anecdote is a sample size of one, and we should collect more data points if possible. The exception is when one result indicates something is possible. The first person to survive a heart transplant was more than an anecdote.

Thinking about your samples also teaches that sometimes what you need to do to see the world in a more accurate way is to obtain a larger or more representative sample. Traveling, living in a big city, or otherwise finding a way to meet more diverse people may make you more tolerant. Exposing yourself to a broader range of ideas through interdisciplinary, far-reaching reading may make you more open-minded. Learning more about the history of your industry and accumulating more experience may make you more risk-aware as you discover rarer and more extreme possibilities.

Defining a Language

It is important to recognize when one measurement isn't enough. The making of the first *Oxford English Dictionary* (*OED*) is a story that demonstrates the value of increasing sample size, in terms of the increased accuracy many measurements can bring.

It's hard to imagine the effort required for the first dictionary of a language to be created. We have grown up in a post-dictionary world, where all words are cataloged with their definitions and history. In looking through any dictionary, it's easy to find words that have multiple meanings. Does "dove" refer to a bird or the past action of jumping into a pool? To capture the entire history and use of a language, the first dictionaries must consider hundreds of thousands of data points. The *OED,* although not the first English dictionary, was the first to accomplish the feat of a thorough cataloging of the English language.

Talk of the *OED* first got underway in 1856. At the outset, the purpose of the OED was described thus: "A dictionary should be a record of all words that enjoy any recognized lifespan in the standard language." The group initiating the task felt that a proper dictionary should not just show contemporary usage of words, but "had to have, for every word, a passage quoted from literature that showed where each word was used first."[8]

What would producing this kind of record entail? As Simon Winchester explains in *The Professor and the Madman,* it "would mean the reading of everything and the quoting of everything that showed anything of the history of the words that were to be cited. The task would be gigantic, monumental, and—according to the conventional thinking of the times—impossible."[9] Essentially, to produce the *OED,* all books ever written in the English language would have to be read in order to pull out not only all the words the language has ever produced, but their first instances, their multiple uses, and their evolutions.

At what can be regarded as the kick-off meeting, Winchester describes that, with a sensibility that was out of step for their place and time, the group of men who sought to produce a dictionary of the English language realized the only way it would ever be achieved would be to enlist the help of large numbers of people "to peruse all of English literature—and to comb the London and New York newspapers and the most literate of the magazines and journals."[10] Production of the dictionary would require combing through millions of pages of words.

Why wasn't it enough to just note the common usage of a word and carry on? Let's briefly consider the word "take." It's fairly common and likely one we use every day. But to define it based on one example of usage would be a mistake. It has at least four definitions:

1. To remove something (e.g., I take that away from you)
2. To hold something (e.g., I take my mother's hand)
3. A recorded scene from a movie (e.g., We shot that in one take)
4. The amount of something gained from a source (e.g., taxation or being paid off; he was on the take)

To get a complete understanding of the word "take," you need to factor in all these possible uses. In order to include "take" in the dictionary, all these uses need to be found. And you need to make sure there aren't any more.

An army of volunteers read through every book in the English language, preparing submissions for the editorial group. As Winchester describes, "Each volunteer would take a slip of paper, write at its top left-hand side the target word, and below, also on the left, the date of the details that followed: these were, in order, the title of the book or paper, its volume and page number, and then, below that, the full sentence that illustrated the use of the target word."[11]

Entries poured in from across the world. Winchester states, "In the end more than six million slips of paper came in from the volunteers."[12] The vast numbers of books and magazines being investigated meant not only that the entirety of the language was being covered but also that the accuracy of the history and definitions of each word were quite refined. The editors could cross-reference ideas and sources to produce a final product verified against all written sources of English.

The first OED was finished on December 31, 1927. It contained 12 volumes with 414,835 words defined and 1,827,306 illustrative quotations. It is the most complete chronicle of the English language ever produced. It is also a testament to the value of considering what sample size you need to get accurate results.

Insurance

Insurance, as a concept, is predicated on the idea of reducing uncertainty by spreading the cost of adverse events between groups of people, companies, and other entities, and across time. It's impossible to predict if a given individual will get their laptop stolen or break their leg, or if a particular company will have a factory burn down or cause an oil spill, and so on. But with a large enough sample size, it's possible to predict with reasonable accuracy the expected number of payouts per year. Insurance companies use this to calculate how much to charge. Each customer pays much less than they would if they were to face a calamity uninsured, but most never receive a payout.

Insuring a small group of customers tends to be high risk, and a big group is usually low risk. With enough customers, an insurance company can effectively eliminate the uncertainty. Individual risks are uncertain; aggregate risks are predictable.[13] In order for a risk to be safely insurable, it must show some uniformity across the population.

Occasionally insurers are blindsided by extreme or unforeseen events. The 1906 San Francisco earthquake was one of the most severe natural disasters in US history, leading to insured losses of more than $6.3 billion in today's money. Such an earthquake (with an estimated magnitude of 7.7 to 8.3) is expected only every two hundred years, making it a surprise for insurers. Around fourteen insurance companies went bankrupt as a result of the payouts, and the losses were equal to all profit the industry earned over the prior forty-seven years.[14] Due to the earthquake's rarity and the extent of the damage, much of it caused by subsequent fires, sample size didn't help in this case.

In other cases, an event can essentially be the first of its kind and be so extreme and rare that no sample size makes it safe to insure. Following the 9/11 terrorist attacks, which led to payouts of $31.6 billion, the US government had to intervene to ensure companies continued offering terrorism risk insurance.[15]

Not All Sample Sizes Are Created Equal

One of the most important considerations with sample sizes is their representative diversity. The insights you get from a large number of data points are only going to be as good as the range of possibilities they cover. If, for example, you want to know how effective airbags are in preventing serious injury in car passengers, but you've collected information only on drivers, no amount of that data will give you a useful answer.

The authors of "The Weirdest People in the World?" explain, "Behavioral scientists routinely publish broad claims about human psychology and behavior in the world's top journals based on samples drawn entirely from Western, Educated, Industrialized, Rich, and Democratic (WEIRD) societies."[16] They go on to demonstrate that the people in WEIRD societies are outliers in many ways; therefore, we probably shouldn't be using studies based entirely on the behavior of WEIRD subjects as representative of the entire human population.

If we want to uncover universals about the behavior of human three-year-olds, we don't need to study more children in California. Adding to the numbers we already have with more studies using the same subject set is not going to help us gain insights with broad applicability. If we want to say something meaningful about human nature, then our data set ought to contain information from a sample of humans who represent the diversity found on the planet.

In the book *Invisible Women,* author Caroline Criado Perez explores how data sets often used to make decisions that impact women don't actually contain any information about women. She argues, "When your Big Data is corrupted by big silences, the truths you get are half-truths, at best."[17]

It is important to study samples representative of the overall population. However, it can also be important to study subsets with different features that might not be apparent from averages.

Data needs to be collected in order to be analyzed, so you need to ask yourself if you have the right mechanisms to collect the data that will give you the fullest picture possible—or at least enough to make a good decision with the potential for good outcomes. Perez reports that more than 90 percent of people who experience unwanted sexual behavior on public transport in New York and London don't report it. Nor do female metro users in Azerbaijan. So if someone were to conclude, based on official police reports, that safety for women isn't an issue in these places, they would be dead wrong.[18] Therefore, those making rules and changes based on data need to look hard at the data being used.

Not including women creates a data set that eliminates half the human race. Perez gives examples of when this is annoying, like phones too big for the average female hand, and when it creates serious negative outcomes for women, such as in medical treatment.

She explains, "Nearly all pain studies have been done exclusively on male mice," and many clinical trials done exclusively on men will have their results applied equally to women, despite women having different physiognomies.[19]

The majority of clinical trials (at least for prescriptions used by everyone) produce results applicable to a two-hundred-pound adult. There's also ethnicity to consider in the sample size: for example, African American, Latino, Asian, and Caucasian populations have their own unique metabolic and enzymatic profiles, thus leading to many medications behaving differently in each population. To obtain sufficient diversity in a sample size is often far too costly for pharmaceutical companies. Therefore, many medications are launched with suboptimal data or never reach the market because a subset of the larger sample showed unexpected adverse events.

One of the problems with assuming that a large sample size alone gives us a good data set is that we can undermine the problems we are trying to solve. For example, no number of samples will be sufficient if you can't acknowledge that you have biases, and volume on its own won't help you overcome them. Perez writes, "If you aren't aware of how those biases operate, if you aren't collecting data and taking a little time to produce evidence-based processes, you will continue to blindly perpetuate old injustices."[20]

Perez argues, "The introduction of Big Data into a world full of gender data gaps can magnify and accelerate already-existing discriminations."[21] It is not a big leap to conclude that Big Data based on narrow data sets can exacerbate many different forms of discrimination. As the authors of "The Weirdest People in the World?" conclude, "We need to be less cavalier in addressing questions of human nature on the basis of data drawn from this particularly thin, and rather unusual, slice of humanity."[22] The lesson is that deep data on a homogeneous population is relevant only to that population. If a data set is being used to describe the broad category of "human," then it needs to be representative of the diversity of the species.

Why should we care about the quality of our sample sizes? Because, as Perez explains, "having an accurate measure is important because data determines how resources are allocated."[23] We tend to draw conclusions from samples not for fun but to make meaningful, sometimes critical decisions that can have a wide impact. You will reduce your chances of a good outcome if the data you collect is not representational of the people affected by the decisions you make. Yes, large sample sizes are better than small sample sizes for decision making, but it's critical to remember that not all data sets are created equal.

Conclusion

Sample size is about how much of the world you're looking at. It's the number of data points you're using to draw conclusions. Like trying to guess the average height of people in a city by measuring a few folks on the street. The more people you measure, the more confident you can be in your estimate.

One of the biggest mistakes we can make is drawing conclusions from too small a sample size—like trying to guess a puzzle picture from only a few pieces. In most instances, increasing our sample size gives us valuable information that lets us see our situation in a new light. The catch is that large sample sizes are expensive. It takes time and money to collect all that data. So practitioners and researchers are always balancing the need for precision with the constraints of budget and deadline. They'll often settle for the smallest sample size that can still give them a statistically significant result.

Using this model means taking the time to explore what isn't obvious and being aware of how easy it is to corrupt our samples with bias.

The next time you hear a statistic, think about the sample size. It'll give you a clue about how seriously to take it. Remember: the larger the sample, the closer to the truth.

Randomness

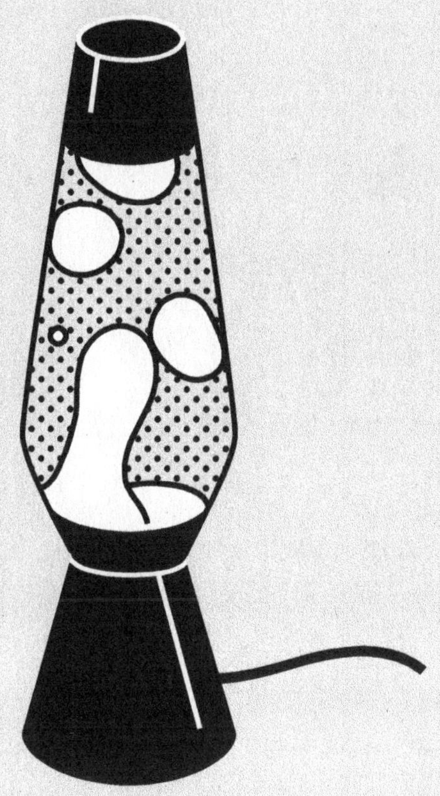

Predictability is often an illusion.

The human mind is built to identify for each event a definite cause and can, therefore, have a hard time accepting the influence of unrelated or random factors.

—LEONARD MLODINOW[1]

Randomness can be a hard model to use because humans aren't great at comprehending true randomness. When we look at the world, we tend to see order. We notice patterns and sequences, like thinking the world is out to get us because a few bad things happened in a row. Yet our sense of predictability and order is an illusion. Much of what we encounter day-to-day is random; we just don't perceive that. Using randomness as a model means being willing to accept that it exists and looking for situations in which it can help us.

A dictionary definition of randomness is "proceeding, made, or occurring without definite aim, reason, or pattern."[2] It is the opposite of predictability and order, something we aren't wired to conceptualize. Randomness goes against the way we like to view the world. Yet it's not an anomaly or a rarity; randomness is the rule, not the exception. We misunderstand randomness anytime we attribute causality where none exists. Although we cannot tame it, we can learn to work with—not against—randomness.

One reason randomness can be challenging is that it makes the universe seem less friendly and comprehensible than we might wish. It's hard to accept that much of what happens in our lives is chance, not ordained in any way. It's like the world throws random dots at us, and humans are constantly trying to draw lines between them, even if none exist. Randomness thus forces us to confront our lack of control over outcomes in many situations.

> The history of ideas is a history of gradually discarding the assumption that it's all about us.
>
> —PAUL GRAHAM[3]

Similarly, we can forget that the past was as random as the future will be. In hindsight, history can seem ordered and logical. When we open a history book, we see structured narratives. Events have a beginning, a middle, and an end. It only seems this way in retrospect. Not only are past events random, so is the information we have about them. Historical documents survive at random, and it's also up to chance whether a particular researcher comes across them or even how they interpret them.[4] Documents get lost, destroyed by fire or water, or thrown away because no one recognizes their value. Others get ignored or are hard to interpret. The further back in time we look, the more incomplete the information we have becomes.

Randomness is not something to be afraid of. It's a tool at our disposal. For example, our immune systems have to contend with a vast variety of possible pathogens. To deal with new and varied threats, our bodies produce different-shaped lymphocytes at random, meaning each has the potential to fight different pathogens.[5] Similarly, when ants forage for food, they all move around at random. If one finds food, it leaves a pheromone trail to it. Other ants will find that trail at random and follow it, making it stronger. Without any central control, this enables ants to coordinate themselves.[6] "It appears that such intrinsic and probabilistic elements are needed in order for a comparatively small population of simple components to explore an enormously large space of possibilities, particularly when the information to be gained from such explorations is statistical in nature and there is little a priori knowledge about what will be encountered."[7]

Randomness is a fundamental part of the universe, and embracing it instead of trying to fit order where it doesn't belong can help us do two things: be less predictable and be more creative.

> Making use of chance can be a deliberate and effective part of approaching the hardest sets of problems.
>
> —BRIAN CHRISTIAN AND TOM GRIFFITHS[8]

What Are the Odds?

One situation in which we misunderstand randomness is when equally likely random events happen in a sequence. We sometimes think what happened last time dictates what will happen next time. For instance, in a sequence of random events, we may think it is unlikely for the same thing to happen multiple times in a row. If you flip a coin six times and it's heads every time, it might seem like it's not a fair coin. But seeing as the outcome of each flip is equally likely to be heads or tails regardless of the previous result, HHHHHH is as probable as any other specific sequence, say, HTTHTH.

Casinos take advantage of this principle, getting people to bet on random events while ensuring the odds are always to their benefit. Whether a given gambler wins any particular round is random, but on average everyone loses. One major fallacy casinos profit from is the mistaken belief that what happened in the previous round affects what happens in the next one. Assuming no tampering, any particular outcome of a roll of the dice or a spin of a roulette wheel is equally likely each time. The past does not influence it.

In 1913, the roulette wheel in a Monte Carlo casino landed on black twenty-six times in a row. Gamblers lost millions when they kept betting large sums of money on it being red next. The fallacy was that each time the wheel landed on black, the chances of the next spin being red increased. But the probability of getting red is always 50 percent, and the previous results have no impact on that. The gamblers had no reason to bet more in that situation than in any other. While a roulette wheel landing on black so many times in a row is remarkably unlikely, it doesn't change the probability of any given spin being black.

Serendipity and Creating

A question authors always seem to be asked in an interview is, "Where do you get your ideas?" More than a few have gone on record stating how much they hate this question. Why? Because it implies there is an idea bank, or a creativity app, or some defined source authors can access—that when they are faced with a blank page, they can purchase or otherwise pull out an idea from this source, and away they go.

The reality is far messier. Ideas come from everywhere with great inconsistency. What is inspiring to one author one day may not inspire them the next time they are looking for an idea. And a particular source of inspiration is unlikely to work for another author in the same way. When one's creativity feels blocked or interesting ideas seem inaccessible, the introduction of randomness can come to the rescue.

Author Jane Smiley, in her book *13 Ways of Looking at the Novel,* reflects on her creative process in developing her works of fiction.

> I hadn't ever had much of a theory of creativity beyond making a cup of tea or opening a can of Diet Coke and sitting down at the typewriter or computer. The first and last rules were "get on with it." But perhaps that getting on with it that I had taken for granted for so many years was dependent upon those half-attentive ruminations during diaper changes and breadmaking and driving down the road?[9]

Smiley makes it clear that although ideas definitely come from somewhere, an author can never know precisely where that might be. And so randomness—in this case understood as unpredictability—is a very useful tool when trying to create.

The writing process for fiction is far from formulaic. Sometimes you start with the whole plot in your head, and sometimes you don't. Sometimes you plan out every chapter before you start writing, and sometimes your characters unexpectedly steer your story in a different direction. Sometimes you have enough ideas to give you momentum to reach the end, and sometimes you get stuck halfway through. Smiley recalls how she dealt with a challenging time writing a story: "Rather than planning and working out in advance, as I had done with most of my earlier novels, I willingly entered a zone of randomness."[10]

Making your characters do something unexpected by writing a scene you hadn't planned is one way to work around a creative block. These scenes aren't always amazing, and you may cut them later. But sometimes just seeing your characters having an unplanned experience can give you insight into how to use their attributes to keep your story going.

Writing a work of fiction is not a linear process. As Smiley describes in one experience, "One day I waited for inspiration, got some, went off in a completely new direction, then had second thoughts the next day and tried something new."[11] Often an author will have to try a variety of options for a particular scene to determine the best way forward.

When you begin a novel, where you start is often not where you end up. You may have certain ideas going into it, but your research demonstrates you've made some erroneous assumptions, and you have to change your plot or your setting. Or a character turns out to be more interesting than you imagined, and they end up carving out a bigger role for themselves.

In Smiley's description of the novel-writing process, she makes it clear that there are very few universals. "Some novelists write by obligation, others by desire. These are questions of temperament.

There is no intrinsically better way, since the only standard of achievement to begin with (and for quite a long time) is the accumulation of pages."[12] Which brings up another important point about the value of randomness in novel writing: authors are by no means universal themselves. The experiences, desires, assumptions, and goals of those telling the stories are just as varied as the stories themselves.

In exploring the history of the novel, Smiley looks at the works of Daniel Defoe, like *Robinson Crusoe*, and says, "Defoe's Nonconformist religious training gave him a sense of sympathetic connection with subjects not previously given serious literary treatment—prostitutes, servants, criminals, working men and women, courtesans, adventurers of all stripes."[13] And Defoe is but one example. We can imagine that all novelists draw on their own lives for inspiration, and their particular backgrounds determine what they see in the world around them. The unique intersection of experience and temperament, combined with the unpredictability of how one feels at any given moment when writing, means that it is very hard to trace a line of cause and effect in the writing of a story.

Even with an interesting story developing in the brain, with plot points and characters pushing to get out and onto the page, sometimes authors get stuck. Instead of waiting to get unstuck as if by magic, the better solution is to add an element of randomness and see where it takes you.

Smiley advises as a remedy to "find out more—read more, travel to the spot where your novel is set and spend a few days there, ask questions, look for original documents, engage your senses to gain more knowledge of what you are writing about. If you are bored with your subject, it is fatal to try to think your way out of it."[14] Instead you must experience your way out of it. If you are stuck, it means that everything you currently think cannot help you. You must get out into the world and experience the serendipity of stumbling into new things. One of these new things will help you continue your story, and you have no way of knowing in advance which thing it will be. So get out there and see what you run into.

Although it's impossible to know for sure, it seems unlikely that all great novels haven't benefited from their authors' exposure to random events. Why? Great novels aren't a formula. You cannot copy exactly what others have done and achieve the same results.

Perhaps most important, there is no precise definition of what makes a novel great anyway. As Smiley explains to a novelist as they begin their creation, "As you aim for perfection, don't forget that there is no perfect novel, that because every novel is built out of specifics, every novel offers some pleasures but does not offer some others, and while you can try to achieve as many pleasures as possible, some cancel out others."[15] A particular novel cannot be all things to all people.

One of the greatest and most frustrating elements of creativity is its imprecision. One can neither master creativity nor be creative all the time. When you are stuck while pursuing the nebulous task of trying to achieve creative output, introducing an element or two of randomness can help you make new connections to move past the block you are pushing against.

Two Perspectives on Randomness

To understand true randomness, we need to distinguish it from pseudorandomness.

Pseudorandomness is the appearance of randomness due to our inability to predict or detect a pattern although there are underlying causal influences.

True randomness is different. It is still coupled with probability distributions but is completely detached from any causal factor, meaning there's no explanation that we could apply to even approximately guess a more or less likely outcome for the next trial.

Our tendency to create a narrative to order and organize the world makes us predictable. We are also highly suggestible, remembering the most recent things we were exposed to. Thus, humans often behave in a pseudorandom manner, a fact that can be exploited.

Professional magicians exploit our availability bias and narrative tendencies in some of their tricks. If you're asked to think of a random number or pick out a random card from a pack, you might not realize there is an order to your choices. Your choice is not truly random, merely pseudorandom.

Chananel Mifelew, better known by his stage name, Chan Canasta, became famous for his magic tricks in the 1950s and '60s. His tricks were typically simple, performed using little more than a pack of cards or a book, but with a flair that earned him the nickname "a remarkable man." Canasta's tricks had an experimental air, as they tended to rely on taking chances. It was not unusual for them to go wrong during live performances.

Yet failures only highlighted Canasta's lack of trickery. Sometimes he took wild chances if he believed it was worth the risk. In one trick, Canasta asked a panel to each come up with a random word and then combine them into a sentence that he would predict in advance. Canasta was completely wrong, but he explained that it was worth trying. The chance of him getting it right was higher than you might imagine because of the way we misinterpret pseudorandomness as randomness. When someone picks a "random" word, the chances of them picking any particular word in the dictionary are not equal. In reality, certain words are much more likely to come up than others.

Unlike many modern magicians, Canasta didn't pretend he was performing magic. Instead, he took advantage of his impressive memory and his ability to give the impression of randomness.[16] For instance, in one trick, he would ask a volunteer to pick three random cards from a pack and then place each in a different pocket, again at random. He was able to subtly influence which cards they took and where they placed them. But the volunteer felt it was random and was unaware of his influence. Even if it didn't always work perfectly, it was impressive when it did.[17]

Canasta went on to inspire other mind readers, who took advantage of the same psychological trick—making people think their choices were random when they were pseudorandom.

When we're asked to make a random choice, especially if we're under pressure, we tend to fall into certain patterns.[18] Asked to name a random vegetable, most people say carrot. After George H. W. Bush declared his hatred of broccoli, that briefly became the more popular choice. Asked to name a shape, mentalist Banachek writes that most people will opt for a square. For a flower, they will usually say a rose. For a number between 1 and 5, most will name 3, and for 1 to 10, the usual choice is 7. The typical "random" color people name is blue, and the piece of furniture is a chair.[19] Performed with enough flair, simple tricks like this can seem like mind reading. It works because we don't recognize we're not making random choices.

Our inability to predict in Canasta's type of magic tricks comes from seeing only one instance of the trick instead of seeing hundreds. The magician takes advantage of the seeming randomness of a single trial, while few people would think it was purely random if they watched it performed a thousand times with different audiences. That's because it's not truly random; it's only pseudorandom.

Generating randomness is hard. Ask someone to give you a

string of random numbers and they'll end up following a form of order. Generating genuine disorder for things like data encryption requires unpredictable physical processes, like radioactive decay, atmospheric noise, and the movement of lava lamps.[20] When generating true randomness is essential, we have to find a method that overrides the way our brains work. One way that people throughout history have achieved this is through divination rituals that provide random data. Although people attributed the success of these practices to magic or divine wisdom, that's not why they worked. Rather, despite the narrative of divination, the rituals generated truly random results that were far more useful than the pseudorandom data our brains often generate.

The Naskapi foragers in Labrador, Canada, needed a way to come up with hunting paths at random so the caribou wouldn't learn to anticipate their routes and avoid them.[21] They achieved this through a ritual involving heating the shoulder bone of a caribou over hot coals until the surface was covered in cracks. Then they used the cracks as a map to tell them where to hunt. Beaver pelvises, skinned otters, and fish jaws also served similar purposes.[22] Although they saw it as a form of divination, it worked by giving them hunting routes more random than any human could manage.

True randomness is detached from any causal factor, which is why no one could predict where the next hunting area was going to be before the bones were heated.

Conclusion

Randomness is the chaos that underlies the cosmos. It's the unpredictable, the uncontrollable, the stuff that doesn't follow any discernible pattern.

Randomness is what makes life surprising. It's why you can't predict the future with certainty. You might make plans, but there's always the possibility of a random event throwing a wrench in the works. A flat tire, a chance encounter, a sudden inspiration. Randomness is the spice that keeps things interesting.

The tricky thing about randomness is that humans are terrible at recognizing it. We see patterns where there are none. We attribute meaning to coincidence. We think we can beat the odds. But true randomness is immune to our predictions and superstitions. It doesn't care about our theories or desires.

SUPPORTING IDEA:

Pareto Principle

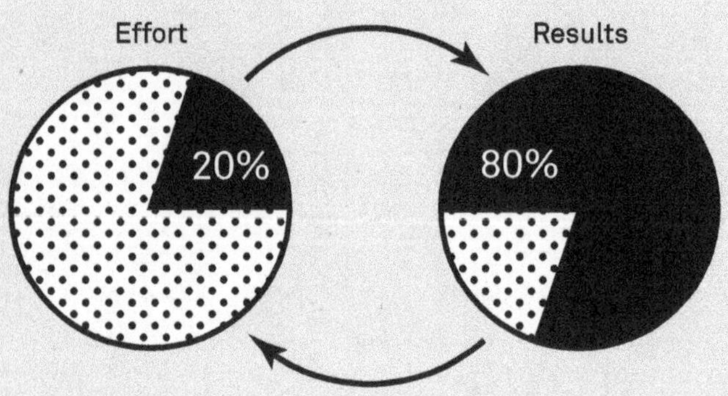

IN 1906, THE ITALIAN POLYMATH VILFREDO PARETO WAS RESEARCHing wealth distribution in Italy. He noticed that 20 percent of the population owned 80 percent of the land and wealth. He is also said to have observed the same distribution in the pea plants he grew, wherein 20 percent of plants produced 80 percent of the peas. In the 1940s, quality control consultant and engineer Joseph M. Juran noted that 80 percent of manufacturing defects were the result of 20 percent of production issues. Juran applied Pareto's name to the principle he defined as a result: In systems, 80 percent of outputs are typically the result of 20 percent of inputs. The other 20 percent of outputs are the result of the remaining 80 percent of inputs.

We can apply the Pareto principle to numerous areas where

this type of distribution holds roughly true: 20 percent of researchers in a field produce 80 percent of published research; 20 percent of words in a language are used 80 percent of the time; 20 percent of the population use 80 percent of healthcare resources and public services; 20 percent of a company's customers create 80 percent of its profits. We often generate 80 percent of our personal results from 20 percent of our efforts. Of course, such distributions tend to be approximate, not precise. The Pareto principle is a rule of thumb, not a law of nature. However, the true split is often surprisingly close to 80-20.

Inputs and outputs are not evenly distributed. Not all inputs lead to the same sort of output. Not all the time you put into a project will be equally productive. Not all the money you put into a retirement fund will have the same impact on the final amount. Not all the employees in a company will be responsible for the same amount of its annual profits. Knowing this can teach us where to focus time and energy. If a company knows 80 percent of users of a piece of software will only ever touch 20 percent of its features, they know to make those as effective and user-friendly as possible.

> That is all there is to the 80/20 rule. We tend to assume that all items on a list are equally important, but usually, just a few of them are more important than all the others put together.
>
> —HANS ROSLING[23]

Regression to the Mean

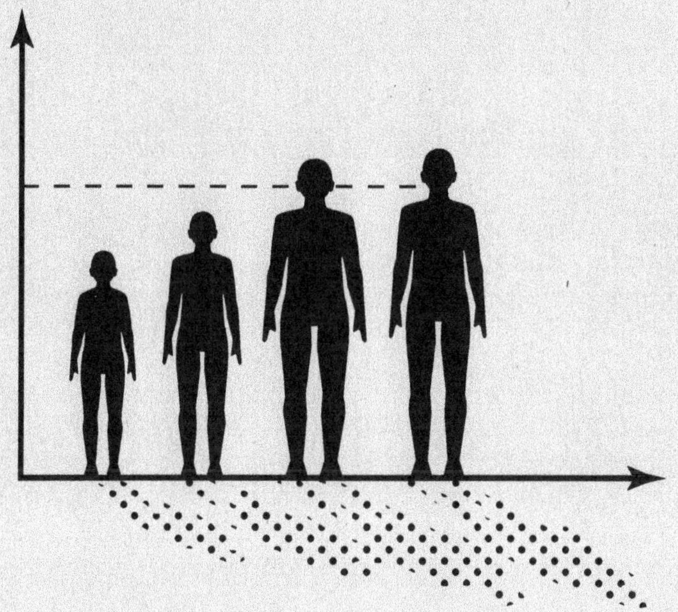

Moderate outcomes follow extreme ones.

When the gods intend to make a man pay for his crimes, they generally allow him to enjoy moments of success and a long period of impunity, so that he may feel his reverse of fortune, when it eventually comes, all the more keenly.

–JULIUS CAESAR[1]

Things often even out over time. When we have success in life, we are typically faced with a challenge. Successes are great, and no doubt we want to repeat them, but we have to consider how much of our initial success was skill and how much was luck. Did we succeed mostly on our own merit, thanks to preparation and hard work? Or was our success the result of a massive stroke of luck, such as our competitors making poor choices? If we had faced stronger competition, would we have had more average results? The model of regression to the mean is a tool to understand where individual experiences fit on the spectrum of possibility.

Even when success is entirely the result of hard work and preparation, it often sows the seeds of its own destruction. When things are going really well, a few things tend to naturally happen: we get overconfident, more opportunities come our way, we get complacent, and we get greedy. The skills we need to be successful are different from the skills needed to stay successful. When things are going badly, complacency falls to the wayside and we get back to what made us successful.

Luck is random. So outlier results with a luck component are probably followed by more moderate ones. This is regression to the mean: when data far above or below the mean is more likely to be followed by data close to it. Outlier results in situations like exam scores tend to normalize if measured multiple times as we perform to what is average for us over multiple iterations. Where luck is a factor, some successes and failures always come down to randomness.

The statistician Francis Galton identified the concept of regression to the mean in the late nineteenth century while comparing the heights of parents and their children. He found that unusually tall or short parents tended to have children of a more average height. It was as if nature were trying to maintain an average height by returning to the average after outlier results.[2]

The same is true for other phenomena we experience in our lives. Extreme events and results tend to be balanced out. Extraordinary successes are often followed by average results as we perform to our true capabilities. From a single result, we can't distinguish luck from skill. An athlete who bombs one competition will likely perform at their regular skill level in the next one. A warm day in the winter might be followed by an average cold one. You will make both profitable and poor investment decisions, with most generating average returns corresponding to your knowledge and experience.

Failure or success is usually followed by a result closer to the mean, not the other extreme.

> The larger the influence of luck in producing an extreme event, the less likely the luck will repeat itself in multiple events.
>
> **—WIKIPEDIA**

Regression to the mean is beneficial for differentiating between luck and skill. As you progress through any venture, be it investing in stocks, reading minds, or growing vegetables, it is inevitable you will have both good and bad luck. With repeated iterations, results will converge more toward your true ability level. It's unwise to place too much emphasis on the initial few outcomes because they're unlikely to be truly representative. Beginner's luck is a real thing, because beginners who fail spectacularly are less inclined to continue.

A further lesson from regression to the mean is that if you keep trying something, most of your results will be average, but with repetition you might get an exceptional outlier. For example, if you write a blog post every week for years, most will get roughly the same number of readers, yet you might end up writing one that attracts a lot of attention. Your skill will have improved, and you'll have more chances for luck to play a role too. Just as one extreme result is not always the start of a new pattern, lots of average results do not preclude the occasional big success.

The *Sports Illustrated* Curse

Athletes refer to the "*Sports Illustrated* curse," wherein those who appear on the cover of the magazine experience a sudden decline in their performance afterward. Regression to the mean offers an explanation. Athletes featured tend to be at the very top of their game—something that is partly due to skill and partly due to luck. From there, they're most likely to regress to the mean and return to more average performance.[3]

An athlete who reaches the level of success necessary to appear on the magazine's cover probably has nowhere to go but down. It's usually outlier success that gets athletes on the covers of magazines, and outlier success always has a component of unreliable good luck to it. An athlete will probably regress to their mean in the next season, while someone else will have some lucky success.

Serious injuries bring an end to many athletic careers. Again, the more times someone plays a sport, the more opportunities they have to sustain an injury. Age-related wear and tear from doing something so physically demanding further compounds the role of bad luck. Just as good luck might lead an athlete to do exceptionally well one season, bad luck may lead them to break a bone the next. In baseball, players who win the Cy Young Award for pitching tend to later experience a downward turn for the same reason.[4]

The best way to assess someone's abilities is to consider their track record, not their greatest achievements. An extreme result is not necessarily the start of a new trend; we need a larger sample size to make an accurate assessment. While an athlete achieving something incredible during one season or game is for sure impressive, it doesn't mean they'll keep performing like that forever.

The same is true in our lives outside the sports world, and for both positive and negative events. After having a bad experience in a job at a company with a terrible culture, the company you work at next is likely to have a more normal, reasonable culture. After being in an amazing relationship, you might find that your next one is less extraordinary. The key is to recognize when luck is a factor. Whether things are going better than normal or worse than normal, they may well not continue that way. Life has its ups and downs, but most of the time you'll find yourself somewhere around the mean.

The Ford Edsel Was Just a Car

Not every effort we make is going to produce rare and spectacular results. There's always an average. So often we put so much pressure on ourselves to knock it out of the park all the time that average results can seem like failures. Regression to the mean is a useful model for helping us put our averages in perspective. We have some influence over what our personal average is. We can work hard to get that mean comparatively high. But we will always have an average and cannot expect outlier success all the time. Appreciating the average is one way to consider the story of the Ford Edsel.

In 1957, sixteen-year-old Don Mazzella skipped class for a rather unusual reason. He wasn't off to smoke cigarettes in the local park or meet a girlfriend. Mazzella and a couple of friends were sneaking off to see a car.[5] They didn't plan to buy or joyride it. They just wanted to know what it looked like.

Why were they so excited about this particular car? The vehicle in question was the Edsel, launched dramatically by Ford on what the company dubbed "E-day." Named after Henry Ford's son, it might well have been the most hyped product released during the 1950s.

Everyone knew about the Edsel before its release; no one knew what it looked like. Ford preceded its release with a lavish two-year advertising campaign. Its name was everywhere, but none of the ads depicted the car itself.[6] Aiming to build anticipation by shrouding the vehicle in mystery, they showed only small details or unrelated images accompanied by bold claims.

Ford made big promises about the Edsel. They said it was to be the greatest car ever made. Cars were a huge deal for Americans in the 1950s. In the post-war era, owning one went from being a luxury to being attainable for the average person. Mainstream car ownership literally changed the landscape of America with the construction of motorways and surrounding infrastructure like gas stations and motels. People took pride in their vehicles, viewing them as the linchpin of a new form of freedom and prosperity. So the Edsel captured their imagination, and the notion of it being something revolutionary seemed plausible. If cars had already changed the country, why couldn't a new car model prove transformative again?

Millions were spent on the Edsel's advertising. Ford's initial idea was to make a strategic move into the new market for medium-priced cars, which their main competitors dominated at the time. Following the wild success of the Thunderbird a couple of years earlier, Ford management was confident they couldn't fail with the Edsel. If the Thunderbird had sold so well, surely the Edsel could only sell better with a bigger advertising budget.[7] They already had the brand name and the trust of consumers.

There was a queue at the local showroom to see the Edsel. Mazzella and his friends waited in line to peek around a corner. As soon as their eyes fell on the Edsel, they went through the same realization as the rest of America. The Edsel was just a car. For many who saw it, it wasn't a particularly attractive one at that. Its huge, vertical front grille looked odd and distorted, like a grimacing mouth.[8] The excitement bubble popped. Americans viewed the Edsel as a disappointment and didn't buy it in anywhere near the expected numbers.

Part of the problem was that the Edsel was so overhyped, it could only ever fall short. Too much advertising drummed up so much excitement that it made the car seem worse than it was in comparison to people's expectations. In addition, its launch wasn't flawless. Early vehicles had some technical issues that, though minor, tarnished its image. When Ford hadn't managed to invent something truly revolutionary, it settled for marketing the Edsel as something it wasn't.

Within two years, Ford stopped selling the Edsel.[9] Some—possibly exaggerated—estimates put the total losses at $2 billion in today's money. Ford had tried to make it more desirable than it was through advertising. They ended up making it less desirable. As David Gartman writes in *Auto-Opium: A Social History of American Automobile Design,* "The Edsel was indeed different, but it protested its novelty so loudly that its exhortations rang hollow."[10]

Thomas E. Bonsall, writing in *Disaster in Dearborn: The Story of the Edsel,* takes a similar view: "People are mesmerized by the mighty brought low. . . . The *Titanic* became a modern morality play. Man had reached too far, gotten too arrogant, and had, inevitably, been given a comeuppance. So it was with the Edsel."[11] People reveled in the schadenfreude of seeing Ford fail at last. (Ford didn't stay down for long, following up the Edsel with the Mustang in 1964.)

Many car models have failed over the decades, many in an even more spectacular fashion than the Edsel. Yet it remains the most famous car failure of all. In an ironic twist, today surviving Edsels are worth a great deal due to small production numbers. Failure made Edsels more popular among collectors of 1950s vehicles, some of whom delight in the almost comically distorted front grille.

The story of the Edsel is complicated. There wasn't one reason for its failure. There is no doubt that the prerelease hype caused consumer expectations to be high. And the higher expectations are, the harder it is to fill them. But there were also issues within the Ford Motor Company during the development of the Edsel that contributed to many poor decisions.

One way to understand the enduring fascination with the story of the Edsel is through the lens of regression to the mean. Businesses are under constant pressure to have every release achieve a new level of success. But sometimes new products are just average. Ford had spectacular success with the Thunderbird before the Edsel and the Mustang after. When judged against those vehicles, the Edsel seems like a massive failure. It wasn't really, though. It ran OK. Some people liked it. It was just an average car useful for a mother taking her kids to baseball practice or an insurance salesman headed to work.

When you look at the spectrum of cars produced by Ford over time, some sold amazingly and others hardly registered, with everything else falling in the range in between. The more cars the company releases, the more it is statistically likely that some will be average sellers. The problem for the Edsel was that the investment made in the marketing suggested brilliance. When the result turned out to be average, the disappointment was in the contrast.

Fighting Back

Throughout history, extreme and unusual events have often been followed by more average ones. The highlights are what we study, with the many more mundane occurrences not even recorded. Regression to the mean is thus an interesting lens to use to look at historical change, because it suggests that we be cautious about making assumptions about the future based on the immediate past.

History is far too complicated to use a simple statistical concept to try to demonstrate a definitive pattern in complex and often random interactions. Rather, using regression to the mean as a model helps you put extremes of success and failure into perspective. An extreme event is not necessarily the start of a new trend. Dramatic events do not always change what follows them.

The Trung sisters, Trung Trac and Trung Nhi, were born in rural Vietnam. While we don't know exactly when they were born or died, they are best known for their activities between 39 and 43 CE, when they earned a lasting legacy as Vietnamese national heroines. As daughters of a lord at a time when women in their country enjoyed unusual freedom, they experienced a relatively privileged upbringing.[12] Vietnamese women were able to inherit property and take on political, legal, commercial, and military roles. By some accounts, Vietnam at the time might even have been a matriarchy, although this may be an exaggeration to highlight the contrast with patriarchal China.[13]

At the time, Vietnam had been under Han Chinese rule since 111 BCE—a period of control that would last more than a thousand years, with just a few intermissions of independence. The Chinese attempted to enforce their way of life based on Confucian philosophy, alongside other unpopular measures like harsh taxation. In 39 CE, Thi Sach, lord of Chau Dien and Trung Trac's husband, protested the rising taxes and was executed as a result. Rather than going into mourning as expected, Trung Trac turned her anger and grief into fuel. Together with her sister, she rallied an army of eighty thousand, consisting mostly of ordinary Vietnamese people without training or much equipment. The sisters assigned mostly women as generals and are often depicted riding elephants into battle.

According to legend, Trung Trac killed a man-eating tiger and wrote her intentions on its skin. Then their army fought back against the Chinese. Another legend tells of a soldier who went into battle nine months pregnant, gave birth on the field, then strapped her baby to her back and continued fighting. While the story is not altogether plausible, it says a lot about how the army was viewed.[14]

Their attack was so unexpected that they succeeded in pushing the Chinese from sixty-five cities and establishing an independent state.

For three years the sisters ruled together and helped restore fairer conditions for the Vietnamese people—including doing away with the heavy taxes that had led to their rebellion. In addition they revived aspects of Vietnamese culture the Chinese had replaced with their own, such as the traditional language and literature. However, their rebellion proved to be an outlier. The Chinese were initially taken by surprise, so part of the sisters' success was due to the poor preparation of the Chinese. Because they were still far more powerful, the Chinese rebounded quickly. Their next efforts against the Vietnamese were more in line with the Chinese mean for military capability.

In 43 CE, the Chinese took back full control of the country and violently punished the rebels. In addition to slaughtering supporters of the Trung sisters, they sought to override Vietnamese culture with their own. Devastated by the loss and seeing no hope, the sisters are said to have leapt into a river together. Their army didn't have the strength to hold off the Chinese long-term. China would ultimately control Vietnam for nearly a thousand years, but by some accounts, Vietnam wouldn't still exist as a country without the Trung sisters. Today they're commemorated throughout Vietnam and remain a source of inspiration.[15]

> All the male heroes bowed their heads in submission / Only the two sisters proudly stood up to avenge the country.
>
> —FIFTEENTH-CENTURY VIETNAMESE POEM[16]

Using regression to the mean as a metaphorical lens, rather than pure math, can provide the insight that great, unusual success isn't usually followed by more of the same. The actions of the Trung sisters were outliers in their time. What they accomplished was not the start of a new standard. When you are new to something, it's a good idea to try to ascertain where the mean lies so you know whether your early results are representative.

Conclusion

Regression to the mean is the universe's way of saying "not so fast." It's the tendency for extreme outcomes to be followed by more average ones. Extreme results are rarely repeated.

The next time you see something extraordinary, enjoy it. But remember, it probably won't last. Sooner or later, regression to the mean will come calling and eventually pull the exceptional back to ordinary. That's the way the universe keeps things in check.

Multiplying by Zero

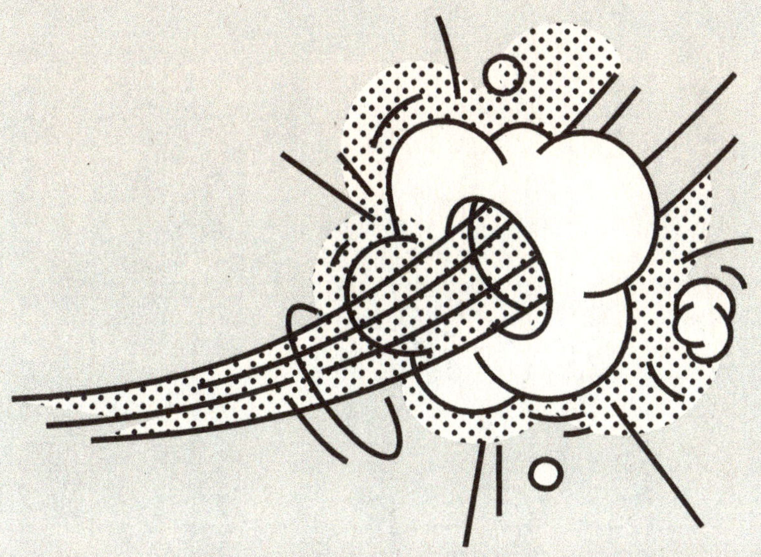

The ultimate destroyer.

Multiplication by zero destroys information. This means there cannot be a reverse process. Some activities are so destructive they cannot be undone.

—PAUL LOCKHART[1]

Any number multiplied by zero equals zero. This is basic math we all learn early in life. This mental model is useful for teaching us to look for the zero—the weak part of any system that threatens to bring the whole thing down.

Within a multiplicative system, there is no point in optimizing the other components if we ignore the zero. It's always worth investing effort in the weakest part because nothing else can compensate for it. It doesn't matter if you multiply zero by 100 or 285,490,940, you still get the same result.

As commonplace as zero might seem now, it's extremely easy to forget it is a remarkable number. Without it much of modern mathematics would be impossible. Early numerical systems couldn't progress further without a means of representing nothing—a number that you can multiply by another number and still get nothing.

It doesn't matter if you have two zeros or five billion zeros. See, in multiplicative systems each number says something about the properties of the other numbers in that system. For example, 2 × 3 says of the number 2 that there are 3 of them (2 + 2 + 2), and of the number 3 that there are 2 of them (3 + 3). It follows that 2 × 0 says of the 2 that there are none of them, and of the 0 that there are 2 of them. Zero twos is nothing. Two zeros is also nothing. So in a multiplicative system with a zero, you will always have a total of zero. No matter how many zeros you add together, they will always add up to zero. And the rest of the numbers in that system are effectively nothing.

The principle of multiplying by zero applies outside math. Any multiplicative system is only as strong as its weakest link. A zero in a system has the power to negate everything that comes before it. For instance, in a competent, well-organized team, one unmotivated person who complains nonstop can bring everyone else down. A company might have strong branding, a large user base, and a useful product, but a CEO who publicly makes racist comments has a good chance of canceling all that out. You might have a fancy security system in your house, but it's useless if you leave the front door open.

The value of this mental model is in learning to identify where the zero might be, how to avoid introducing one, or how to transform an existing one. Imagine you're trying to design an ideal dining experience for customers of a restaurant. What would create a zero for you as a customer? You go to a restaurant to eat. The most important component of the restaurant system for the customer is good food. Beautiful decor, attentive service, good atmosphere—none of these will compensate for tomato-soup pasta sauce or fish that has spoiled. This restaurant could serve the water in gold glasses and be located in a charming French chateau, but if the food is tasteless and unimaginative, you will never go back. Bad food is the zero of the restaurant's system. Great food can compensate for slow service. But the sexiest, most attentive server will not make up for undercooked chicken.

East German Technology Theft

We all work in systems. Whether they're large or small organizations employing thousands of people or just one, we spend most of our time trying to make our systems better. Many of the decisions we make at work are about improving our system, whatever that means for us: higher sales, more flexibility, better outcomes for our clients. Deciding where to invest, what to research, how to develop ourselves and others—these can be done by evaluating the strength of the components of our system.

Work environments are multiplicative systems. Whether you work for the government, a local brewery, or a high-tech multinational, or as a freelance artist, the properties of each component of your system interact in the whole. Understanding sales means understanding marketing, which necessitates a firm grasp of R&D, which in turn draws from finance. If any one of these isn't working, there will be a negative impact on the rest of the system.

Therefore, you have to be able to identify if there are any zeros in your system—a part of the system that isn't producing at all. Putting time, effort, and resources into the other elements of a system will produce no results if any part of the system is a zero. Having a zero in a multiplicative system creates a mirage. You see all these other big numbers and think they are strong enough to compensate for this zero, but they aren't.

A great example of ignoring a zero is the East German quest to build a computer at the end of the Cold War. In the 1970s and '80s, the computer was seen, understandably, as an important technology, a critical element in the ongoing technological development race between East and West. The East Germans had a goal, which was, as Kristie Macrakis explains in *Seduced by Secrets*, "nothing less than constructing an indigenous self-sufficient computer industry."[2]

However, they were nowhere near developing computer technology for themselves. Decades into a social experiment that eventually proved untenable, they had created a system that punished creativity, innovation, and collaboration. It was hardly ideal for developing a computer industry.

In addition, because of the political climate, the East Germans couldn't partner with Western technology companies to build their computer industry either. By the late 1970s, most Western technology was under embargo; it could not be sold or distributed to Eastern Bloc countries.

The East German solution was to steal what they wanted, continuing as they had for much of the Cold War. The theft was carried out by the Ministry for State Security, commonly referred to as the Stasi. Using their networks of agents, Stasi officials worked around the embargo and proceeded to steal the information and technology required to build computers. They obtained everything from blueprints to hardware and reverse-engineered the technology in order to build it themselves. The East Germans spent billions of marks on theft, illegal smuggling, and espionage.[3]

In one example, "rather than conducting its own research and development work, East Germany would import the know-how and production facilities of a complete factory to produce 20 to 30 million 256K RAM circuits yearly."[4] "Import" here meant paying far more than the market price to try to bring in embargoed technology through elaborate illegal routes. This factory never came to pass.

Overall the attempt to build a computer industry in East Germany was a complete failure. Why? Because they didn't develop anything on their own. They didn't let their scientists travel to participate in research efforts or to obtain knowledge to build the desired technology in-house. Their whole computer industry was to be built on a foundation of theft. Money that could have been spent on research and development was instead poured into elaborate schemes to bring in embargoed technology. As Macrakis sums up,

"That was the main contradiction the Stasi presents us with: On the one hand, they vigorously supported state programs by acquiring the needed embargoed or secret technology. On the other hand, security concerns made them work against their own interests by restricting the needed international travel of scientists and by imposing other harmful security measures."[5] Consequently, despite years of trying, the East Germans never met their technology production goals.

We can understand their failure by considering that innovation does not just happen out of thin air. The history of invention shows us that smart people fail dozens of times before they succeed. They build on the failures of others by testing their own hypothesis, tinkering and refining, and learning a remarkable amount in the process. They learn not only how to make things work but why those things work in the first place. Therefore, when things go wrong, they have a deep store of earned knowledge to draw on. They can troubleshoot, adapt, and ultimately improve.

The East Germans had none of the knowledge that is earned in development and failure. "Even with their highly perfected espionage system and seasoned embargo smuggling operations, East Germany forgot one thing: A scientific establishment based on pirated and cloned technology can never be a leader." Because they didn't develop the knowledge themselves, they were not able to troubleshoot, adapt, and most importantly innovate. Macrakis says, "Often machinery did not work when it arrived. Because it was acquired illegally, calling a service repairman was a problem. Sometimes only bits and pieces of information were available, when the whole puzzle was needed intact. But more fundamental problems arose because of secrecy. The [Stasi's] cult of secrecy clashed with the scientific ethos of openness."[6]

The lack of collaboration and knowledge gained from experience was the East Germans' zero, the part of their system that reduced the rest of it to nothing. More spies, more theft, and more money were thrown at the problem, but increasing the value of the rest of the properties in a multiplicative system does nothing if that system contains a zero.

How do you find the zeros in your system? Zeros don't hide. In fact they are usually quite obvious when you draw your perspective back, allowing you to see your system as a whole. They are usually what we deliberately ignore, naively hoping that they will "fix themselves" or that someone might come along who can magic a solution. Zeros are persistent structural flaws that intimidate us. If we avoid them, this is when we fall prey to snake oil salesmen who promise they have an easy (and often expensive) solution based on the latest technology/psychology/accidental success of someone else.

Changing a zero to a one is not going to happen overnight. But for all required components, all zeros can be turned into ones. In trying to build the computer, what the Stasi were missing was at least one person who had earned the knowledge required for the endeavor, someone who had studied, apprenticed, or worked beside others who knew what they were doing. Why didn't they have that one person?

They didn't have that one person because they hadn't created a culture that would allow someone like that to exist. Inventors ask questions, explore options, and challenge the status quo. These were all behaviors that were not encouraged in Cold War East Germany. For the Stasi to have turned their zero into a one, they would have had to modify their culture to support innovation. They would have had to build a team or an organization that would support the development of the creative people they needed. In effect, they would have produced more than one person to solve their problem. And this is the magic of changing your zero into a one. The result is a capitalization of all the other strong numbers you have in place.

It is hard. For the Stasi to implement structural changes of this sort would have amounted to an acknowledgment of the failures of their particular brand of socialism. It's understandable that they didn't own this and instead threw money at the other components of their system.

However, most people understand that success is complex and has many contributing factors. There is no one secret to a good marriage or a profitable business. These systems have many components, all of which have to be working to some degree of efficiency to achieve success. But critically it can often be just one thing that determines failure. If one essential component of the system is neglected, then the whole thing breaks down.

Crop Diversity

When the consequences of failure are high, it's important to do everything you can to avoid multiplying by zero and negating your prior efforts. One place where this is apparent is in agriculture, where maintaining crop diversity is vital.

"Crop diversity" refers to the practice of using a variety of plants in agriculture, both in terms of different species of the same plant as well as variations within species. It applies to individual farmers, to communities, to nations, and to the world as a whole. Crop diversity is also relevant in terms of both the plants we are currently growing and those we have the capacity to grow, as well as domesticated and wild strains. Being dependent on a single crop is a bad idea because something could go wrong and leave you with no harvest, such as a plant disease, a parasite, or unfavorable weather conditions. For a subsistence farmer, that means having nothing to eat. On a larger scale, if most people in the world eat the same thing, a crop failure could mean widespread hunger or even political instability. There are other risks to crop homogeneity, like soil depletion and erosion.

Unfortunately crop diversity is decreasing over time as more of the world comes to depend on wheat, rice, and potatoes.[7] The mental model of multiplying by zero helps illustrate the importance of not creating situations in which one thing going wrong could wipe everything else out. Having crop diversity is like having multiple different equations: if one is multiplied by zero, it doesn't negate the others.

The Irish potato famine, beginning in 1845, is a classic example of the risks of lacking crop diversity. When a fungus affecting potato plants spread throughout the country, more than a third of the population were without their main food source for up to five years.[8] Not only were many people dependent on potatoes alone, there was also a lack of genetic variation within the species. Propagating these vegetatively meant the plants were all clones–that is, genetically identical. When a fungus came along targeting this particular plant, all were equally susceptible. There was no genetic diversity to ensure some plants had resistance.[9]

The mental model of multiplying by zero highlights the importance of not creating excessive dependency on one thing that could fail.

Transforming Zeros

Sometimes we feel like we have a zero in our personal equations: a characteristic, quality, or condition that serves to undermine our efforts in other areas. It can be frustrating when we work hard to develop skills and capabilities only to feel like they are negated by just one part of who we are. This feeling is common for stutterers. Sometimes it can seem like their struggle to verbalize words reduces the perception of the value of their knowledge and experience. In overcoming the limits that stuttering may place on them, many have found varied techniques and treatments to effectively manage their stuttering. Dealing with a stutter is often not just about addressing the condition itself but about overcoming the sense of inadequacy other people place on those who stutter early in life. There are many fascinating stories of the various ways people have turned their perceived zero of stuttering—and all its often-negative consequences—into a one.

Stuttering is defined as "a speech condition that disrupts the normal flow of speech.... With stuttering, the interruptions in flow happen often and cause problems for the speaker."[10] Stutterers may repeat words or syllables, or have a hard time articulating certain sounds. One of the major frustrations for stutterers is that their difficulty in speaking is not at all representative of what is going on in their head or of their intelligence. They know what they want to say. It is the disconnect between having an idea and being able to express it in the course of conventional conversation that causes issues. There is nothing intrinsically wrong with stuttering. It's just a different way of talking and therefore harder for other people to understand.

For many stutterers the physical condition has further consequences. It can lead to poor self-esteem and increased anxiety as everyday situations become huge challenges due to the judgment of other people. The Mayo Clinic says, "Stuttering may be worse when the person is excited, tired, or under stress, or when feeling self-conscious, hurried, or pressured. Situations such as speaking in front of a group or talking on the phone can be particularly difficult for people who stutter." Daily interactions that most of us don't even register can become ongoing sources of stress and tension for stutterers, which can lead them to avoid needed social interaction and relationships.

There is no cure for stuttering. It is a condition that can be greatly improved by speech therapy and other types of therapy, such as cognitive-behavioral. But stuttering never goes away completely and thus must always be managed.

One result of stuttering is often the feeling that regardless of the effort you put into other areas of your life, the condition negates them all. No matter how much you know, how witty you are, or how much wisdom you've gained from your experiences, the struggle to verbally articulate negates the value of anything you have to say.

Stuttering affects millions of people. What many find surprising is the list of stutterers who have achieved success in very public speech roles. From James Earl Jones to King George VI of England, Carly Simon to Winston Churchill, many stutterers have found ways to effectively manage their stuttering in certain public situations.

Marilyn Monroe was one of the first famous people to talk openly about how stuttering affected her life. In a 1955 discussion with the American columnist Maurice Zolotow, Marilyn recalled, "I guess you could say I gave up talking for a long while. I used to be so embarrassed in school. I thought I'd die whenever a teacher called upon me. I always had the feeling of not wanting to open my mouth, that anything I said would be wrong or stupid."[11] Yet she worked through this limitation to achieve success in the film industry.

Many actors who stutter have spoken about how the notion of taking on a role helps them step away from their speech impediment and thus helps them manage it. For example, Emily Blunt is described in an article in *W Magazine* as developing a stutter "so debilitating that she could barely hold a conversation, let alone elbow her way into the limelight. 'I was a smart kid, and I had a lot to say, but I just couldn't say it. . . . It would just haunt me. I never thought I'd be able to sit and talk to someone like I'm talking to you right now.'"[12] Then one of her teachers at school suggested acting lessons, and it was this experience that helped her manage her stutter.

Another fascinating thing about stuttering is that it often goes away while singing. Many stutterers find the words come much easier if they are put to sound. In his 1996 autobiography B. B. King wrote:

> I struggle with words. Never could express myself the way I wanted. My mind fights my mouth, and thoughts get stuck in my throat. Sometimes they stay stuck for seconds or even minutes. As a child, I stuttered. What was inside couldn't get out. I'm still not real fluent. I don't know a lot of good words. If I were wrongfully accused of a crime, I'd have a tough time explaining my innocence. I'd stammer and stumble and choke up until the judge would throw me in jail. Words aren't my friends. Music is. Sounds, notes, rhythms. I talk through music.[13]

Singing also played a role in how Rubin "Hurricane" Carter was able to, over time, effectively manage his stutter. The Stuttering

Foundation has a profile on Carter, among many other stutterers, that tells us, "From an early age, Rubin Carter had to fight so much due to abuse he received because of his stuttering that he developed into a great fighter and was urged by people to consider a career as a boxer."[14] In a 2006 interview with Nicholas Ballasy on his show *On the Issues*, Carter said, "My first eighteen years of my life, I couldn't talk. I stuttered very badly. So fighting became just a natural thing for me because if you are going to attack people when they laugh at you, you better damn well know how to fight or you're gonna get your butt whooped. So that's what got me into fighting."[15]

In his 1974 autobiography, *The Sixteenth Round: From Number 1 Contender to Number 45472*, which was written in prison, Carter writes openly about his stuttering. He says, "I couldn't speak to save my life. I had always been told that as I became older, my speech would eventually straighten itself out, but it did not happen that way with me. Any effort I made to talk made my speech worse, and therefore my habit was to speak as little as possible."[16]

His speech began to change when he discovered that he didn't stutter while singing. The Stuttering Foundation shares a summary from the book *Hurricane: The Miraculous Journey of Rubin Carter*, by James S. Hirsch: "Carter . . . worked hard on trying to replicate that relaxed fluidity from singing into his everyday speaking patterns. Over time he also diligently practiced cadences and forced himself to speak before groups, becoming a compelling speaker." Relaxing while speaking and changing up the cadence of one's speech are two of the core practices of speech therapy, which has helped millions of stutterers gain a measure of control over their stuttering.

Managing a stutter will not always lead to such visible success, but that isn't the point. Too often we think of certain conditions as inherently limiting, zeros that will always render the rest of our personal equations useless. Zeros, however, can form us and challenge us to develop new skills and qualities. How some people have managed their stuttering is a great example of the power of transforming a zero. As stuttering can never be completely "cured," it is not about getting rid of the zero. Stutterers have found many ways to shift the zero just enough to turn it into a one, thereby activating the power of the rest of their equation.

Conclusion

Multiplying by zero is the mathematical version of the Midas touch in reverse. Everything it touches turns to nothing. No matter how big or small a number is, when you multiply it by zero, you get zero. It's the ultimate reset button.

Multiplying by zero shows us that we have to be mindful of the zeros that will negate our other efforts. Just as in engineering, where one faulty component can make an entire system fail, not being reliable can have the same effect in life.

When you multiply by zero everything else becomes irrelevant.

Equivalence

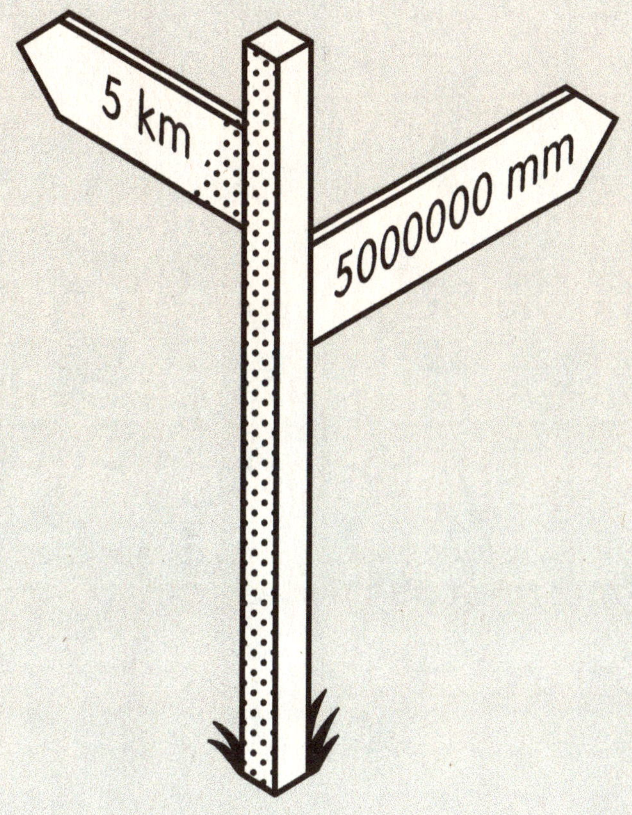

Equal doesn't mean same.

The art of doing mathematics consists in finding that special case which contains all the germs of generality.

—DAVID HILBERT[1]

Things do not have to be the same to be equal. Equivalence as a model helps us see that there are usually many paths to success.

One of the ways equivalence is most useful as a model is when our traditional solution to a problem is no longer viable. We know we must now do things differently, yet we wish to achieve an equivalent result. It also reminds us not to focus on apparent differences but to look for the underlying equality of experiences if we want to better connect with others.

In math, one of the most basic equivalency concepts is "If A = B and B = C, then C = A." We can infer that A, B, and C need not be the same; after all, they are represented by different symbols. But for the purposes of comparison, in at least one aspect they are equivalent. It is often true in mathematics that different symbols can provide an equal answer to a question.

The world is full of things that seem different yet are in some way equivalent. Take the case of human universals. We are, as a species, unimaginably diverse. Despite this, cultures across the world often solve the same problems in equivalent ways.[2] According to anthropology professor Donald Brown, these universals include taboo language, a distinction between how people behave when they are in full control of themselves and when they are not, making promises, rules surrounding inheritance, attempts to predict and influence the weather, and bodily adornments. While these features and behaviors manifest in different ways, they have equivalent purposes across cultures.[3]

Sometimes things recur in equivalent yet different ways. Historical recurrence is the phenomenon wherein seemingly equivalent events happen more than once at varying points throughout history. It's a cliché that history repeats itself, but the similarities can be uncanny in events like the assassinations of Lincoln and Kennedy and the invasions of Russia by both Napoleon and Hitler. People in similar situations facing similar incentives are likely to behave in similar ways.

> History, we know, is apt to repeat herself, and to foist very old incidents upon us with only a slight change of costume.
>
> —GEORGE ELIOT[4]

Multiple Discoveries

There's a powerful myth surrounding scientific discoveries and inventions. We imagine a solitary genius toiling away in their laboratory or workshop, performing experiment after experiment. Then one day, lightning strikes. They shout "Eureka!" as a new idea is born and the sum of human knowledge grows in one swoop. The idea gets named after them, they receive awards and patents, and their name goes in the history books. Should they have been felled by a falling piano a day prior, the idea may never have come into existence.

Except invention and discovery rarely work that way in reality.

Most discoveries are the product of the cumulative work of many people inching toward the conclusion. Often multiple people or teams reach an equivalent result independently at around the same time. In the past it was possible for this to occur even without them being aware of one another's work. Steel, slingshots, and the abacus are some of the many examples of inventions and discoveries that occurred in multiple places and multiple times in history.

> Because everything arises from steps, not leaps, most things are invented in several places simultaneously when different people walk the same path, each unaware of the others.
>
> —KEVIN ASHTON[5]

None of us live in full isolation from the ideas of others or the context of our time. New discoveries are the product of broad scientific and cultural landscapes, and often of recombining existing ideas.[6] We all draw upon what we are exposed to. The work of a researcher is the product of a lifetime spent absorbing the work of others.[7]

To give some of the many, many examples of simultaneous discovery, both Charles Darwin and Alfred Russel Wallace conceived of natural selection without knowledge of each other's work. Chemist Carl Wilhelm Scheele discovered oxygen in 1772 but didn't publicize his discovery for three years, by which point two other chemists, Joseph Priestley and Antoine Lavoisier, knew of its existence.[8] Both Louis Ducos du Hauron and Charles Cros presented similar methods for color photography in the 1860s.[9] Their work differed, as du Hauron used pigments and Cros favored dyes. Nettie Stevens and Edmund Beecher Wilson independently demonstrated that specialized chromosomes (X and Y) determine biological sex.[10] Takaaki Kajita and Arthur B. McDonald's research ended up sharing the 2015 Nobel Prize in Physics for demonstrating that neutrinos have mass.[11]

A misunderstanding of how invention truly works is apparent in patent law, which suggests a patent should go to the inventor of something nonobvious.[12] The implication is that, as the patent's source, the inventor deserves to profit from it. So it's often the case that the person who profits isn't truly the sole source of innovation. They're one of many; they just happen to be the one who files a patent first or gets it accepted. The components of a steam turbine were described by Taqī al-Dīn in 1551 in Syria, long before the first patent was awarded in England for an early steam engine in 1698.[13]

The phenomenon of multiple discoveries shows us how things can be equivalent even if not precisely identical. While they may differ in their details, the underlying principles and concepts are the same. They solve the same problem. In most cases, we credit a well-known discovery or invention only to the person who popularized it. We thus miss out on a rich understanding of the full process of innovation and often fail to hear the stories of those working outside the mainstream. In particular, female and minority scientists and inventors often have a hard time publicizing their work. Credit may go to someone else at a later date. Once a particular individual becomes well-known, they're yet more likely to receive credit, even if someone else had the same idea previously.

Madeleine Vionnet and the Bias Cut

Up until the early twentieth century, for many Western women corsets were part of their standard daily attire. Often containing boning, corset design evolved over the centuries to shape the female body to whatever was considered attractive at the time. Gradually corsets became less fashionable, partly driven by the restriction on material during World War I. In response to the changing trends, designer Madeleine Vionnet came up with a truly novel approach to dressmaking and demonstrated that there is more than one way to look good in clothes. "Vionnet's unique solution was to make the movement of the body part of the movement of the remarkably fluid shapes she was working on. No more boning, no more rubber, no more elastic to give support."[14]

As most of us can verify quite easily in our homes, if you hold a square of fabric–say, cotton–at the center of its edges and pull outward in opposite directions, the material will only stretch a little. However, if you hold it at the corners and pull, the material will stretch significantly more. In 1922 Vionnet exploited this property of fabrics, called the bias cut, to stunning effect in the design and construction of clothes.

As J. E. Gordon describes in *Structures*: "She realized intuitively that there are more ways of getting a fit than by pulling on strings or straining at hooks and eyes [of corsets]. The cloth of a dress is subject to vertical tensile stresses both from its own weight and from the movements of the wearer; and if the cloth is disposed at 45 degrees to this vertical stress, one can exploit the resulting large lateral contraction so as to get a clinging effect."[15]

As explained by Colin McDowell in his online biography of Vionnet, "Starting with studying classical Greek statues, she became obsessed with the soft flattery of clothes that 'moved like water.' From there, she made her great step forward by cutting fabric on the bias (previously used only for collars) and, by doing so, created a completely new shape, which could be called free-form geometric. In her own words, it was 'to free fabric from the constraints that other cuts imposed on it.' She had found her road and, for the rest of her design life, she tackled the whole question of dress with an almost scientific rigor."[16]

The bias cut has become a staple of fashion. It looks nice, it easily clings to different body shapes, and it uses less fabric to achieve its effects. Vionnet's bias cut demonstrated that there is more than one way to shape a silhouette in fashion.

How We Deal with the Universal of Death

Death is a reality all humans have in common. We know our lives will one day be over, and at some point we will have to process the death of a loved one. Due to our social natures, we form strong attachments to people in our lives. Our families and friends mean a lot to us, and when they go, it hurts. The need to process the death of someone we care about is a state all of us experience. How we choose to go about that processing varies widely across cultures. Equivalence is a useful lens through which to look at the various death rituals that exist in the world because it demonstrates just how many ways there are to get the same outcome.

Writing in *Do Funerals Matter?,* William G. Hoy says, "Just as death is a universal event, the desire of groups to make sense of death through ceremonies seems also to hold a universal appeal."[17] There is a wide variety of after-death practices in the world. Some are religion-based, such as the Jewish custom of sitting with the body until burial or the Hindu tradition of constructing a pyre on which the deceased is cremated. Other practices are community-centered, such as sharing food and drink at a gathering or parading with the deceased in a procession. Hoy continues, "Humans have an undeniable need to make sense of death; funeral rituals are created by social groups as potential scripts to achieve this end."[18]

> When Darius was king, he summoned the Greeks who were with him and asked them what price would persuade them to eat their fathers' dead bodies. They answered that there was no price for which they would do it. Then he summoned

> those Indians who are called Callatiae, who eat their parents, and asked them (the Greeks being present and understanding by interpretation what was said) what would make them willing to burn their fathers at death. The Indians cried aloud, that he should not speak of so horrid an act.
>
> —**HERODOTUS, *THE PERSIAN WARS***[19]

Losing someone you love is painful. Across all human culture, crying, anger, and fear are standard reactions. We grieve for the life that is over, and we mourn their loss from our lives. Rarely do we deal with this pain alone; the ceremonies we perform, diverse as they are, serve the function of helping us deal with death. In "How Death Imitates Life," James Gire explains, "In whatever form they may take within a given culture, funerals and burial rituals are ways that each society tries to help the bereaved with the death of a loved one."[20] Or as Colin Murray Parkes, Pittu Laungani, and Bill Young put it in *Death and Bereavement Across Cultures,* "Time of death and bereavement are times when people need people."[21] We all have the same needs when processing the death of a loved one. There are just many different ways of meeting them.

One further aspect of death that the accompanying ceremonies address can be thought of as the closure of the deceased's experience of life. Parkes, Laungani, and Young conclude, "All societies see death as a transition for the person who dies."[22] The way we engage with that transition is varied, but the fact of engaging with it is pretty much ubiquitous across cultures. Hoy summarizes, "The concepts of eventual rest and reward for the dead are common in death rituals, transcending religious beliefs and cultural customs."[23]

The funeral is one such death ritual. Gire explains, "Funeral and burial rites vary significantly across cultures and are influenced by each culture's conceptions of death and dying."[24] Some funerals are somber affairs, with everyone dressed in dark colors and voices kept to a murmur. Others are lavish and colorful. Some include singing, others dancing. Still others incorporate stories of the deceased. And the ways in which funerals treat the body are just as varied. Some end in burial, others in cremation. Tibetan Buddhists chop human remains and leave them on a mountain to return to the elements, and South Koreans turn the ashes into colorful beads. What ties together the variety of traditions is the intent behind them: consoling the living and dealing with the dead. On the subject of the funeral, Gire concludes, "Death is the final life transition. The funeral is often considered as a celebration of a rite of passage for both the deceased and the living."[25]

We all have a need to process death. The traditions and ceremonies we practice are a means of activating that process, allowing us to grieve for lost loved ones as well as have reassurance in what will happen after our passing. The lens of equivalence shows that there are many ways to meet our need. None are the same, but all are equal in the ways they help people.

Conclusion

Equivalence is the art of making things interchangeable. It's the idea that two things can be swapped out without changing the essence of what they're a part of. Like swapping a red Lego brick for a blue one. The color changes, but the structure remains the same.

Being equal doesn't mean being the same. Different inputs can produce identical results, and there is more than one way to solve most problems.

Equivalence lets us simplify complex systems. Instead of getting bogged down in details, we can focus on the essentials. We can see the forest for the trees. And we can make changes without fear of breaking the fundamental structure.

Of course, equivalence has its limits. Not everything is interchangeable. You can't swap out a car's engine for a hamster wheel and expect the car to run. The art is in knowing where equivalence applies and where it doesn't. It's in recognizing the essential differences that matter, and the superficial differences that don't.

The next time you're faced with a complex problem, try thinking in terms of equivalence. Look for the underlying patterns. See if there are components you can swap out or simplify. You might just find a solution that's been hiding in plain sight all along.

SUPPORTING IDEA:

Order of Magnitude

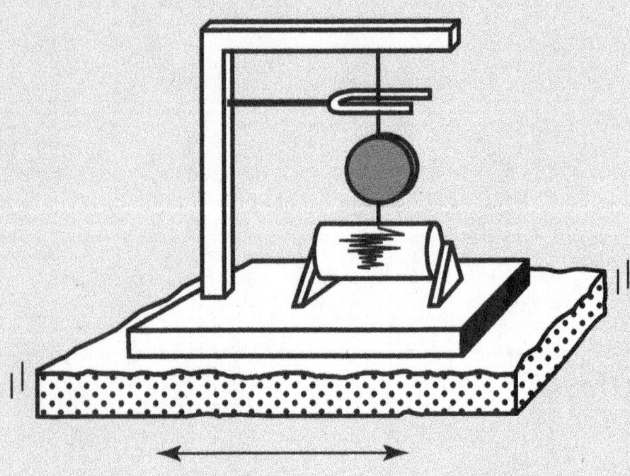

REPRESENTING VERY LARGE OR VERY SMALL NUMBERS CAN BE A challenge. Our brains struggle to conceptualize them. Writing them out can be unwieldy. Primitive counting systems past and present sometimes progress from one and two to "many" because those are the figures needed for day-to-day life.[26] But today we also sometimes need to handle numbers on scales that aren't straight-forward to depict. Science is essentially all about measurements. As it advances, its scale expands to include values like the weight of a cell and the size of a galaxy.

Orders of magnitude are a form of notation used to represent large or small numbers in a compact fashion. To say a number is an order of magnitude larger than another number is to say that it is 10 times larger (a power of 10). To say it is an order of magnitude smaller means it is .10 the size. So, 10 is an order of magnitude smaller than 100, and 1,000 is an order of magnitude larger. We represent numbers between 0 and 1 with negative orders of magnitude. We write out orders of magnitude using the smallest possible power of 10. Science, mathematics, and engineering are disciplines for which this form of notation can be crucial.

One reason orders of magnitude are useful is that they enable us to make comparisons between numbers to give them context, such as stating how many orders of magnitude greater the weight of Earth is than the weight of a car. We also use powers of ten when handling imprecise numbers and making estimations.

In our day-to-day lives, we might easily be able to imagine a group of twenty people, but what would a crowd of one million look like? We can picture a thousand dollars in one-dollar or one-hundred-dollar bills, but how big would a stack of a billion dollars be? If we sacrifice perfect accuracy, learning to conceptualize orders of magnitude can help us compare numbers. For instance, spending a dollar a second, it would take you just over eleven days to spend a million dollars and about thirty-two years to spend a billion. The difference between the two is three orders of magnitude.

The Richter scale is an earthquake measurement system using orders of magnitude. Created by seismologists Charles F. Richter and Beno Gutenberg, it measures the size and destructive power of earthquakes and was designed with the Southern California region in mind.[27] Although other systems are in use, "Richter scale" tends to serve as an umbrella term for any means of categorizing and comparing earthquakes by magnitude. Using orders of magnitude is a shortcut for showing the size difference between seismic events.

The Richter scale ascends from 0 (with negative numbers being available on more advanced seismometers) to 10. In theory it could continue higher, but there has never been a recorded earthquake measuring 10 or more. Each step on the scale means an earthquake has ten times the ground motion effect of the prior step, which in turn means it releases thirty-two times as much energy. The largest earthquake recorded to date occurred in Chile in 1960, reaching 9.5 on the Richter scale. Most earthquakes are at the bottom end of the scale, too small for anyone to notice or measure them. Each year there are about 1.3 million measuring between 2 and 2.9, but only one at 8 or higher.[28]

As Richter himself explained in his original paper on the topic:

> Precision in this matter was neither expected nor required. What was looked for was a method of segregating large, moderate, and small shocks, which should be based directly on instrumental indications, and thus might be freed from the uncertainties of personal estimates or the accidental circumstances of reported effects.[29]

Comparing the destructive potential of earthquakes going up the Richter scale is one tool for understanding orders of magnitude.

Surface Area

Know your exposure.

We can think of surface area as the amount in contact with, or able to react to, the outside world. A teaspoon of loose sugar will dissolve much faster than a cube because the surface area is larger. You need more wrapping paper for a large gift than a small one, because the surface area is larger.

As a model, surface area is about recognizing when increasing our exposure will help us and when it will cause us problems. Sometimes we want a large surface area, such as when we are trying to increase our exposure to new ideas. But large areas come with risks, so when we want to protect ourselves, shrinking our surface area might be the answer.

In chemistry, the greater a reactant's surface area, the faster a reaction is likely to occur, as there are more collisions between particles. So the same material in powdered form will produce a faster reaction than when in lumps. It's easier to start a fire with many small sticks than a few logs.

In biology, living things evolve to have a greater or smaller surface area for achieving different aims, either on the whole or in different parts of their bodies. Our lungs and intestines have a huge surface area to increase the absorption of oxygen and nutrients. Animals living in cold regions tend to have a lower surface-area-to-volume ratio than those in warmer regions to reduce heat loss, and vice versa. When you're cold, you probably scrunch up your body without thinking about reducing your surface area.

Surface area is useful when considering the amount of dependencies or assumptions something has. A program whose code has little surface area is much more likely to age well and be robust than a piece with many dependencies. The same goes for projects. If a project depends on ten teams, it's much less likely to finish on time than one with less surface area.

Surface Area

As a rule, the larger your surface area, the more energy you have to expend maintaining it. Of course, when most of us think of surface area, we think of a rectangle or how much grass we have to mow. But there is a surface area of life, and most of us never realize how much it consumes.

If you have one house, you have a relatively small surface area to maintain (depending on the size of the house, of course). If you buy another one, your surface area expands. But it doesn't expand linearly–it expands slightly above that. It's all the same work plus more.

Friends are another type of surface area. You have a finite amount of time to spend with friends before you die. The more friends you have, the less time you can spend with each one individually.

Wealth is another form of surface area. The more money you have, the more you have to keep track of different types of assets and investments.

When your surface area expands too much, you hire people to help you scale–assistants, property managers, family offices, and so on. They're scaling you–but they're also scaling the surface area of responsibility. This, of course, only masks the rapidly expanding surface area by abstracting it.

Beliefs are another type of surface area.

The thing about surface area is that the more you have, the more you have to defend and maintain. The larger your surface area, the more you are burdened with, mentally and physically.

If you think in terms of surface area, it's easy to see why we are so anxious, stressed, and constantly behind. We feel like we need more time, but what we're really craving is more focus on things that are important. What we need is a smaller surface area.

Surface area becomes part of your identity. She's the "busy person" with her hand in every project. He's the guy with four houses.

Competition can drive expansion. Most people want a bigger house to compete with someone else who has a nicer house. We are animals, after all. On a group level, this causes great benefits. On an individual level, it can cause unhappiness.

Most of the really happy people I know have a relatively small surface area. I know billionaires with two houses. Most of my close friends have only four or five close friends—everyone else is a friend in the loose sense of the word. Most of the productive people I know at work are focused on one or two things, not five.

The way to maximize your enjoyment in life is to keep your surface area small. It's a lot of work but if the happiest people I know are any indication, it's a lot less work to keep it small than to maintain it when it's large.

Circus Schools and Increasing Creativity

Sometimes, as individuals or as organizations, we have a creativity problem. We need some fresh ideas but have a hard time coming up with them. We rely on what we already know and often end up with more of the same. When we need to spur innovation we can try increasing our surface area of exposure to new disciplines. More surface area can give us more diversity, which is sometimes what we need in order to innovate and create.

One short period in the history of circus development provides an excellent example of why multidisciplinary learning can be so powerful. The circus has been around for a long time in various forms. Records of people juggling or doing acrobatics in a public space go back to the Middle Ages. The circus has evolved since then in response to changes in the social environment, and eventually it coalesced into the form that seems to represent the archetype: the big tent with a ringmaster, animals, clowns, and the flying trapeze.

Iconic circuses like Barnum & Bailey, with trains traveling around the country and setting up the big top for a few days of shows at every stop, became the definition of "circus." The performers would live in the circus and raise their kids in the circus environment, and often those children would grow up to become circus performers. Duncan Wall explains in *The Ordinary Acrobat*, "During the eighteenth and nineteenth centuries, well after the rise of public education, circus performers continued to educate their children themselves." This resulted in a situation in which "they didn't just learn their skills, they *lived* them, an intuitive experience that translated into astonishing ability."[1] From very young ages, circus performers could accomplish the amazing feats presented in a circus show.

However, this family system led to a problem. Circus acts became predictable. They may have required great athleticism, but they were always the same. As Wall describes, "Beholden to tradition, each generation mindlessly duplicated the work of the last," creating an artistic bubble in which "technical ability continued to rise, but the art as a whole stagnated. A cheap uniformity ensued."[2]

Eventually the circus became synonymous with nostalgia and directed its marketing at children because they were the only group to whom the circus was new and exciting. Overall ticket sales went down, and the circus was well on its way to becoming history.

How did this decline happen? One of the reasons was that, as Wall explains, "the family system defined the circus for centuries. But while it provided the source for much of the circus's strength and allure, it also had a fundamental flaw. Ruled by families, the circus was what physicists call a closed system. Although the troupes traveled widely, they remained almost totally isolated from the outside world."[3] The surface area of the circus community was small. The borders were not around individuals but the whole unit. Interactions with anyone outside the circus were kept to a minimum. Thus there were minimal opportunities for creative reactions to occur.

Today it's a different story. Circuses are vibrant and diverse. Commercially, companies like Cirque du Soleil have wide appeal and earn into the billions of dollars. The shows are nothing like the traditional circus. In many, the animals have disappeared. Circuses are performed in a variety of venues, from stand-alone theaters to open-air spaces under the stars. Audiences go to see what is new and dynamic in both tricks and artistry. The creativity has exploded in the past fifty years. And one of the reasons is the increased surface area of the new circus education.

Duncan Wall writes, "The story of how the circus finally extracted itself from [its] creative hole is, in large part, the story of the development of circus education. It begins in Russia."[4] After the Russian Revolution in 1916, many of the circus families left due to the political uncertainty. Russians, however, still wanted to go to the circus. So the Russian government, deciding that maintaining and improving the circus could improve the people, re-created the Russian circus and opened a school.

These actions proved momentous in the evolution of the circus. Wall explains how circus performer education was changed by the Russians: "Based largely on Russia's famous ballet schools, the program took an interdisciplinary approach to education." Students learned traditional techniques, but they also learned philosophy, physics, math, and chemistry, which "develop[ed] their intellects" and served as sources of inspiration.[5]

To complement this new education, the Russians took a fresh look at other aspects of the circus. "To encourage innovation, the state invited revered artists from other disciplines" to develop circus content, and "in circus 'labs' around the country, artists and scientists developed new circus methods and equipment."[6]

The results were incredible. "During the fifties and sixties, while the critics were lamenting the death of the circus in the West, the Soviet circus was soaring. . . . They developed what was known as 'the Studio,' a sort of circus production house, in which artists from all disciplines . . . teamed up to devise original circus material. The work coming out of such institutions was unparalleled in artistry and professional polish." Eventually the shows filtered out from behind the Iron Curtain. Soviet circuses toured abroad to critical acclaim and sold-out shows wherever they went. They established dozens of permanent circus theaters at home, selling a hundred million circus tickets every year.[7]

The new multidisciplinary approach to circus education did not go unnoticed, and many countries started their own schools. One of the most notable is the national circus school in France. They too teach a wide variety of subjects to their students. The French school culminates with the creation of an original work, giving students experience in all facets of a production. Wall explains why: "It trained the students to *create* new work, not just *perform* work, in order to keep the circus evolving."[8]

Therein lies the difference between the family approach that almost rendered the circus obsolete and the way circus education is taught now. Students are expected to come up with innovations to move the art in new directions. It is no longer enough to repeat what came before. Both audiences and performers expect new ideas to push the art forward.

Making the core of circus education multidisciplinary is effectively increasing the surface area to promote more creative reactions, increasing the pace of innovation. When you have a narrow knowledge set to draw on, it's harder to come up with new ideas. Exposure to different disciplines sets up circus performers to be creative in the execution of their art. Increasing our own knowledge surface area is a solution when lack of creativity or fresh ideas is a problem.

Guerrilla Warfare

Sometimes reducing your surface area is important. Decreasing your exposure can make you less vulnerable to influence, manipulation, or attack. Designing security measures is one area where surface area needs to be as small as possible without compromising functionality.

In internet security, surface area refers to the number of opportunities an attacker has to gain unauthorized access. Every additional entry point increases the surface area. For instance, employees who have access to important information in a company increase the surface area, as an attacker could gain control of their accounts. Or the more connection points your network has to the internet, the more attack vectors an adversary has. While perfect security is impossible, having the smallest possible surface area reduces the risk of breaches.

Far from being a modern concept, the application of reduced surface area for security is also evident in the narrow slit windows of medieval fortifications and walled cities with only a few guarded entrances. There is a natural relationship between surface area and defense. The smaller your area of exposure to an adversary, the more you can concentrate your resources on a powerful defense of those exposure points.

A small surface area is not only a defensive strategy but also a possible offensive one. Guerrilla warfare is essentially the use of small attack groups against larger, more conventional standing armies. Those who engage in guerrilla warfare reduce their surface area in two dimensions. First, they operate in small autonomous units, and second, they aren't attached to occupying and holding a given territory. Both factors provide little surface area for their adversaries to attack.

The use of guerrilla warfare can be traced back to ancient times, when the guerrillas were nomads fighting against the rulers in a particular region. In *Invisible Armies,* Max Boot explains one of the advantages that small, mobile bands of attackers had: "Having no cities, crops, or other fixed targets to defend, nomads had little cause to worry about enemy attack, making them hard to deter."[9] When you aren't defending a territory or other fixed structures, you give your adversary far fewer points of vulnerability.

As nomads evolved into more contemporary guerrilla warriors, the basic principle of reduced surface area continued to define their tactics. As Robert Greene explains in *The 33 Strategies of War*, "Early guerrilla warriors learned the value of operating in small, dispersed bands as opposed to a concentrated army, keeping in constant motion, never forming a front, flank, or rear for the other side to hit."[10] It's harder to attack small groups of people with no attachment to the territory they occupy.

Guerrilla warriors keep their infrastructure to a minimum, as mobility is always a factor. Although a guerrilla organization has leaders, they tend to organize offensive efforts around small groups that can act independently. Guerrilla warfare maintains such a small surface area because it is critical if they are to have any success. As Boot explains, guerrilla tactics "always have been the resort of the weak against the strong. That is why insurgents wage war from the shadows; if they fought in the open . . . they would be annihilated."[11]

Perhaps one of the most famous examples of successful guerrilla warfare was that carried out under the leadership of Fidel Castro in Cuba in the 1950s. His rebel group operated out of mobile bases in the highest mountains in Cuba and was dedicated to overthrowing the regime of Fulgencio Batista. Their eventual success came as a result of more than just the guerrilla warfare tactics they employed, but those were textbook.

Castro started out in the mountains with only about twenty men. The United States Army Special Operations Command produced a document titled *Case Studies in Insurgency and Revolutionary Warfare: Cuba 1953–1959*. The report makes it clear that Castro's available manpower was only ever a small fraction of Batista's: "Castro has revealed that he had only 180 men with him in April 1958" (Batista's regime fell on January 1, 1959), and that "the two columns that were given the single biggest operation in August 1958 [by Castro] amounted to only 220 men."[12] Contrast these numbers with the thousands of trained military personnel Batista commanded and the surface area of the Cuban rebels seems incredibly small.

This small number of guerrillas operated in tiny tactical units that, in classic guerrilla warfare style, chipped away at Batista's infrastructure. They obviously never attacked the Cuban military directly; they didn't have the manpower for that. Instead they went after vulnerable, isolated units or relatively unguarded parts of the communications infrastructure or supply chains.

Castro's rebels were also mobile. They operated out of bases deep in the heart of mountainous territory that was hard to access. But they were not attached to any particular piece of territory. Thus they could easily move around, evading capture and giving their adversary minimal surface area to attack.

The lens of surface area demonstrates how a small one can be both a defensive and offensive strategy. One of the most famous guerrilla warriors, T. E. Lawrence—who led small groups of Bedouins against the Turks, wrote foundational literature on guerrilla warfare, and became famous as Lawrence of Arabia—explained the essence of the strategy thus: to become "a thing intangible, invulnerable, without front or back."

When You Can't Tell the Whole Truth

Maps are a great example of both the dangers and opportunities of reducing a surface area. All maps present "a chosen aspect of reality."[13] No map can represent everything in a territory. When we choose which details to include, we are deciding which view of the territory to present. Thus all maps show a smaller surface area than the corresponding territory they represent. We are not talking about a geographical surface area but rather a conceptual one. Maps cannot capture every point of detail in a territory, nor is that their function. By necessarily omitting some details, a map reduces the number of information points about a given area.

In *How to Lie with Maps*, Mark Monmonier explains, "A good map tells a multitude of little white lies; it suppresses truth to help the user see what needs to be seen. . . . Reality is three-dimensional, rich in detail, and far too factual to allow a complete yet uncluttered two-dimensional graphic scale model. . . . But the value of a map depends on how well its generalized geometry and generalized content reflect a chosen aspect of reality."[14]

A clear example of the need to simplify a territory in order to make a useful map is the London Underground (known as the Tube) map. It's instantly recognizable, popping up on T-shirts, mugs, posters, and souvenirs. It's been the inspiration for countless underground maps across the world. For Londoners, becoming fluent in reading it is an important rite of passage and a point of pride. As a design, it's beautiful and elegant. Yet part of what makes it so successful is the fact that it doesn't represent reality.

The original design for the Tube map comes from Harry Beck, a humble electrical draftsman. Lacking any relevant formal design training, Beck took his knowledge of drawing circuit diagrams and applied it to a new domain. As an outsider, he was able to approach the problem of conveying the relative locations of stations and lines in a fresh manner. Ignoring geographical accuracy, he portrayed the tube lines as simple colored lines, with circles representing stations.[15] In reality, neither is laid out in a logical manner.

Beck unveiled his radical design in 1933 and was met with unequivocal derision. The Underground's publicity department couldn't imagine commuters using it. After all, it wasn't a map in the usual sense of the word. Beck ignored the actual scale of the city. He portrayed the distance between stations as almost exactly equal. He conveyed the Tube lines as a grid, ignoring the true way they twist and turn beneath the ground. He showed the line intersections as forty-five-degree angles to indicate where to change trains.

Yet as soon as they made a trial print run of the Tube map, people fell in love with it. Harry Beck opened up the city in a new way. The first prints were snapped up by commuters, for whom the simplicity mattered far more than geographical accuracy. Despite numerous changes to the transport system, the modern map retains the spirit of Beck's original design. It now also indicates certain landmarks and other forms of transport, like overground trains and the Docklands Light Railway.

Seeing as a map is always a simplification, it must omit a large amount of unnecessary detail and nuance. It may match the territory in some details but not all. It can never be an exact representation. The London Underground map excludes a number (some estimates run as high as fifty) of abandoned stations that were closed due to low passenger numbers or never opened in the first place. There isn't any real need to include these on the general public's map. It would just confuse people and prompt more requests to visit them, which isn't allowed. A few can be briefly glimpsed if you look out the window at the right moment.

The Tube map reduces the surface area of London to a few points of information to communicate for a single purpose. Thus, when we communicate, it might be helpful to reduce surface area to provide useful content. We cannot cover everything at once. Monmonier writes, "The map must omit details that would confuse or distract."[16] We want Tube travelers to get to Piccadilly Circus if they need to.

Conclusion

Surface area is what determines how much an object interacts with its environment. The more surface area the more contact. Surface area can be good and bad. Sometimes keeping it small is favorable and sometimes increasing our exposure is beneficial.

Surface area teaches us that increasing cognitive diversity can give us fresh ideas and help us innovate. The model also reminds us, however, that in many ways, the more we expose ourselves, the more vulnerable we are. Different situations require different surface areas.

Global and Local Maxima

Embrace the peaks and valleys.

The maxima and minima of a mathematical function are the largest and smallest values over its domain. Although there is one maximum value—the global maximum—there can be smaller peaks of value in a given range: the local maxima. Global maxima are like the highest mountain peak in the world—the ultimate point you can reach on Earth. Local maxima, on the other

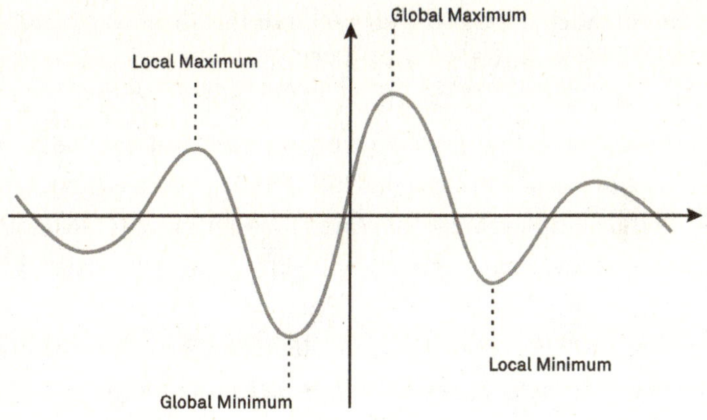

The hill-climbing graph looks much like our experience of life: a lot of time spent navigating between highs and lows.

hand, are like the highest hills in your neighborhood; they're the top points in their immediate area, but they might not be the highest points when you look at the bigger picture.

Using global and local maxima as a model is about knowing when you have hit your peak, or if there is still potential to go higher. It reminds us that sometimes we have to go down to go back up. The model can also help us understand that to optimize and reach our peaks, we need to align the large components before we refine the details.

> We may need to temporarily worsen our solution if we want to continue searching for improvements.
>
> —BRIAN CHRISTIAN AND TOM GRIFFITHS[1]

One of the characteristics of maxima is that there is an increase before and a decrease afterward. Thus, they occur at a critical point of change.

The algorithm that produces the global and local maxima graph is known in computer science as "hill climbing," because, as Christian and Griffiths explain, "the search through a space of solutions, some better and some worse, is commonly thought of in terms of a landscape with hills and valleys, where your goal is to reach the highest peak."[2] We go up and down hills and valleys our entire lives as we work through challenges and develop new expertise.

One of the challenges with climbing a hill is how to know we are climbing the highest peaks. The value of using global and local maxima as a model is that it pushes us to consider if and how we could do better. Even when things are going well, we are often just at a local maximum. In the article "Escaping Local Maxima," Dave

Rael explains that the "chasms between where we are and where we could be [are] opportunities to improve by finding ways of moving from a place where progress is flat to find a new slope to climb."

Getting to a new peak means change—changing what you know, changing the way you are doing things. At a local maximum, things are as good as they can get with the current structure. To get to the peak of a higher hill requires us to walk through a valley as we go back to being neophytes in some ways. Or it requires us to step back, broaden our view, and determine if we are heading in the right direction. But as we learn new skills, partner with new people, or make big jumps in our optimization, we start climbing back up to reach the next maximum.

Navigating the Hills

The story of a new product, from conception to widespread use and high market share, is usually one of ups and downs. There are so many facets of business to learn, from production to sales to marketing, that for novice businesspeople trying to turn their great idea into a successful sales story, there are usually a few mistakes along the way. In addition, we often have to manage traversing our own peaks and valleys while trying to ensure that our current capacities don't limit our ability to climb a higher peak. Using the lens of global and local maxima shows that in bringing a new product to market, there are many times when the owners reach a peak of success only to have to go down to a local minimum as they take on the next challenging climb.

The story of the development of the sports bra in 1977 is a great example of the hills and valleys one is likely to experience taking a product from conception to market success. Lisa Lindahl loved running, but she had a problem. The motion of running caused her breasts to hurt, but she didn't want to give up on a pastime she found so physically and psychologically rewarding. So she and her friend Polly Smith designed the first sports bra based on the requirements Lindahl noted when running: straps that don't dig in, seams that don't rub, and support that minimizes breast movement.[3] Forty years later, sports bras were everywhere. Reading Lindahl's story makes it clear that a graph of the eventual success of the sports bra looks less like a forty-five-degree line that just keeps climbing up and more like the hills and valleys of reaching and moving past local minima and maxima.

After many experiments with different designs and fabrics, Smith constructed a one-off sports bra. Lindahl wore it running, and it worked. But as anyone who has prototyped a new product knows, what you do to get the first one isn't scalable to turning it into a business.

Lindahl entered into a partnership with another woman who had been around during the initial design phase, Hinda Schreiber. Together they tried to develop the sports bra prototype into a business. Calling it the Jogbra, Lindahl and Schreiber had to figure out production, sales, logistics, and marketing. Where could they source the very specific material needed? Where could they get the bras sewn? How would they bring them to market? Who would sell them? How would they let women know the product was available?

Lindahl reflects in her memoir, *Unleash the Girls*, "Starting and running this business was always about learning, gaining information, then accruing the knowledge to apply it correctly."[4] This cycle is often filled with mistakes, as part of accruing knowledge is learning what doesn't work as much as figuring out what does.

Part of what makes Lindahl's story interesting is that the development of the Jogbra company required her to work through personal local maxima and minima to reach a higher global maximum.

Lindahl describes how growing the Jogbra company required her to push herself out of the comfort zones of early security. She went back to college in her late twenties, despite being intimidated, because she realized that in a sense, she had maxed out atop the hill she was on. In order to go higher, she had to start climbing another hill, "challenging many old, ingrained limitations that had held [her] back in the past."

Another factor that required dedicated effort to address was her epilepsy, which she'd had since childhood. She writes of how it shaped her early choices and understanding of her capabilities. For instance, she was conditioned to be afraid of living alone due to the risks associated with having a seizure, and thus she chose early marriage as a result. Part of Lindahl's attachment to running was the better connection it gave her to her own body. It was this connection that helped her not to let her epilepsy stop her from looking for ways to reach her global maxima. Her epilepsy was a factor in her life, but she recounts how she often made decisions so that it wasn't a limiting one (it became a one instead of being a zero).

When it came to the Jogbra business, Lindahl's description of some of the early choices she made makes it clear that she was looking at what was needed to scale the highest peak. For example, she decided to sell it in sporting goods stores as a piece of sports equipment instead of the more obvious choice of the lingerie section of department stores. She recounts how during the late 1970s, women in the United States were starting to get into sports in unprecedented numbers due to legislative changes that mandated equal access to athletics. And the Jogbra was the only product on the market to give women the flexibility and support needed to participate. She felt that putting the Jogbra out there as lingerie would limit its sales, especially because bra sales in general were on a downward trend. It was, however, by no means obvious to the mostly male sales reps and owners of sports stores that the Jogbra was a piece of athletic equipment. She and her small team had to work hard to convince them that Jogbras for women were as essential as jockstraps for men.

She recounts their first full year of business:

> Already articles had been written about the product, about us, and there was never a lack of orders. So, yes, the perception, both publicly and personally, that Jogbra was a success came right away. Right. Away. And the perception was supported by some impressive numbers. We were profitable in our first full year in business and had no idea that this was unusual.[5]

It was an awesome start, and very quickly they hit a local maximum. The end of their first year, though, wasn't a global maximum, and Lindahl often references the learning she had to do to keep the company growing.

Do you go back down a hill when you learn something new? In a lot of ways, yes. If you've never done marketing, you're probably going to have to be bad at it for a while before you get good at it. And before your company can leverage marketing to reach a new local maximum, you're going to have to start near the bottom of that hill.

Lindahl describes the many mistakes the company made as they were developing both their product line and their brand. There were poor naming choices, awful colors, styles that didn't sell. She says, "In those early years, we got off track quite a bit. But we were learning. We were learning the importance of *not* being a one-product company." She describes the Jogmit—mitts to wear while jogging—as a failure but the foray into a men's line as a success. "The line evolved over time, some products came and went;

some became staples. And some... some should have just stayed on the drawing board."[6] Using the lens of global and local maxima, we can see that experimentation, with its inevitable failures, is part of achieving success. Going down sometimes is a part of going up, but if you can improve, you know you haven't reached your global maximum.

Product failures taught the Jogbra team to be aware of their niche, and over time they got better and better at exploiting it. As the company grew, there were continued downs and ups. Expansion required new expertise—and often new capital. The partnership went through challenges. Competition increased. Eventually, as Lindahl describes, "the looming need for capital to fund our continually climbing sales growth" led to her and Schreiber selling the Jogbra company to Playtex.[7] For Lindahl, this was just another hill and valley that led to her exploring other life maxima.

Reflecting on her experience with the invention of the sports bra and the development of the Jogbra company, Lindahl writes, "You make your plans looking upward toward your goal, only to reach it and find that what you thought was the pinnacle, the ceiling of your endeavor, was in fact only the floor of your next level."[8]

Using the model of global and local maxima helps us remember that we often cannot reach our full potential if we aren't willing to stretch ourselves, take risks, and fail once in a while.

Optimization

Another use of the global and local maxima model is in optimization. It helps you know how and when to optimize, and when to avoid overoptimization.

This is actually easier to explain if we start by talking about minima instead.

Let's suppose you want to identify the lowest point in your hometown (the point from which everywhere else is uphill). How would you go about doing so?

One way to solve this problem could be to take a ball (let's pick a basketball), set it down, and watch where it rolls. We expect it to roll downhill, at least if it's on a hill, but since your town is probably pretty large and the ball is unlikely to navigate all the routes, it's improbable that it will stop at the absolute lowest point. Instead it might stop on the lowest point of your street—a local minimum. Could we improve this?

What if we took a giant ball, say, a quarter mile in diameter. Forget for a minute the liability of such a plan and the cost of producing it. How would it roll? With such a large size, it could easily roll over houses, and it's much more likely to find something approaching the global minimum, but it'll never find the global minimum itself. Why is that?

The scale is simply too large. The true global minimum probably fits underneath such a large object, which never quite gets down there. Now that we're close, though, we could switch back to our basketball. Finally we may have found the true global minimum (or at least we're close enough—we've already destroyed a lot of houses in our pursuit).

This story tells a lesson about scale in optimization. We need to make the big changes first, before we try to optimize the details. There is just no other practical way to do it. We also need to be mindful of the directionality of the changes. The feedback mechanism of the ball rolling tells us which way to look. We're not just randomly sampling different locations to try to predict which way will give us the greatest optimization. The other major lesson in this thought experiment is that local minima (or maxima) act as a sort of trap. Our little basketball gets stuck too soon. Stepping back and making a bigger jump by using a bigger ball gives us a better indication of where the global minimum is.

Using New Partnerships to Optimize

We don't have mathematical functions to determine subjective states in our life, such as whether we've reached a global or local maximum on our success potential. We have to perform an analysis of events to determine if we've gone as far as we can within the parameters we've set up, or if we need to regroup and change the scale of how we're optimizing in order to find a higher peak.

Using the model of global and local maxima helps us identify when and how to find a higher peak. Sometimes we know we're close and just need to fine-tune, like rolling the basketball in the sidebar example. And sometimes we need to get out the giant ball because we have the feeling we're not in the right place at all. Changing the scale at which we are optimizing gives us perspective on where to go and how to get there. For example, with a rock band, we can think of its members like the giant balls and individual chords like the basketballs. There is no point in changing the chord in one particular song to get out of a local minimum if your guitar player isn't a good fit and is leading you in the wrong direction. Before bands start tinkering with their image or style, they first need to have the optimal people in the group.

Who hasn't heard of the band Queen? Who can't sing along to at least one of their multiple top-ten hits? They are a rock band who unequivocally made it. They seemed to create hit after hit, entertaining millions and inspiring many musicians. It's easy to think it was all luck, but it wasn't. Queen was the product of years of experimentation and development, and many failed bands. Before they came together as Queen, each member of the band spent years learning how to try to optimize for success in the music business.

All of the members of Queen—Freddie Mercury, Brian May, John Deacon, and Roger Taylor—were members of bands before.

Many of these bands weren't total failures. They had gigs in decent-size venues, fans, and even a record contract. However, we can look back and see that each band before Queen was a local maximum.

John Deacon, the bassist, "who had been strumming the acoustic guitar he bought with his early morning paper round wages since the age of twelve," formed a band called the Opposition with some friends before he turned fourteen.[9] They played together for four years, and during that time they went through ten members. Some left to pursue other interests; some were asked to leave on account of inferior playing or not gelling with the rest of the group. Deacon was noted as a perfectionist in both playing and arranging, and the Opposition had many gigs in their home region of Leicester. As Mark Hodkinson writes in *Queen: The Early Years*, "This was John Deacon's musical apprenticeship, and it was extraordinarily thorough."[10] In addition, just before joining Queen, he briefly formed another band with some friends simply called Deacon.

Roger Taylor started out on guitar before settling on the drums. He was part of three bands. His third band, the Reaction, had some longevity. With six different members over the years, this band too experimented with group dynamics. It was a learning process, a continual effort to understand what promoted cohesion and creativity as well as what undermined group success. Taylor "evolved into the natural leader. He was barely seventeen years old . . . but he willingly shouldered most of the responsibility for running the group."[11] These were lessons that he applied later to success with Queen.

Brian May also started strumming guitar in his school days. Captivated by science as well as music, "it was fated that Brian would fuse his interest in music and technology, and along with a school friend . . . he began to record songs." He and friends formed a band called 1984, which over the years had eight members. With one of them, Tim Staffell, he wrote songs. These were harmonies that later turned into Queen songs, and "during these raw formative days, there was already evidence of ideas which would be developed many years later."[12] The band didn't have the right members to help the sound take off, but the process of trying to write songs gave May an indication of the type of people who might be needed to optimize the music.

May played guitar and did backing vocals on the recordings of other groups, and with 1984 he gained exposure to some of the components that are required of a successful band: stage setup, sound checks, band etiquette and industry quirks, and the need for patience. This was information that was useful for figuring out the essentials of the minimum needed for success: who a band needed to develop style, sound, and songs.

In the late 1960s, Brian May and Roger Taylor formed the band Smile with Tim Staffell. Smile worked hard to try to put together what each member had learned to find a higher peak. "The coyness and ready conformity was gone forever, and Brian May and Tim Staffell's ideology reflected these changes. Individuality was everything and in support of this free expression, their new group would mainly write their own material, or interpret others from a unique panorama."[13]

Smile got a record deal and steady gigs—definitely a local maximum in the music business. They recorded tracks and tried to be an "albums band," but they found their record deal was going nowhere. They pivoted, and "with laudable fortitude, resolved to find a niche as a live band."[14] Smile learned there is little predictability in the music business, and their studio-recorded album was never released. However, "elements which were later brilliantly realized by Queen were already present."[15]

Freddie Mercury, who became the legendary front man of Queen, was born Farrokh Bulsara and grew up in Zanzibar and India before moving to England in his late teens. Although he loved music and sang covers as part of his school's unofficial band, Mercury also cultivated a prescient understanding of another key component of musical success: image. The Freddie Mercury who rocked Live Aid in 1985 spent years, like every other member of the band, developing as an artist. He was a member of the group Ibex and then joined the band Sour Milk Sea. Playing with these groups helped him refine and polish both his vocals and his stage presence. Mercury was described as having "a certain tenacity, a single-mindedness,"[16] and reading his story reveals a man who paid a lot of attention to the details, absorbing the dynamics of the environment he intended to succeed in.

Before Queen could start producing hits, the members had to find one another.

Changing who you play with in a band is like rolling the big ball. You already have a decent sense of the territory and can make an educated guess about which direction the ball is likely to roll. But the emergent properties of playing music as a group mean that you can never exactly predict what sound certain individuals will make when they come together. You don't know if a group might have settled over the global maximum at least until they start playing together.

In 1970 May, Taylor, and Mercury, who had been friends for a while, decided to form a new band. Putting in all the knowledge they had gained over the years, they first had to roll that big ball to find a bass player. They went through three bassists before they found John Deacon, who turned out to be an excellent fit.

Once they thought they were in the general territory of the global maximum, they refined element by element. They played shows. They wrote music. "They openly solicited their friends' comments about performances and were not afraid of criticism."[17] Through constant learning and a willingness to incorporate feedback into developing new functions aimed at optimizing to reach their global maxima, the members of Queen became one of the most dynamic and memorable rock bands of all time.

Conclusion

Global and local maxima as a model can be used in different ways to help us make the changes we need for success. It encourages us to see achieving our goals not as a steady upward trajectory but as a path full of peaks and valleys. Understanding that sometimes we have to go down in order to climb even higher helps us make short-term sacrifices to play the long game. In engineering, you might be trying to maximize efficiency. In life, you might be trying to maximize happiness. But in all these cases, it's easy to get stuck on a local maximum. You find a pretty good solution, and you stop looking for a better one.

The next time you're trying to optimize something, remember the concept of global and local maxima. Don't just settle for the first peak you find. Keep exploring. Keep searching for that global maximum. It might be a tough climb, but the view from the top is worth it.

Afterthoughts

You've finished reading the third volume of *The Great Mental Models* series. You now have almost fifty models from these books in your toolkit. We hope you have found our exploration of each model interesting and insightful. But now you may be wondering, what next? How can you take these seeds of ideas about timeless knowledge and grow them to make improvements in all areas of your life?

Exposing yourself to new ideas is always the first step in learning. But to develop wisdom, what you learn needs to be put to the test. When it comes to mental models, you can't just passively read about them and hope that one day you will notice a positive change in your life. You need to use them.

Pick a model, maybe one per week, and start looking at your life through that lens. What do you notice? What looks different? Write down or record your observations. Take the time to reflect on your experiences using each model, because it is through reflection that the most valuable knowledge builds. Note where you make a different choice based on the insight provided by the model. Pay attention to what worked and improved your outcomes. Learn from your mistakes. Over time you will build knowledge of where each model is most useful and most likely to help you.

As you practice using more models, you will begin to build a latticework. You will see connections and notice that some models give the best insight when paired with certain others. Eventually your latticework will be comprehensive enough that you will be able to use it in every situation, reducing your blind spots and preventing problems.

Using mental models is a lifelong journey, and this book is just one step on that road. The next volume in the series will cover the foundational ideas from economics and military strategy, which will give you another set of tools for your toolbox.

Improving our lives means seeing the world as it is and learning to work with the fundamental principles that govern it. Having a diverse set of thoughtful mental models that reflect how the world works is a critical component of making better decisions and ultimately living a more meaningful life.

As *The Great Mental Models* goes out into the world, we will continue to create and update resources on fs.blog/tgmm to help you integrate these models into your thinking. As we wrote in the previous volume, before long, when it comes to using mental models, you will be capitalizing on the powerful momentum you have created. These ideas will become such an integral part of the fabric of your thinking that it will be impossible to view any situation without the valuable lenses they provide.

Acknowledgments

I'm forever indebted to Charlie Munger, Peter D. Kaufman, Warren Buffett, and Peter Bevelin, who, to varying degrees, started me down the path of multidisciplinary thinking. I owe them a huge debt of gratitude.

Thank you to my coauthor Rhiannon Beaubien for making this series possible. It's impossible to overstate her contributions to this volume and the entire series. Without her, you would not be holding this book in your hands. And thank you to my other coauthor, Rosie Leizrowice, for her substantial contribution to this book.

This series would be lost without our talented illustrator, Marcia Mihotich. Thank you for seeing these words and ideas and bringing them to life in simple and exceptional ways.

While this is a revised volume 3, I wanted to give a special mention to Garvin Hirt and Morgwn Rimel for shaping the creativity of the original version. Working with you both has encouraged me to make things beautiful and timeless. And thank you to our OG editor Kristen Hall-Geisler for her willingness to dive in and ensure the material flows and comes together in the end.

The original version of this series would not have been possible without our partnership with Automattic and their incredible CEO, Matt Mullenweg. Thank you to Niki Papadopoulos and the entire team at Portfolio for rereleasing this series and supporting my efforts to make it as beautiful and timeless as we can.

Thank you to Simon Hørup Eskildsen, Zachary Smith, Paul Ciampa, Devon Anderson, Alex Duncan, Vicky Cosenzo, Laurence Endersen, David Epstein, Ozan Gurcan, Will Bowers, Sanjay Bakshi, Jeff Annello, Tara Small, Tina Cantrill, Nathan Taggart, Tim Bragassa, Yves Colomb, Rick Jones, Ran Klein, Maria Petrova, and Dr. Gregory P. Moore for taking the time to review various books in this series. Your comments and contributions have helped make everything better.

Thank you to my sons for reminding me to continue to learn and grow along with them. This series was largely written for you and future generations.

Thank you to the entire FS team for your hard work and dedication over the years to bring this series to life.

And finally, thanks to you, the reader. I continue to be amazed by how many of you want to take this mental models journey with me. I hope this book is one you can reference time and again as you seek to better understand the world.

Notes

Introduction

1. Howard Gardner, *The Disciplined Mind: What All Students Should Understand* (New York: Simon & Schuster, 1999).
2. Hilde Østby and Ylva Østby, *Adventures in Memory* (Vancouver, Canada: Greystone Books, 2018).
3. Marc N. Kleinhenz, "Doctor Strange Advisor Explains the Science behind Marvel's Multiverse," ScreenRant, March 2, 2017, screenrant.com/doctor-strange-multiverse-science.
4. Peter M. Senge, *The Fifth Discipline* (London: Random House Business, 2006).

SYSTEMS

1. Donella H. Meadows, *Thinking in Systems* (White River Junction, VT: Chelsea Green, 2008).

Feedback Loops

1. James Clear, "The 1 Percent Rule: Why a Few People Get Most of the Rewards," James Clear, jamesclear.com/the-1-percent-rule, accessed June 15, 2023.
2. Jack Russell Weinstein, "Adam Smith (1723–1790)," *Internet Encyclopedia of Philosophy*, accessed August 14, 2019, iep.utm.edu/smith.
3. Russ Roberts, *How Adam Smith Can Change Your Life: An Unexpected Guide to Human Nature and Happiness* (New York: Portfolio, 2015).
4. Adam Smith, *The Theory of Moral Sentiments* (London: Printed for A. Millar, A. Kincaid, and J. Bell in Edinburgh, 1761).
5. Ibid.
6. Ward Farnsworth, *The Legal Analyst* (Chicago: University of Chicago Press, 2007).

7. Ibid.
8. Ibid.
9. Ibid.
10. Ibid.
11. Ibid.
12. Ibid.
13. Donella H. Meadows, *Thinking in Systems* (White River Junction, VT: Chelsea Green, 2008).
14. Anthony Bourdain, *Kitchen Confidential* (New York: Bloomsbury, 2000).
15. Farnsworth, *The Legal Analyst*.
16. Ibid.
17. Ibid.
18. Ibid.
19. Some of the material on the Prisoner's Dilemma appears on the *Farnam Street* blog: fs.blog/2020/02/prisoners-dilemma.
20. Farnsworth, *The Legal Analyst*.
21. Kevin Ashton, *How to Fly a Horse* (New York: Anchor Books, 2015).

Equilibrium

1. Kelvin Rodolfo, "What Is Homeostasis?" *Scientific American*, January 3, 2000, scientificamerican.com/article/what-is-homeostasis.
2. Antonio Damasio, *The Strange Order of Things* (New York: Vintage Books, 2018).
3. Arabella L. Simpkin and Richard M. Schwartzstein, "Tolerating Uncertainty: The Next Medical Revolution?" *New England Journal of Medicine* 375, no. 18 (2016): 1713–5.
4. Cathy Charles, Amiram Gafni, and Tim Whelan, "Shared Decision-Making in the Medical Encounter: What Does It Mean?" *Social Science and Medicine* 44, no. 5 (1997): 681–92.
5. David S. Walonick, "General Systems Theory," Parkoffletter, 1993, accessed February 28, 2024, parkoffletter.org/general-system-theory-by-walonick.
6. Annie Janvier and John Lantos, "Ethics and Etiquette in Neonatal Intensive Care," *JAMA Pediatrics* 168, no. 9 (2014): 857–8.
7. Daniel C. Dennett, *Intuition Pumps and Other Tools for Thinking* (New York: W. W. Norton & Company, 2014).
8. John Northern Hilliard et al., *Greater Magic: A Practical Treatise on Modern Magic* (Silver Spring, MD: Kaufman and Greenburg, 1994).
9. Dennett, *Intuition Pumps*.
10. William F. Dempster, "Biosphere 2 Engineering Design," *Ecological Engineering* 13 (1999): 31–42, ecotechnics.edu/wp-content/uploads/backup/2011/08/Ecol-Eng-1999-Bio-2-Engineering-Design-Dempster.pdf.
11. *Encyclopedia Britannica*, s.v. "Biosphere 2," by Kara Rogers, accessed November 5, 2020, britannica.com/topic/Biosphere-2.

12. Jordan Fisher Smith, "Life under the Bubble," *Discover*, updated April 12, 2023, discovermagazine.com/environment/life-under-the-bubble.
13. Ibid.
14. Lisa Ruth Rand et al., "Biosphere 2: Why an Eccentric Ecological Experiment Still Matters 25 Years Later," *Edge Effects*, updated October 9, 2021, edgeeffects.net/biosphere-2.
15. Ibid.
16. Smith, "Life Under the Bubble."
17. Rand et al., "Biosphere 2."

Bottlenecks

1. W. Bruce Lincoln, *The Conquest of a Continent* (New York: Random House, 1994).
2. T. R. Reid, *The Chip* (New York: Random House, 2001).
3. Christian Wolmar, *To the Edge of the World* (New York: Public Affairs, 2013).
4. Ibid.
5. Ibid.
6. Ibid.
7. Encyclopedia.com, s.v. "The Invention of Nylon," by Peter J. Andrews, accessed January 31, 2020, encyclopedia.com/science/encyclopedias-almanacs-transcripts-and-maps/invention-nylon.
8. Audra J. Wolfe, "Nylon: A Revolution in Textiles," Science History Institute, October 2, 2008, sciencehistory.org/distillations/nylon-a-revolution-in-textiles.
9. Jon Marmor, "Waldo Seman: He Helped Save the World," *Columns*, September 1999, washington.edu/alumni/columns/sept99/semon.html.
10. "US Synthetic Rubber Program," American Chemical Society, August 1998, acs.org/content/acs/en/education/whatischemistry/landmarks/synthetic rubber.html.
11. Edward Tenner, *Why Things Bite Back: Technology and the Revenge of Unintended Consequences* (New York: Vintage Books, 1997).
12. Ibid.
13. Neetha Mahadevan, "100 Years Legacies: The Lasting Impact of World War I," *Wall Street Journal*, updated October 31, 2018, graphics.wsj.com/100-legacies-from-world-war-1.

Scale

1. Miyamoto Musashi, *Honor: Samurai Philosophy of Life: The Essential Samurai Collection* (Somerville: Bottom of the Hill, 2010).
2. Scott D. Anthony et al., "Corporate Longevity Forecast: Creative Destruction Is Accelerating," Innosight, February 2018, innosight.com/wp-content/uploads/2017/11/Innosight-Corporate-Longevity-2018.pdf.

3. Kim Gittleson, "Can a Company Live Forever?" BBC News, January 19, 2012, bbc.co.uk/news/business-16611040.
4. Joe Pinsker, "Japan's Oldest Businesses Have Survived for More Than 1,000 Years," *The Atlantic*, February 12, 2015, theatlantic.com/business/archive/2015/02/japans-oldest-businesses-have-lasted-more-than-a-thousand-years/385396.
5. "Kongo Gumi Company Profile," TakaMatsu Group, accessed August 15, 2019, takamatsu-cg.co.jp/eng/about/group/takamatsu/kongogumi.html.
6. Mariko Oi, "Adult Adoptions: Keeping Japan's Family Firms Alive," BBC News, September 19, 2012, bbc.co.uk/news/magazine-19505088.
7. Joanna Gillan, "Kongo Gumi: Oldest Continuously Operating Company Survives 1,400 Years before Crash," Ancient Origins, September 5, 2015, ancient-origins.net/history/kongo-gumi-oldest-continuously-operating-company-survives-1400-years-crash-003765.
8. Irene Herrera, "Building on Tradition—1,400 Years of a Family Business," Works That Work, accessed August 15, 2019, worksthatwork.com/3/kongo-gumi.
9. Geoffrey West, *Scale* (New York: Penguin, 2017).
10. Jane Brox, *Brilliant: The Evolution of Artificial Light* (London: Souvenir, 2012).
11. Ibid.
12. Ibid.
13. Ibid.
14. Ibid.
15. Wolfgang Schivelbusch, *Disenchanted Night* (Oakland: University of California Press, 1988).
16. Brox, *Brilliant*.
17. Schivelbusch, *Disenchanted Night*.
18. "Frederick Albert Winsor (Winzer) Biography (1763–1830)," How Products Are Made, accessed August 11, 2020, madehow.com/inventorbios/79/Frederick-Albert-Winsor-Winzer.html.
19. Brox, *Brilliant*.
20. Schivelbusch, *Disenchanted Night*.
21. Brox, *Brilliant*.
22. Ibid.
23. Jennifer Latson, "How Edison Invented the Light Bulb—and Lots of Myths about Himself," *Time*, October 21, 2014, time.com/3517011/thomas-edison.
24. Brox, *Brilliant*.
25. Schivelbusch, *Disenchanted Night*.
26. Brox, *Brilliant*.
27. Jason Donev et al., "Electrical Grid," Energy Education, 2020, energyeducation.ca/encyclopedia/Electrical_grid.
28. Schivelbusch, *Disenchanted Night*.

Margin of Safety

1. Arthur Conan Doyle, *Tales of Terror and Mystery* (London: Pan Books, 1978).
2. Benjamin Graham, *The Intelligent Investor* (New York: HarperCollins, 2006).
3. David Bjerklie, "The Hidden Danger of Seat Belts," *Time*, November 30, 2006, content.time.com/time/nation/article/0,8599,1564465,00.html.
4. Chris Hadfield, *An Astronaut's Guide to Life on Earth* (Toronto: Vintage Canada, 2013).
5. Ibid.
6. Ibid.
7. Ibid.
8. Ibid.
9. Ibid.
10. Ibid.
11. Ibid.
12. Ibid.
13. Ibid.
14. William McDonald, *The Obits: Annual 2012* (The New York Times, November 2011), 110.
15. "Jacques Jaujard (1895–1967)," Monuments Men and Women Foundation, accessed August 19, 2019, monumentsmenfoundation.org/the-heroes/the-monuments-men/jaujard-jacques.
16. Agnès Poirier, "Saviour of France's Art: How the Mona Lisa Was Spirited Away from the Nazis," *Guardian*, November 22, 2014, theguardian.com/world/2014/nov/22/mona-lisa-spirited-away-from-nazis-jacques-jaujard-louvre.
17. Agnès Poirier, *Left Bank: Art, Passion, and the Rebirth of Paris 1940–1950* (London: Bloomsbury, 2016).
18. Poirier, "Saviour of France's Art."
19. Noah Charney, "Did the Nazis Steal the Mona Lisa?" *Guardian*, November 12, 2013, theguardian.com/artanddesign/2013/nov/12/nazis-steal-mona-lisa-louvre.
20. Aurelien Breeden, "Art Looted by Nazis Gets a New Space at the Louvre. But Is It Really Home?" *New York Times*, February 8, 2018, nytimes.com/2018/02/08/world/europe/louvre-nazi-looted-art.html.
21. Gerri Chanel, *Saving Mona Lisa: The Battle to Protect the Louvre and Its Treasures from the Nazis* (London: Icon Books, 2018).
22. "Rose Valland (1898–1980)," Monuments Men and Women Foundation, accessed May 26, 2020, monumentsmenfoundation.org/valland-capt-rose.
23. Chanel, *Saving Mona Lisa*.
24. Poirier, *Left Bank*.
25. Naomi Rea, "Less Than a Month after the Louvre Hired a Nazi Loot Expert to Investigate Its Collection, She Found 10 Ill-Gotten Works Hiding in Plain Sight," Artnet, January 22, 2020, news.artnet.com/art-world/restitution-nazi-loot-louvre-france-1758900.

Churn

1. Lawrence Van Gelder, "Charles Dederich, 83, Synanon Founder, Dies," *New York Times*, March 4, 1997, nytimes.com/1997/03/04/us/charles-dederich-83-synanon-founder-dies.html.
2. Jyotsna Sreenivasan, *Utopias in American History* (Santa Barbara, CA: ABC-CLIO, 2008).
3. Hillel Aron, "The Story of This Drug Rehab–Turned–Violent Cult Is *Wild, Wild Country*–Caliber Bizarre," *Los Angeles*, April 23, 2018, lamag.com/citythinkblog/synanon-cult.
4. Sreenivasan, *Utopias in American History*.
5. Ibid.
6. "Like a duck on a pond . . ." AZ Quotes, accessed January 9, 2024, azquotes.com/quote/1384792#google_vignette.
7. Encyclopedia.com, s.v. "Bourbaki, Nicolas," by Leo Corry, accessed August 19, 2019, encyclopedia.com/people/science-and-technology/mathematics-biographies/nicolas-bourbaki.
8. Marjorie Senechal, "The Continuing Silence of Bourbaki," *Mathematical Intelligencer* 1 (1998): 22–8, accessed August 19, 2019, at ega-math.narod.ru/Bbaki/Cartier.htm.
9. Amir D. Aczel, *The Artist and the Mathematician* (London: High Stakes, 2007).
10. Ibid.
11. Maurice Mashaal, *Bourbaki: A Secret Society of Mathematicians* (Providence, RI: American Mathematical Society, 2006).
12. J. J. O'Connor and E. F. Robertson, "Bourbaki: The Pre-War Years," Mac Tutor, accessed August 19, 2019, mathshistory.st-andrews.ac.uk/HistTopics/Bourbaki_1.html.

Algorithms

1. Yuval Noah Harari, *Homo Deus: A Brief History of Tomorrow* (New York: Harper Perennial, 2018).
2. Daniel Dennett, *Intuition Pumps and Other Tools for Thinking* (New York: W. W. Norton and Company, 2013).
3. Ibid.
4. Ibid.
5. Ibid.
6. "What Is a Constitution?" The Constitution Unit, University College London, accessed June 7, 2019, ucl.ac.uk/constitution-unit/what-uk-constitution/what-constitution.
7. Peter T. Leeson, *The Invisible Hook: The Hidden Economics of Pirates* (Princeton, NJ: Princeton University Press, 2011).
8. Ibid.
9. Ibid.

10. James Surowiecki, "The Pirates' Code," *New Yorker*, July 2, 2007, newyorker.com/magazine/2007/07/09/the-pirates-code.
11. Leeson, *The Invisible Hook*.
12. David D. Friedman, Peter T. Leeson, and David Skarbek, *Legal Systems Very Different from Ours* (self-pub., 2019).
13. Ibid.
14. "Pirate Code of Conduct and Pirate Rules," The Way of the Pirates, accessed February 17, 2020, thewayofthepirates.com/pirate-life/pirate-code.
15. Peter T. Leeson, "An-*arrgh*-chy: The Law and Economics of Pirate Organization," *Journal of Political Economy* 115, no. 6 (2007): 1049–94.
16. Ibid.
17. Ibid.
18. Surowiecki, "The Pirates' Code."
19. Anita Sarkeesian and Ebony Adams, *History vs Women: The Defiant Lives That They Don't Want You to Know* (London: Faber and Faber, 2020).
20. This is based on the estimates of Richard Glasspoole, a hostage on one of her ships for two months.
21. "Queen Anne's Revenge Conservation Lab," Queen Anne's Revenge Project, accessed January 13, 2020, qaronline.org/history/blackbeard.
22. Urvija Banerji, "The Chinese Female Pirate Who Commanded 80,000 Outlaws," Atlas Obscura, updated June 15, 2022, atlasobscura.com/articles/the-chinese-female-pirate-who-commanded-80000-outlaws.
23. Paul Lockhart, *Arithmetic* (Cambridge, MA: Belknap Press, 2017).
24. Thomas Hager, *The Demon under the Microscope* (New York: Harmony Books, 2006).
25. Ibid.
26. Ibid.
27. Ibid.
28. Ibid.
29. Ibid.
30. Ibid.
31. Ibid.
32. Scott E. Page, *Diversity and Complexity* (Princeton, NJ: Princeton University Press, 2011).
33. Serena Chan, "Complex Adaptive Systems" (research paper, ESD.83 Research Seminar in Engineering Systems, Cambridge, Massachusetts Institute of Technology, 2001), web.mit.edu/esd.83/www/notebook/Complex%20Adaptive%20Systems.pdf.
34. Melanie Mitchell, *Complexity: A Guided Tour* (New York: Oxford University Press, 2011).
35. Garrett Hardin, *Living within Limits: Ecology, Economics, and Population Taboos* (New York: Oxford University Press, 1993).
36. Nate Silver, *The Signal and the Noise: The Art and Science of Prediction* (London: Penguin 2013).

37. Joachim P. Sturmberg and Carmel M. Martin, eds., *Handbook of Systems and Complexity in Health* (New York: Springer, 2013).

Critical Mass

1. Morton Grodzins, "50 Years Ago in Scientific American: 'Metropolitan Segregation,'" *Scientific American,* September 18, 2007, scientificamerican.com/article/50-years-ago-in-scientific-american-white-flight-1.
2. Allen Downey, "Self-Organized Criticality and Holistic Models," *Probably Overthinking It* (blog), February 24, 2012, allendowney.blogspot.com/2012/02/self-organized-criticality-and-holistic.html.
3. Steven H. Strogatz, *Sync: How Order Emerges from the Chaos in the Universe, Nature, and Daily Life* (New York: Hyperion, 2003).
4. Rutger Bregman and Elizabeth Manton, *Utopia for Realists: And How We Can Get There* (London: Bloomsbury, 2018).
5. Nathan J. Russell, "An Introduction to the Overton Window of Political Possibilities," Mackinac Center for Public Policy, January 4, 2006, mackinac.org/7504.
6. "Women and the Vote," New Zealand History, updated September 19, 2023, nzhistory.govt.nz/politics/womens-suffrage.
7. Katie Pickles, "Why New Zealand Was the First Country Where Women Won the Right to Vote," *Conversation,* September 18, 2018, theconversation.com/why-new-zealand-was-the-first-country-where-women-won-the-right-to-vote-103219.
8. "NZ in the 19th Century," New Zealand History, December 11, 2019, nzhistory.govt.nz/media_gallery/tid/2219.
9. "Story: Dalrymple, Learmonth White," The Encyclopedia of New Zealand, accessed May 26, 2020, teara.govt.nz/en/biographies/1d2/dalrymple-learmonth-white.
10. Patricia Grimshaw, *Women's Suffrage in New Zealand* (Auckland, NZ: Auckland University Press, 2013).
11. Ibid.
12. Ibid.
13. "Temperance Movement," New Zealand History, updated March 13, 2018, nzhistory.govt.nz/politics/temperance-movement/beginnings.
14. Grimshaw, *Women's Suffrage.*
15. Ibid.
16. "Minority Rules: Scientists Discover Tipping Point for the Spread of Ideas," *ScienceDaily,* July 26, 2011, sciencedaily.com/releases/2011/07/110725190044.htm.
17. Ed Yong, "The Tipping Point When Minority Views Take Over," *Atlantic,* June 7, 2018, theatlantic.com/science/archive/2018/06/the-tipping-point-when-minority-views-take-over/562307.
18. Christopher Alexander, *A City Is Not a Tree* (Portland, OR: Sustasis Foundation, 2015).

19. Jane Jacobs, *The Death and Life of Great American Cities* (New York: Random House, 1961).
20. Ibid.
21. Ibid.
22. Ibid.
23. Ibid.
24. Ibid.
25. Charles Montgomery, *Happy City: Transforming Our Lives through Urban Design* (London: Penguin, 2015).
26. "The World's Longest Pedestrian Street—'Strøget'—Copenhagen," Copenhagen-Portal.dk, accessed February 3, 2020, copenhagenet.dk/cph-map/CPH-Pedestrian.asp.
27. Montgomery, *Happy City.*
28. Alexander, *A City Is Not a Tree.*
29. Jordi Sanchez-Cuenca, "Uneven Development of Planned Cities: Brasília," Smart Cities Dive, accessed February 3, 2020, smartcitiesdive.com/ex/sustainablecitiescollective/uneven-development-planned-cities-brasilia/121571.
30. James C. Scott, *Seeing Like a State* (New Haven: Yale University Press, 1998).

Emergence

1. Robert M. Pirsig, *Zen and the Art of Motorcycle Maintenance: An Inquiry into Values* (London: Vintage Books, 2008).
2. Susan Ratcliffe, *Oxford Essential Quotations* (Oxford, UK: Oxford University Press, 2018).
3. Lisa Margonelli, "Collective Mind in the Mound: How Do Termites Build Their Huge Structures?" *National Geographic,* August 1, 2014, nationalgeographic.com/news/2014/8/140731-termites-mounds-insects-entomology-science.
4. "The Incredible Termite Mound," PBS, October 28, 2011, pbs.org/wnet/nature/the-animal-house-the-incredible-termite-mound/7222.
5. Mark A. Bedau, "Weak Emergence," *Noûs* 31, s11 (1997): 375–99, doi.org/10.1111/0029-4624.31.s11.17.
6. Diana Taylor, *Disappearing Acts: Spectacles of Gender and Nationalism in Argentina's "Dirty War"* (Durham, NC: Duke University Press, 2005).
7. Uki Goñi, "Forty Years Later, the Mothers of Argentina's 'Disappeared' Refuse to Be Silent," *Guardian,* April 28, 2017, theguardian.com/world/2017/apr/28/mothers-plaza-de-mayo-argentina-anniversary.
8. Lester Kurtz, "The Mothers of the Disappeared: Challenging the Junta in Argentina (1977–1983)," International Center for Nonviolent Conflict, July 2010, nonviolent-conflict.org/mothers-disappeared-challenging-junta-argentina-1977-1983.
9. Lyn Reese, "Speaking Truth to Power: Madres of the Plaza De Mayo," Women in World History Curriculum, accessed August 23, 2019, womeninworldhistory.com/contemporary-07.html.

10. Goñi, "Forty Years Later."
11. Taylor, *Disappearing Acts.*
12. Erin Blakemore, "30,000 People Were 'Disappeared' in Argentina's Dirty War. These Women Never Stopped Looking," History, updated August 24, 2023, history.com/news/mothers-plaza-de-mayo-disappeared-children-dirty-war-argentina.
13. Ibid.
14. "Another Grandson Recovers His Identity and His Life Story," Abuelas de Plaza de Mayo, August 3, 2018, abuelas.org.ar/resources/ABUELAS-La%20historia%20de%20abuelas.pdf.
15. "World Report 2019: Rights Trends in Argentina," Human Rights Watch, January 17, 2019, hrw.org/world-report/2019.
16. Joseph Henrich, *The Secret of Our Success* (Princeton, NJ: Princeton University Press, 2016).
17. Ibid.
18. Ibid.
19. Robert Boyd and Peter J. Richerson, "Culture and the Evolution of Human Cooperation," *Philosophical Transactions of the Royal Society B: Biological Sciences* 364, no. 1533 (2009): 3281–8.
20. Ibid.
21. Ibid.
22. Charles Perreault, "The Pace of Cultural Evolution," *PLoS ONE* 7, no. 9 (2012): e45150, doi.org/10.1371/journal.pone.0045150.
23. Henrich, *Secret of Our Success.*
24. Ibid.
25. Steven Strogatz, *Sync: How Order Emerges from Chaos in the Universe, Nature, and Daily Life* (New York: Hachette Books, 2015).
26. Peter Dizikes, "When the Butterfly Effect Took Flight," *MIT Technology Review,* February 22, 2011, technologyreview.com/s/422809/when-the-butterfly-effect-took-flight.
27. "Sensitivity to Initial Conditions," Vanderbilt University, accessed January 15, 2020, vanderbilt.edu/AnS/psychology/cogsci/chaos/workshop/Sensitivity.html.
28. Melanie Mitchell, *Complexity: A Guided Tour* (New York: Oxford University Press, 2011).
29. Albert Einstein is often quoted as saying, "As far as the laws of mathematics refer to reality, they are not certain, and as far as they are certain, they do not refer to reality." This statement reflects Einstein's views on the relationship between mathematical abstractions and physical reality, although the exact source of this specific wording is unclear.
30. Étienne Ghys, "The Butterfly Effect," *Proceedings of the 12th International Congress on Mathematical Education* (2015): 19–39.
31. John Gribbin, *Deep Simplicity* (London: Penguin Books, 2005).

Irreducibility

1. Andrew Robinson, "Did Einstein Really Say That?" *Nature,* April 30, 2018, nature.com/articles/d41586-018-05004-4.
2. "Abram Games and the Power of the Poster," National Army Museum, accessed November 12, 2020, nam.ac.uk/explore/abram-games-designer.
3. Ibid.
4. Joseph Jon Kaminski, "World War I and Propaganda Poster Art: Comparing the United States and German Cases," *Epiphany* 7, no. 2 (2014): 64–81.
5. Eric Gill, *An Essay on Typography* (London: Penguin Modern Classics, 2013).
6. Ibid.
7. Ibid.
8. Ibid.
9. Ibid.
10. Ibid.
11. Paul Felton, *The Ten Commandments of Typography: Type Heresy* (London: Merrell, 2006).
12. Ibid.

The Law of Diminishing Returns

1. Darrell A. Russel and Gerald G. Williams, "History of Chemical Fertilizer Development," *Soil Science Society of America Journal* 41 no. 2 (1977): 260–5.
2. Paul M. Johnson, "Diminishing Returns, Law Of," A Glossary of Political Economy Terms, accessed August 15, 2019, auburn.edu/~johnspm/gloss/diminishing_returns_law_of.
3. John Pencavel, "The Productivity of Working Hours," *Economic Journal* 125, no. 589 (2015): 2052–76, doi.org/10.1111/ecoj.12166.
4. Alexander Mikaberidze, *Atrocities, Massacres, and War Crimes: An Encyclopedia* (Santa Barbara, CA: ABC-CLIO, 2013).
5. Neil Oliver, *The Vikings* (London: Weidenfeld & Nicolson, 2012).
6. Joshua J. Mark, "Viking Raids on Paris," World History Encyclopedia, November 13, 2018, ancient.eu/Viking_Raids_on_Paris.
7. Martina Sprague, *Norse Warfare: The Unconventional Battle Strategies of the Ancient Vikings* (New York: Hippocrene Books, 2007).
8. Ibid.
9. James T. Palmer, *The Apocalypse in the Early Middle Ages* (Cambridge, UK: Cambridge University Press, 2014).
10. Simon Coupland, *Carolingian Coinage and the Vikings: Studies on Power and Trade in the 9th Century* (Burlington, VT: Ashgate, 2007).
11. Ibid.
12. Angus A. Somerville and R. Andrew McDonald, *The Vikings and Their Age* (Toronto: University of Toronto Press, 2013).

13. Sprague, *Norse Warfare.*
14. John Haywood, *Northmen: The Viking Saga, AD 793–1241* (New York: Thomas Dunne Books, 2016).
15. Ibid.
16. Ben Hubbard, *Bloody History of Paris: Riots, Revolution and Rat Pie* (London: Amber Books, 2018).
17. Mark Kurlansky, *Salt: A World History* (London: Vintage, 2003).
18. Hubbard, *Bloody History of Paris.*
19. John Locke, *An Essay Concerning Human Understanding* (Oxford, UK: Clarendon Press, 1979).
20. Steven Pinker, *The Better Angels of Our Nature: Why Violence Has Declined* (New York: Penguin Books, 2012).
21. Walter A. Lunden, "Pioneers in Criminology XVI: Emile Durkheim (1858–1917)," *Journal of Criminal Law, Criminology, and Police Science* 49, no. 1 (1958): 2–9.
22. Warren Buffett and Lawrence A. Cunningham, *The Essays of Warren Buffett: Lessons for Corporate America* (Durham, NC: Carolina Academic Press, 2013).
23. Ric Meyers, *For One Week Only: The World of Exploitation Films* (Guilford, CT: Emery Books, 2011).
24. Ibid.
25. Ibid.
26. Ibid.
27. Ibid.
28. Ibid.
29. Ibid.
30. Feona Attwood et al., eds., *Controversial Images: Media Representations on the Edge* (Basingstoke, UK: Palgrave Macmillan, 2013).
31. Meyers, *For One Week Only.*
32. Joseph A. Tainter, *The Collapse of Complex Societies* (Cambridge, UK: Cambridge University Press, 2017).
33. Ibid.

MATHEMATICS

1. Shakuntala Devi, *Puzzles to Puzzle You* (India: Orient Paperbacks, 2005).
2. "Statistical Distributions," accessed October 2020, New York University Stern School of Business, people.stern.nyu.edu/adamodar/New_Home_Page/StatFile/statdistns.htm.
3. Ibid.
4. Leonard Mlodinow, *The Drunkard's Walk: How Randomness Rules Our Lives* (New York: Pantheon Books, 2009).
5. Brian Christian and Tom Griffiths, *Algorithms to Live By* (Toronto: Penguin, 2016).
6. Ibid.

7. Epicurus, "Letter to Menoeceus," in *Classics of Western Philosophy*, 4th ed., ed. Steven M. Cahn (Indianapolis: Hackett, 1995).
8. Daniel Klein, foreword to *Epicurus: The Art of Happiness*, by Epicurus, trans. George K. Strodach (New York: Penguin Books, 2012).
9. Ibid.
10. George K. Strodach, trans., introduction to *Epicurus: The Art of Happiness*, by Epicurus (New York: Penguin Books, 2012).
11. Epicurus, "Letter to Menoeceus."
12. Catherine Wilson, *How to Be an Epicurean: The Ancient Art of Living Well* (New York: Basic Books, 2019).
13. Ibid.

Compounding

1. Naval (@naval), Twitter, May 31, 2018, 1:26 a.m., twitter.com/naval/status/1002103908947263488?lang=en.
2. Bill Fay, "Compound Interest: How It Works," Debt.org., updated December 1, 2023, debt.org/blog/compound-interest-how-it-works.
3. C. S. Lewis, *The Complete C. S. Lewis Signature Classics* (London: HarperCollins, 2012).
4. Maristella Botticini and Zvi Eckstein, *The Chosen Few: How Education Shaped Jewish History, 70–1492* (Princeton, NJ: Princeton University Press, 2012).
5. Ibid.
6. Ibid.
7. Ibid.
8. Ibid.
9. Ibid.
10. Ibid.
11. Mireya Mayor, *Pink Boots and a Machete* (Washington, DC: National Geographic, 2011).
12. Ibid.
13. Ibid.
14. Ibid.
15. Ibid.
16. Michael J. Mauboussin, *The Success Equation: Untangling Skill and Luck in Business, Sports, and Investing* (Boston: Harvard Business Review Press, 2012).
17. William D. Cohan, *Money and Power: How Goldman Sachs Came to Rule the World* (New York: Anchor Books, 2012).
18. Adam Baldwin, *Heroes and Villains of Finance: The 50 Most Colorful Characters in the History of Finance* (Hoboken, NJ: John Wiley & Sons, 2015).
19. Jonathan A. Knee, *The Accidental Investment Banker: Inside the Decade That Transformed Wall Street* (New York: Random House, 2007).
20. Cohan, *Money and Power*.

21. Baldwin, *Heroes and Villains of Finance.*
22. Charles D. Ellis, *The Partnership: The Making of Goldman Sachs* (London: Penguin, 2009).
23. "How Goldman Sachs Landed on Top," *The Week*, updated January 11, 2015, theweek.com/articles/502831/how-goldman-sachs-landed.
24. "Business: Everybody's Broker Sidney Weinberg," *Time*, December 8, 1958, content.time.com/time/subscriber/article/0,33009,864550,00.html.

Sampling

1. *Oeuvres illustrées de Balzac* (1852), Vol. 3, Louis Lambert, 28. As translated in Robert and Mary Collison (eds.), *Dictionary of Foreign Quotations* (London: Palgrave Macmillan 1980), 223.
2. Morgan Housel, *The Psychology of Money: Timeless Lessons On Wealth, Greed, and Happiness* (Chicago: Harriman House, 2020).
3. Supriya Bhalerao and Prashant Kadam, "Sample Size Calculation," *International Journal of Ayurveda Research* 1, no. 1 (2010): 55–7.
4. Ibid.
5. Ibid.
6. David Spiegelhalter, *The Art of Statistics: Learning from Data* (London: Pelican Books, 2019).
7. Divyang Shah, "Healthy Worker Effect Phenomenon," *Indian Journal of Occupational and Environmental Medicine* 13, no. 2 (2009): 77–9.
8. Simon Winchester, *The Professor and the Madman* (New York: Harper Collins, 2005).
9. Ibid.
10. Ibid.
11. Ibid.
12. Ibid.
13. Parimal Kumar Ray, *Agricultural Insurance* (Oxford, UK: Pergamon Press, 1966).
14. "The San Francisco Earthquake of 1906: An Insurance Perspective," Insurance Information Institute, accessed January 27, 2020, iii.org/article/san-francisco-earthquake-1906-insurance-perspective.
15. "The Impact of 9/11 on Business," *Investopedia*, September 11, 2023, investopedia.com/financial-edge/0911/the-impact-of-september-11-on-business.aspx.
16. Joseph Henrich, Steve J. Heine, and Ara Norenzayan, "The Weirdest People in the World?" *Behavioral and Brain Sciences* 33, no. 2–3 (2010): 61–83.
17. Caroline Criado Perez, *Invisible Women* (New York: Abrams Press, 2019).
18. Ibid.
19. Ibid.
20. Ibid.

21. Ibid.
22. Henrich, Heine, and Norenzayan, "The Weirdest People in the World?"
23. Perez, *Invisible Women*.

Randomness

1. Leonard Mlodinow, *The Drunkard's Walk: How Randomness Rules Our Lives* (New York: Pantheon Books, 2009).
2. Dictionary.com, s.v. "randomness," accessed August 23, 2019, dictionary.com/browse/randomness.
3. Paul Graham, "See Randomness," April 2006, paulgraham.com/randomness.html.
4. "Professor Chris Wickham," University of Oxford, accessed August 23, 2019, ox.ac.uk/research/research-in-conversation/randomness-and-order/chris-wickham.
5. Melanie Mitchell, *Complexity: A Guided Tour* (New York: Oxford University Press, 2011).
6. Ibid.
7. Ibid.
8. Brian Christian and Tom Griffiths, *Algorithms to Live By* (Toronto: Penguin, 2016).
9. Jane Smiley, *13 Ways of Looking at the Novel* (New York: Alfred A. Knopf, 2005).
10. Ibid.
11. Ibid.
12. Ibid.
13. Ibid.
14. Ibid.
15. Ibid.
16. "Chan Canasta," Roberto Forzoni Mind-Reader & Magician, accessed November 17, 2020, forzonimagic.com/mindreaders-history/chan-canasta.
17. David Britland, "Chan Canasta Triple Card Coincidence," *Cardopolis* (blog), January 27, 2010, cardopolis.blogspot.com/2010/01/chan-canasta-triple-card-coincidence.html.
18. Banachek, *Psychological Subtleties* (Houston: Magic Inspirations, 1998).
19. Ibid.
20. Mads Haahr, "True Random Number Generators (TRNGs)," Random.org, accessed August 23, 2019, random.org/randomness.
21. Shona L. Brown and Kathleen M. Eisenhardt, *Competing on the Edge: Strategy as Structured Chaos* (Boston: Harvard Business School Press, 1998).
22. Ibid.
23. Hans Rosling, Ola Rosling, and Anna Rosling Rönnlund, *Factfulness: Ten Reasons We're Wrong about the World—and Why Things Are Better Than You Think* (London: Sceptre, 2019).

Regression to the Mean

1. Julius Caesar, *The Conquest of Gaul* (London: Penguin Books, 1982).
2. Stephen Senn, "Francis Galton and Regression to the Mean," *Significance* 8 no. 3 (2011): 124–6.
3. Thomas Gilovich, *How We Know What Isn't So: The Fallibility of Human Reason in Everyday Life* (New York: Free Press, 1991).
4. "Are Cy Young Award Winners Jinxed? Injuries to Cubs' Rick Sutcliffe Seem to [Lend] Credence to the Belief," *Los Angeles Times*, August 11, 1985, latimes.com/archives/la-xpm-1985-08-11-sp-2900-story.html.
5. Peter Carlson, "The Flop Heard Round the World," *Washington Post*, September 4, 2007, washingtonpost.com/wp-dyn/content/article/2007/09/03/AR2007090301419_pf.html.
6. Jamie Page Deaton, "The Ford Edsel Failed, but Why?" How Stuff Works, updated February 21, 2024, auto.howstuffworks.com/why-the-ford-edsel-failed.htm.
7. Mark Rechtin, "The T-Bird: Whoever Did It, Did It Right," *Automotive News*, June 16, 2003, autonews.com/article/20030616/SUB/306160815/the-t-bird-whoever-did-it-did-it-right.
8. Richard L. Oliver, *Satisfaction: A Behavioral Perspective on the Consumer* (Oxfordshire, UK: Routledge, 2010).
9. Eliot A. Cohen, *Military Misfortunes: The Anatomy of Failure in War* (New York: Free Press, 2012).
10. David Gartman, *Auto Opium: A Social History of American Automobile Design* (London: Routledge, 1994).
11. Thomas E. Bonsall, *Disaster in Dearborn: The Story of the Edsel* (Stanford, CA: Stanford University Press, 2002).
12. Lyn Reese, "The Trung Sisters," Women in World History Curriculum, accessed November 18, 2020, womeninworldhistory.com/heroine10.html.
13. Kathleen Barry, *Vietnam's Women in Transition* (London: Macmillan Press, 1996).
14. Paige Whaley Eager, *From Freedom Fighters to Terrorists: Women and Political Violence* (London: Taylor and Francis, 2016).
15. *Encyclopedia Britannica*, s.v. "Trung Sisters," accessed November 18, 2020, britannica.com/topic/Trung-Sisters.
16. Patricia M. Pelley, *Postcolonial Vietnam: New Histories of the National Past* (Durham, NC: Duke University Press, 2002).

Multiplying by Zero

1. Paul Lockhart, *Arithmetic* (Cambridge, MA: Belknap Press, 2017).
2. Kristie Macrakis, *Seduced by Secrets* (Annapolis, MD: Naval Institute Press, 2008).
3. Ibid.
4. Ibid.

5. Ibid.
6. Ibid.
7. Mark Kinver, "Crop Diversity Decline 'Threatens Food Security,'" BBC News, March 3, 2014, bbc.com/news/science-environment-26382067.
8. Jim Donnelly, "The Irish Famine," BBC, February 17, 2011, bbc.co.uk/history/british/victorians/famine_01.shtml.
9. "Monoculture and the Irish Potato Famine: Cases of Missing Genetic Variation," Understanding Evolution, UC Museum of Paleontology, accessed August 12, 2020, evolution.berkeley.edu/evolibrary/article/agriculture_02.
10. "Stuttering," Mayo Clinic, accessed November 18, 2020, mayoclinic.org/diseases-conditions/stuttering/symptoms-causes/syc-20353572.
11. Maurice Zolotow, *Marilyn Monroe* (New York: Perennial Library, 1990).
12. "Putting It Bluntly," *W Magazine*, October 1, 2007.
13. B. B. King and David Ritz, *Blues All Around Me: The Autobiography of B. B. King* (New York: HarperCollins, 1996).
14. "The Turbulent Life of Rubin 'Hurricane' Carter," Stuttering Foundation, accessed November 18, 2020, stutteringhelp.org/content/turbulent-life-rubin-hurricane-carter.
15. Ibid.
16. Rubin Carter, *Sixteenth Round: From Number 1 Contender to Number 45472* (Chicago: Chicago Review Press, 2011).

Equivalence

1. Constance Reid, *Hilbert* (New York: Copernicus, 1996).
2. "Human Nature: Six Things We All Do," *New Scientist*, accessed August 23, 2019, newscientist.com/round-up/human-nature.
3. Donald E. Brown, *Human Universals* (Philadelphia: Temple University Press, 1991).
4. George Eliot, *Scenes of Clerical Life: Janet's Repentance* (Boston: Lauriat Comp, 1908).
5. Kevin Ashton, *How to Fly a Horse* (New York: Anchor Books, 2015).
6. Steven Johnson, *Where Good Ideas Come From: The Seven Patterns of Innovation* (London: Penguin, 2011).
7. William F. Ogburn and Dorothy Thomas, "Are Inventions Inevitable? A Note on Social Evolution," *Political Science Quarterly* 37, no. 1 (1922): 83–98, jstor.org/stable/2142320.
8. Julian Rubin, "The Discovery of Oxygen," February 2018, juliantrubin.com/bigten/oxygenexperiments.html.
9. Saman Musacchio, "The Birth of Color Photography," CNRS News, August 23, 2018, news.cnrs.fr/articles/the-birth-of-color-photography.
10. *Encyclopedia Britannica*, s.v. "Nettie Stevens," accessed November 25, 2020, britannica.com/biography/Nettie-Stevens.
11. Nobel Foundation, "The Nobel Prize in Physics 2015," news release, October 6, 2015, nobelprize.org/prizes/physics/2015/press-release.

12. Mark A. Lemley, "The Myth of the Sole Inventor" (Working Paper No. 1856610, Stanford Law School, Stanford, CA, July 21, 2011),papers.ssrn .com/sol3/papers.cfm?abstract_id=1856610.
13. Salim Ayduz, "Taqi al-Din Ibn Ma'ruf: A Bio-Bibliographical Essay," Muslim Heritage, June 26, 2008, muslimheritage.com/taqi-al-din-bio-essay.
14. Colin McDowell, "Madeleine Vionnet (1876–1975)," Business of Fashion, August 23, 2015, businessoffashion.com/articles/news-analysis/madeleine -vionnet-1876-1975.
15. J. E. Gordon, *Structures or Why Things Don't Fall Down* (Cambridge, MA: Da Capo Press, 1978).
16. McDowell, "Madeleine Vionnet."
17. William G. Hoy, *Do Funerals Matter?* (New York: Routledge, 2013).
18. Ibid.
19. Herodotus, *The Persian Wars*, Volume I: Books 1–2, Translated by A. D. Godley (Cambridge, MA: Harvard University Press, 1920).
20. James Gire, "How Death Imitates Life: Cultural Influences on Conceptions of Death and Dying," *Online Readings in Psychology and Culture* 6, no. 2 (2014), doi.org/10.9707/2307-0919.1120.
21. Colin Murray Parkes, Pittu Laungani, and Bill Young, *Death and Bereavement across Cultures* (London: Routledge, 1997).
22. Ibid.
23. Hoy, *Do Funerals Matter?*
24. Gire, "How Death Imitates Life."
25. Ibid.
26. Tim Radford, "One, Two, . . . Er, Too Many," *The Guardian*, August 19, 2004, theguardian.com/world/2004/aug/20/highereducation.research.
27. "The Richter Scale," Earthquake Magnitude: The Richter Scale (ML), accessed August 23, 2019, scientificamerican.com/article/how-was-the-richter -scale.
28. "Earthquake Facts," US Geological Survey, accessed September 11, 2019, sciencenotes.org/richter-scale-and-earthquake-magnitude.
29. Kirtley F. Mather and Shirley L. Mason, *Source Book in Geology, 1900–1950* (Cambridge, MA: Harvard University Press, 1970).

Surface Area

1. Duncan Wall, *The Ordinary Acrobat* (New York: Vintage Books, 2013).
2. Ibid.
3. Ibid.
4. Ibid.
5. Ibid.
6. Ibid.
7. Ibid.
8. Ibid.
9. Max Boot, *Invisible Armies* (New York: Liveright, 2013).

10. Robert Greene, *The 33 Strategies of War* (New York: Penguin, 2006).
11. Boot, *Invisible Armies.*
12. United States Army Special Operations Command, *Case Studies in Insurgency and Revolutionary Warfare: Cuba 1953–1959* (Washington, DC: Special Operations Research Office, 1963), available at www.soc.mil.
13. Mark Monmonier, *How to Lie with Maps*, 3rd ed. (Chicago: University of Chicago Press, 2018).
14. Ibid.
15. Amar Toor, "Meet Harry Beck, the Genius behind London's Iconic Subway Map," *Verge*, March 29, 2013, theverge.com/2013/3/29/4160028/harry-beck-designer-of-iconic-london-underground-map.
16. Monmonier, *How to Lie with Maps.*

Global and Local Maxima

1. Brian Christian and Tom Griffiths, *Algorithms to Live By* (Toronto: Penguin, 2016).
2. Ibid.
3. Lisa Z. Lindahl, *Unleash the Girls: The Untold Story of the Invention of the Sports Bra and How It Changed the World (and Me)* (Mount Pleasant, SC: Bublish, 2019).
4. Ibid.
5. Ibid.
6. Ibid.
7. Ibid.
8. Ibid.
9. Mark Hodkinson, *Queen: The Early Years* (London: Omnibus Press, 2009).
10. Ibid.
11. Ibid.
12. Ibid.
13. Ibid.
14. Ibid.
15. Ibid.
16. Ibid.
17. Ibid.

Also by Shane Parrish

'A masterwork'
Ryan Holiday

'Indispensable'
James Clear

Clear Thinking

The Art and Science of Making Better Decisions

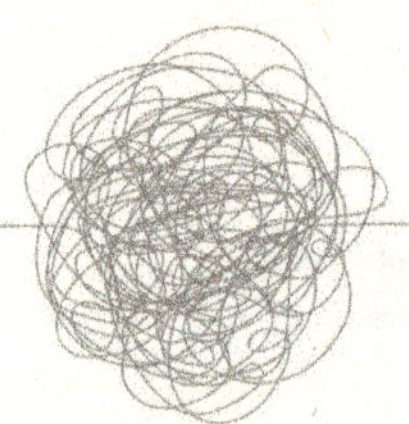
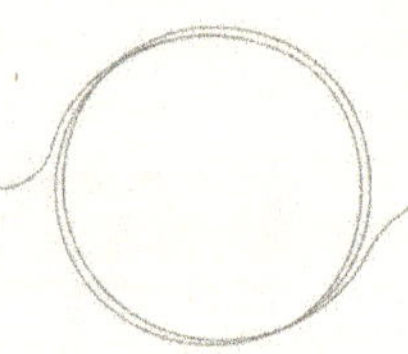

Shane Parrish

The *New York Times* Bestseller

'A must-read' Mark Manson